bedfordstmartins.com/easy

Bedford Integrated Media for *EasyWriter*, Fifth Edition

Lunsford

STUDENT ACCESS CODE

Scratch off to reveal code. Do not peel.

6-USE CARD: This student access code is valid for six users. Each user is granted access for a time period of up to one year.

TEACHERS: To get instructor access, go to bedfordstmartins.com/easy.

For technical support:
• macmillanhighered.com/techsupport

bedfordstmartins.com/easy

Bedford Integrated Media for *EasyWriter*, Fifth Edition

Lunsford

RECORD THE INFORMATION YOU NEED TO ACCESS THE MEDIA. KEEP THIS INFORMATION SECURE.

Student's name: ....
Student's e-mail: ....
Password: ....
Teacher's name: ....
Date activated: ....

Student's name: ....
Student's e-mail: ....
Password: ....
Teacher's name: ....
Date activated: ....

Student's name: ....
Student's e-mail: ....
Password: ....
Teacher's name: ....
Date activated: ....

Student's name: ....
Student's e-mail: ....
Password: ....
Teacher's name: ....
Date activated: ....

Student's name: ....
Student's e-mail: ....
Password: ....
Teacher's name: ....
Date activated: ....

Student's name: ....
Student's e-mail: ....
Password: ....
Teacher's name: ....
Date activated: ....

If an access card is not attached, visit the following site for more information: bedfordstmartins.com/easy

Brief Contents

Integrated media at **bedfordstmartins.com/easy** (more information inside this flap)

◎ video   ⊜ model writing, activity, exercise   ☑ LearningCurve adaptive quizzing

FIFTH EDITION

EasyWriter

A High School Reference

Andrea A. Lunsford
STANFORD UNIVERSITY

Advice for multilingual writers by

Paul Kei Matsuda
ARIZONA STATE UNIVERSITY

Christine M. Tardy
UNIVERSITY OF ARIZONA

BEDFORD/ST. MARTIN'S
Boston ◆ New York

FOR BEDFORD/ST. MARTIN'S

Publisher for High School: Ann F. Heath
Publisher for Composition: Leasa Burton
Executive Editor: Carolyn Lengel
Senior Editor: Nathan Odell
Senior Production Editor: Ryan Sullivan
Senior Production Supervisor: Dennis J. Conroy
Senior Marketing Manager: Lisa Erdely
Editorial Assistant: Leah Rang
Indexer: Melanie Belkin
Photo Researcher: Connie Gardner
Text Design: Claire Seng-Niemoeller
Cover Design: Billy Boardman
Composition: Graphic World, Inc.
Printing and Binding: RR Donnelley and Sons

Manufactured in the United States of America.

1   2   3   4   5   6   18   17   16   15   14

For information, write: Bedford/St. Martin's, 75 Arlington Street, Boston, MA 02116
(617-399-4000)

ISBN 978-1-4576-4252-4

ACKNOWLEDGMENTS

How to Use This Book

Chances are that you're called on to write and do research often, maybe even every day. Whenever you have questions about writing and research, *EasyWriter* offers quick and reliable answers.

Online Tutorials

bedfordstmartins.com/easy
Video Tutorial > What's in a handbook?
Video Tutorial > How to find what you need in your handbook
Video Tutorial > How to use the handbook documentation guidelines

Finding Help in the Print Book

Brief Contents.   The first thing you see when you open the book is a brief table of contents, which lists general contents. If you're looking for advice on a broad topic, just flip to the chapter. The tabs at the top of each page tell you where you are.

Contents.   If you're looking for specific information, the detailed table of contents lists chapter titles, major headings, and media content.

The Top Twenty.   On page 1 is advice on the twenty most common problems teachers are likely to identify in academic writing by first-year students. The Top Twenty provides examples and brief explanations to guide you toward recognizing, understanding, and editing these common errors. Cross-references point to other places in the book where you'll find more detailed information.

Integrated Media References.   The integrated media for this book includes online videos of student writers, exercises, adaptive quizzing, student writing models, and more. Cross-references at the bottom of a page direct you to **bedfordstmartins.com/easy** for media content related to that section of the book.

Documentation Navigation.   Each documentation section has its own color-tabbed pages; look for directories within each section to find models for citing your sources. Color-coded source maps walk you through the process of citing sources.

Glossary/Index. The index lists everything that's covered in the book. You can find information by looking up a topic, or, if you're not sure what your topic is called, by looking up the word you need help with. The index doubles as a glossary that defines important terms. Any **boldface term** you see in the print book is defined in the index.

Revision Symbols. The list of symbols on the last page of the book can help you learn more about any markings an instructor or a reviewer may make on your draft.

Glossary of Usage. This glossary, which appears right before the index, gives help with commonly confused words.

Page Navigation Help

The descriptions below correspond to the numbered elements on the sample pages on the next page.

❶ Guides at the top of every page. Headers tell you what **chapter** or **section** you're in, the **chapter number** and **section letter**, and the **page number**. **Icons** that indicate the name of the section (building blocks for Sentence Grammar, for example) also appear at the top of the page.

❷ Hand-edited examples. **Example sentences** are hand-edited in orange, allowing you to see an error or nonstandard usage and its revision at a glance. Orange pointers and boldface type make examples easy to spot on the page.

❸ Cross-references to integrated media. Cross-references at the bottom of a page point you to video, quizzing, student writing models, and more.

❹ Boxed tips. Many chapters include quick-reference **Checklist** boxes with an overview of important information. **For Multilingual Writers** boxes appear throughout the book, and additional advice can be found in Chapters 33–36. A directory of topics for multilingual writers appears on p. 387.

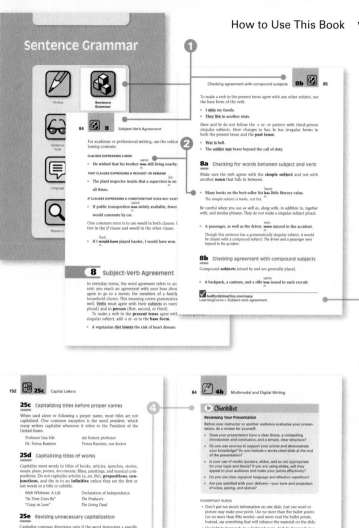

Sentence Grammar

Writing

Sentence Grammar

Sentence Style

Language

Research

---

84 🔲 **8** Subject-Verb Agreement

For academic or professional writing, use the subjur
lowing contexts:

CLAUSES EXPRESSING A WISH

▸ He wished that his brother was still living nearby.

THAT CLAUSES EXPRESSING A REQUEST OR DEMAND

▸ The plant inspector insists that a supervisor is on
all times.

IF CLAUSES EXPRESSING A CONDITION THAT DOES NOT EXIST

▸ If public transportation was widely available, fewer
would commute by car.

One common error is to use *would* in both clauses. U
tive in the *if* clause and *would* in the other clause.

▸ If I would have played harder, I would have won.

---

8 Subject-Verb Agreement

In everyday terms, the word *agreement* refers to an
sort: you reach an agreement with your boss abou
agree to go to a movie; the members of a family
household chores. This meaning covers grammatica
well. **Verbs** must agree with their **subjects** in num
plural) and in **person** (first, second, or third).

To make a verb in the **present tense** agree wit
singular subject, add *-s* or *-es* to the **base form**.

▸ A vegetarian diet lowers the risk of heart disease.

Checking agreement with compound subjects **8b** 🔲 85

To make a verb in the present tense agree with any other subject, use
the base form of the verb.

▸ I miss my family.
▸ They live in another state.

Have and *be* do not follow the *-s* or *-es* pattern with third-person
singular subjects. *Have* changes to *has*; *be* has irregular forms in
both the present tense and the **past tense**.

▸ War is hell.
▸ The soldier was brave beyond the call of duty.

8a Checking for words between subject and verb

Make sure the verb agrees with the **simple subject** and not with
another **noun** that falls in between.

▸ Many books on the best-seller list has little literary value.

The simple subject is books, *not* list.

Be careful when you use *as well as*, *along with*, *in addition to*, *together
with*, and similar phrases. They do not make a subject plural.

▸ A passenger, as well as the driver, were injured in the accident.

*Though this sentence has a grammatically singular subject, it would
be clearer with a compound subject: The driver and a passenger were
injured in the accident.*

8b Checking agreement with compound subjects

Compound **subjects** joined by *and* are generally plural.

▸ A backpack, a canteen, and a rifle was issued to each recruit.

✓ bedfordstmartins.com/easy
LearningCurve > Subject-verb agreement

---

152 🔲 **25c** Capital Letters

25c Capitalizing titles before proper names

When used alone or following a proper name, most titles are not
capitalized. One common exception is the word *president*, which
many writers capitalize whenever it refers to the President of the
United States.

Professor Lisa Ede   my history professor
Dr. Teresa Ramirez   Teresa Ramirez, our doctor

25d Capitalizing titles of works

Capitalize most words in titles of books, articles, speeches, stories,
essays, plays, poems, documents, films, paintings, and musical compositions. Do not capitalize articles (*a*, *an*, *the*), **prepositions**, **conjunctions**, and the *to* in an **infinitive** unless they are the first or
last words in a title or subtitle.

Walt Whitman: A Life   *Declaration of Independence*
"As Time Goes By"   *The Producers*
"Crazy in Love"   *The Living Dead*

25e Revising unnecessary capitalization

Capitalize compass directions only if the word designates a specific
geographical region.

▸ John Muir headed west, motivated by the desire to explore.

🌐 **For Multilingual Writers**

Learning English Capitalization

Capitalization systems vary considerably. Arabic, Chinese, Hebrew,
and Hindi, for example, do not use capital letters at all. English may
be the only language to capitalize the first-person singular pronoun
(*I*), but Dutch and German capitalize some forms of the second-
person pronoun (*you*)—and German also capitalizes all nouns.

📝 **4b** Multimodal and Digital Writing

▶ **Checklist**

Reviewing Your Presentation

Before your instructor or another audience evaluates your presentation, do a review for yourself.

▸ Does your presentation have a clear thesis, a compelling
introduction and conclusion, and a simple, clear structure?

▸ Do you use sources to support your points and demonstrate
your knowledge? Do you include a works-cited slide at the end
of the presentation?

▸ Is your use of media (posters, slides, and so on) appropriate
for your topic and thesis? If you are using slides, will they
appeal to your audience and make your points effectively?

▸ Do you use clear signpost language and effective repetition?

▸ Are you satisfied with your delivery—your tone and projection
of voice, pacing, and stance?

POWERPOINT SLIDES

▸ Don't put too much information on one slide. Just one word or
picture may make your point. Use no more than five bullet points
(or no more than fifty words)—and never read the bullet points.
Instead, say something that will enhance the material on the slide.

▸ Use light backgrounds in a darkened room, dark backgrounds in a
lighted one.

▸ If you include audio or video clips, make sure they are audible.

▸ Use only visuals that are large and sharp enough to be clearly visible
to your audience.

Practice.   Set aside enough time to practice your presentation—
including the use of all visuals—at least twice. You might also record
your rehearsals, or practice in front of a mirror or with friends who
can comment on content and style.

Timing your run-throughs will tell you whether you need to cut (or
expand) material to make the presentation an appropriate length.

e bedfordstmartins.com/easy
Student Writing > Multimedia presentation, Shuqiao Song
Analysis Activity > Analyze Shuqiao Song's genre choices

Contents

ⓔ ⊙ ☑ Icons indicate additional integrated media resources available at **bedfordstmartins.com/easy**.

The Top Twenty

Surface errors—grammar, punctuation, word choice, and other small-scale matters—don't always disturb readers. Whether your instructor marks an error in any particular assignment will depend on personal judgments about how serious and distracting it is and about what you should be focusing on in the draft. In addition, not all surface errors are consistently viewed as errors: some of the patterns identified in research for this book are considered errors by some instructors but stylistic options by others. Such differing opinions don't mean that there is no such thing as correctness in writing—only that *correctness always depends on some context*, on whether the choices a writer makes seem appropriate to readers.

Research reveals a number of changes that have occurred in student writing over the past twenty-five years. First, writing assignments in first-year composition classes now focus less on personal narrative and much more on research essays and argument. As a result, students are now writing longer essays than they did in the 1980s and working much more often with sources, both print and nonprint. Thus it's no surprise that students today are struggling with the conventions for using and citing sources.

What else has changed? For starters, wrong-word errors are *by far the most common* errors among first-year student writers today. Twenty years ago, spelling errors were most common by a factor of more than three to one. The use of spell checkers has reduced the number of spelling errors in student writing—but spell checkers' suggestions may also be responsible for some (or many) of the wrong words students are using.

All writers want to be considered competent and careful. You know that your readers judge you by your control of the conventions you have agreed to use, even if the conventions change from time to time. To help you in producing writing that is conventionally correct, you should become familiar with the twenty most common error patterns among U.S. college students today, listed here in order of frequency. A brief explanation and examples of each error are provided in the following sections, and each error pattern is cross-referenced to other places in this book where you can find more detailed information and additional examples.

> ## ▶ Checklist

The Top Twenty

1. Wrong word
2. Missing comma after an introductory element
3. Incomplete or missing documentation
4. Vague pronoun reference
5. Spelling (including homonyms)
6. Mechanical error with a quotation
7. Unnecessary comma
8. Unnecessary or missing capitalization
9. Missing word
10. Faulty sentence structure
11. Missing comma with a nonrestrictive element
12. Unnecessary shift in verb tense
13. Missing comma in a compound sentence
14. Unnecessary or missing apostrophe (including *its/it's*)
15. Fused (run-on) sentence
16. Comma splice
17. Lack of pronoun-antecedent agreement
18. Poorly integrated quotation
19. Unnecessary or missing hyphen
20. Sentence fragment

1 Wrong word

> Religious texts, for them, take ~~prescience~~ *precedence* over other kinds of
> sources.

Prescience means "foresight," and *precedence* means "priority."

▶ The child suffered from a severe ~~allegory~~ *allergy* to peanuts.

Allegory is a spell checker's replacement for a misspelling of *allergy*.

▶ The panel discussed the ethical implications ~~on~~ *of* the situation.

Wrong-word errors can involve using a word with the wrong shade of meaning, using a word with a completely wrong meaning, or using a wrong **preposition** or another wrong word in an idiom. Selecting a word from a thesaurus without knowing its meaning or allowing a spell checker to correct spelling automatically can lead to wrong-word errors, so use these tools with care. If you have trouble with prepositions and idioms, memorize the standard usage. (See Chapter 32 on word choice and Chapter 36 on prepositions and idioms.)

2 Missing comma after an introductory element

▶ Determined to get the job done, we worked all weekend.

▶ Although the study was flawed, the results may still be useful.

Readers usually need a small pause—signaled by a comma—between an introductory word, **phrase**, or **clause** and the main part of the **sentence**. Use a comma after every introductory element. When the introductory element is very short, you don't always need a comma, but including it is never wrong. (See 19a.)

3 Incomplete or missing documentation

▶ Satrapi says, "When we're afraid, we lose all sense of analysis and reflection." (263).

The page number of the print source for this quotation must be included.

▶   According to one source, James Joyce wrote two of the five

   best novels of all time. ("100 Best").

   The source mentioned should be identified (this online source has no author or page numbers).

Cite each source you refer to in the text, following the guidelines of the documentation style you are using. (The preceding examples follow MLA style—see Chapter 41; for other styles, see Chapters 42 and 43.) Omitting documentation can result in charges of plagiarism. (See Chapter 39.)

4 Vague pronoun reference

POSSIBLE REFERENCE TO MORE THAN ONE WORD

▶   Transmitting radio signals by satellite is a way of overcoming the

   problem of scarce airwaves and limiting how ~~they~~ the airwaves are used.

   In the original sentence, *they* could refer to the signals or to the airwaves.

REFERENCE IMPLIED BUT NOT STATED

▶   The company prohibited smoking, ~~which~~ a policy many employees resented.

   What does *which* refer to? The editing clarifies what employees resented.

A **pronoun** should refer clearly to the word or words it replaces (called the *antecedent*) elsewhere in the sentence or in a previous sentence. If more than one word could be the antecedent, or if no specific antecedent is present, edit to make the meaning clear. (See Chapter 11.)

5 Spelling (including homonyms)

▶   Ronald ~~Regan~~ Reagan won the election in a landslide.

▶   ~~Every where~~ Everywhere we went, we saw crowds of tourists.

The most common misspellings today are those that spell checkers cannot identify. The categories that spell checkers are most likely to miss include homonyms, compound words incorrectly spelled as separate words, and proper **nouns**, particularly names. After you run the spell checker, proofread carefully for errors such as these—and be sure to run the spell checker to catch other kinds of spelling mistakes.

6 Mechanical error with a quotation

▶ "I grew up the victim of a disconcerting confusion,"/

Rodriguez says (249).

The comma should be placed *inside* the quotation marks.

Follow conventions when using quotation marks with commas (19h), colons, and other punctuation. Always use quotation marks in pairs, and follow the guidelines of your documentation style for block quotations. Use quotation marks for titles of short works (23b), but use italics for titles of long works (27a).

7 Unnecessary comma

BEFORE CONJUNCTIONS IN COMPOUND CONSTRUCTIONS THAT ARE NOT COMPOUND SENTENCES

▶ This conclusion applies to the United States/ and to the

rest of the world.

No comma is needed before *and* because it is joining two phrases that modify the same verb, *applies*.

WITH RESTRICTIVE ELEMENTS

▶ Many parents/ of gifted children/ do not want them to

skip a grade.

No comma is needed to set off the restrictive phrase *of gifted children*, which is necessary to indicate which parents the sentence is talking about.

Do not use commas to set off **restrictive elements** that are necessary to the meaning of the words they modify. Do not use a comma before a **coordinating conjunction** (*and, but, for, nor, or, so, yet*) when the conjunction does not join parts of a compound sentence (error 13). Do not use a comma before the first or after the last item in a series, between a **subject** and **verb**, between a verb and its **object** or object/complement, or between a **preposition** and its object. (See 19i.)

8 Unnecessary or missing capitalization

▸ Some ~~Traditional~~ Chinese ~~Medicines~~ containing ~~Ephedra~~
  traditional   medicines   ephedra

remain legal.

Capitalize proper nouns and proper adjectives, the first words of sentences, and important words in titles, along with certain words indicating directions and family relationships. Do not capitalize most other words. When in doubt, check a dictionary. (See Chapter 25.)

9 Missing word

▸ The site foreman discriminated ^against^ women and promoted men with

less experience.

Proofread carefully for omitted words, including prepositions (36a), parts of two-part verbs (36b), and correlative **conjunctions**. Be particularly careful not to omit words from quotations.

10 Faulty sentence structure

▸ ~~The information which~~ ^High^ school athletes are presented with

~~mainly includes~~ information on what credits ~~needed~~ ^they need^ to graduate,

~~and thinking about the college~~ which ~~athletes are trying~~ [colleges to try] to play [how to] for, and apply.

A sentence that starts out with one kind of structure and then changes to another kind can confuse readers. Make sure that each sentence contains a subject and a verb, that subjects and **predicates** make sense together (14b), and that comparisons have clear meanings (14d). When you join elements (such as subjects or verb phrases) with a coordinating conjunction, make sure that the elements have parallel structures (see Chapter 17).

11 Missing comma with a nonrestrictive element

► **Marina, who was the president of the club, was first to speak.**

The clause *who was the president of the club* does not affect the basic meaning of the sentence: Marina was first to speak.

A **nonrestrictive element** gives information not essential to the basic meaning of the sentence. Use commas to set off a nonrestrictive element (19c).

12 Unnecessary shift in verb tense

► **Priya was watching the great blue heron. Then she ~~slips~~ [slipped] and ~~falls~~ [fell] into the swamp.**

Verbs that shift from one **tense** to another with no clear reason can confuse readers (18a).

13 Missing comma in a compound sentence

► **Meredith waited for Samir, and her sister grew impatient.**

Without the comma, a reader may think at first that Meredith waited for both Samir and her sister.

A compound sentence consists of two or more parts that could each stand alone as a sentence. When the parts are joined by a coordinating conjunction, use a comma before the conjunction to indicate a pause between the two thoughts (19b).

14 Unnecessary or missing apostrophe (including *its/it's*)

▶ Overambitious parents can be very harmful to a ~~childs~~ child's well-being.

▶ The library is having ~~it's~~ its annual fund-raiser. ~~Its~~ It's for a good cause.

To make a noun **possessive**, add either an apostrophe and an -s (*Ed's book*) or an apostrophe alone (*the boys' gym*). Do *not* use an apostrophe in the possessive **pronouns** *ours, yours,* and *hers.* Use *its* to mean *belonging to it;* use *it's* only when you mean *it is* or *it has.* (See Chapter 22.)

15 Fused (run-on) sentence

▶ Klee's paintings seem simple, but they are very sophisticated.

▶ ~~She~~ Although she doubted the value of meditation, she decided to try it once.

A **fused sentence** (also called a *run-on*) joins clauses that could each stand alone as a sentence with no punctuation or words to link them. Fused sentences must either be divided into separate sentences or joined by adding words or punctuation. (See Chapter 12.)

16 Comma splice

▶ I was strongly attracted to her, for she was beautiful and funny.

▶ We hated the meat loaf, that the cafeteria served ~~it~~ every Friday.

A **comma splice** occurs when only a comma separates clauses that could each stand alone as a sentence. To correct a comma splice, you can insert a semicolon or period, connect the clauses with a word such as *and* or *because*, or restructure the sentence. (See Chapter 12.)

17 Lack of pronoun-antecedent agreement

> *All students   uniforms.*
> ~~Every student~~ must provide their own ~~uniform.~~
>   ^   ^

> *its*
> Each of the puppies thrived in ~~their~~ new home.
>   ^

Pronouns must agree with their antecedents in gender (male or female) and in number (singular or plural). Many **indefinite pronouns**, such as *everyone* and *each*, are always singular. When a singular antecedent can refer to a man or a woman, either rewrite the sentence to make the antecedent plural or to eliminate the pronoun, or use *his or her*, *he or she*, and so on. When antecedents are joined by *or* or *nor*, the pronoun must agree with the closer antecedent. A collective **noun** such as *team* can be either singular or plural, depending on whether the members are seen as a group or as individuals. (See 11b.)

18 Poorly integrated quotation

> *showed how color affects taste:*
> A 1970s study of what makes food appetizing "Once it became
>   ^
> apparent that the steak was actually blue and the fries were
> green, some people became ill" (Schlosser 565).

> *According to Lars Eighner,*
> "Dumpster diving has serious drawbacks as a way of life"
>   ^
> (~~Eighner~~ 383). Finding edible food is especially tricky.

Quotations should all fit smoothly into the surrounding sentence structure. They should be linked clearly to the writing around them (usually with a signal phrase) rather than dropped abruptly into the writing. (See 39a.)

19 Unnecessary or missing hyphen

▶ This paper looks at fictional and real ‑life examples.

A compound adjective modifying a noun that follows it requires a hyphen.

▶ The buyers want to fix⁄up the house and resell it.

A two-word verb should not be hyphenated.

A compound **adjective** that appears before a noun needs a hyphen. However, be careful not to hyphenate two-word verbs or word groups that serve as subject complements. (See Chapter 28.)

20 Sentence fragment

NO SUBJECT

▶ Marie Antoinette spent huge sums of money on herself and her
                                        Her extravagance
favorites. ~~And~~ helped bring on the French Revolution.

NO COMPLETE VERB

                                was
▶ The old aluminum boat sitting on its trailer.

BEGINNING WITH A SUBORDINATING WORD

                                where
▶ We returned to the drugstore⁄, ~~Where~~ we waited for our

buddies.

A **sentence fragment** is part of a sentence that is written as if it were a complete sentence. Reading your draft out loud, backwards, sentence by sentence, will help you spot sentence fragments. (See Chapter 13.)

▶ Checklist

Taking a Writing Inventory

One way to learn from your mistakes is to take a writing inventory.
It can help you think critically and analytically about how to improve
your writing skills.

1. Collect two or three pieces of your writing to which either your
   instructor or other students have responded.

2. Read through these writings, adding your own comments
   about their strengths and weaknesses. How do your comments
   compare with those of others?

3. Group all the comments into three categories—*broad content
   issues* (use of evidence and sources, attention to purpose
   and audience, and overall impression), *organization and
   presentation* (overall and paragraph-level organization, sentence structure and style, and design and formatting), and
   surface errors (problems with spelling, grammar, punctuation,
   and mechanics).

4. Make an inventory of your own strengths in each category.

5. Study your errors. Mark every instructor and peer comment
   that suggests or calls for an improvement, and put all these
   comments in a list. Consult the relevant part of this book or
   speak with your instructor if you don't understand a comment.

6. Make a list of the top problem areas you need to work on.
   How can you make improvements? Then note at least two
   strengths that you can build on in your writing. Record your
   findings in a writing log that you can add to as the class
   proceeds.

Academic Essentials

As you embark on your academic career, here are some skills, tips, and habits of mind that can help you succeed.

1 Managing your time wisely

With the competing demands of school, clubs, sports, friends, family, and maybe even a job, it's important to plan your time.

- **Know your goals.** Reflect on what you want to accomplish. Consider what's important to you in both the short term and long term.
- **Make a plan to meet your goals.** You can't do it all, so you need to prioritize. Make a daily list of things you need to do, and figure out which are most important or most urgent. If you set a long-term goal, make a list of small, manageable steps with strict deadlines to help you progress toward that goal.
- **Stick to the plan.** Be strict with yourself. Remember that procrastination makes you more miserable than simply getting the work done. Use a calendar or other organizer to structure your time, and set deadlines for yourself. Then stick to them.

2 Participating in class

To take full advantage of your class time, try using the following techniques:

- **Take a seat as close to the front as possible.**
- **Keep your eyes trained on the instructor.** Sitting up front will make this easier to do.
- **Focus on the lecture.** Do not let yourself be distracted. It might be wise not to sit near friends who can distract you.
- **Speak up in class.** Ask a question or volunteer to answer a question or make a comment. This becomes easier every time you

do it. Never feel that you're asking a stupid question. If you don't understand something, you have a right to ask for an explanation.

- **If you have recently read a book or article that is relevant to the class topic, bring it up.** Use it either to ask questions about the topic or to provide information that was not covered in class.

3 Listening critically

Knowing how to listen in class can help you get more out of what you hear, understand better what you have heard, and save time. Here are some suggestions:

- **Be ready for the message.** Prepare yourself to hear, to listen, and to receive the message. If you have done the assigned reading, you will already know details from the text, so you can focus your notes on key concepts during the lecture. You will also be able to notice information that the text does not cover, and you will be prepared to pay closer attention when the instructor is presenting unfamiliar material.

- **Listen to the main concepts and central ideas, not just to any fragmented facts and figures.** Although facts are important, they will be easier to remember and will make more sense when you can place them in a context of concepts, themes, and ideas.

- **Repeat mentally.** Think about what you hear, and restate it silently in your own words. If you cannot translate all of the information into your own words, ask the instructor for further clarification.

- **Ask questions.** Do not hesitate to ask questions if you did not hear or understand what your instructor just said. It is best to clarify things immediately, if possible, and other students are likely to have the same questions. If you can't hear another student's question or response, ask that it be repeated.

- **Sort, organize, and categorize.** When you listen, try to match what you are hearing with what you already know. Take an active role in deciding how best to recall what you are learning. Categorizing information by level of importance will help you take notes and study from them later.

4 Taking effective notes

You can make class time more productive by using your listening skills to take effective lecture notes, but first you have to decide on a system. Any system can work as long as you use it consistently.

- **Cornell format.** Using the Cornell format, one of the best-known methods for organizing notes, you create a "recall" column on each page of your notebook by drawing a vertical line about two to three inches from the left border. As you take notes during a lecture—whether writing down ideas, making lists, or using an outline or paragraph format—write only in the wider column on the right; leave the recall column on the left blank. The recall column is the place where you write down the main ideas and important details for tests and examinations as you sift through your notes as soon after class as possible, preferably within an hour or two.

- **Outline format.** You probably already know what a formal outline looks like, with key ideas represented by Roman numerals and other ideas relating to each key idea represented in order by uppercase letters, numbers, and lowercase letters. If you use this approach, try to determine the instructor's outline and re-create it in your notes. Add details, definitions, examples, applications, and explanations.

- **List format.** This format can be effective in taking notes on lists of terms and definitions, facts, or sequences, such as the body's pulmonary system. It is easy to use lists in combination with the Cornell format, with key terms on the left and their definitions and explanations on the right.

Remember, don't try to write down everything. If you do, you will stop being a thinker and become a stenographer. As you take notes, leave spaces so that you can fill in additional details that you might have missed during class but remember later. Take the time to review and complete your notes as soon after class as possible.

Finally, remember to download any notes, outlines, or diagrams, charts, graphs, and other visuals from your instructor's Web site before class and bring them with you. You might be able to save yourself considerable time during the lecture if you do not have to try to copy complicated graphs and diagrams while the instructor is talking. Instead, you can focus on the ideas being presented while adding your own labels and notes to the visual images.

Writing

Writing

Sentence
Grammar

Sentence
Style

Punctuation/
Mechanics

Language

Multilingual
Writers

Research

Documentation

1 A Writer's Choices

You send a text message to your best friend confirming weekend plans. Later on, you put together an analysis of cost-cutting possibilities for the manager of the company you're interning for. And later still, just before calling it a day, you pull out the notes you took on your biology experiment and write up the lab report that is due tomorrow. In between, you probably do a lot of other writing as well—notes, lists, blog entries, Facebook status updates, and so on.

These are the kinds of writing most of us do every day, more or less easily, yet each demands that we make various important choices. In your text message, you probably use a kind of shorthand, not bothering to write complete sentences or even entire words. For your boss, however, you probably choose to be more formal and "correct." And for your lab report, you probably choose to follow the format your instructor has demonstrated. In each case, the choices you make are based on your **rhetorical situation**—the entire context for the writing.

1a Moving between social and academic writing

Students are doing more writing and reading today than ever before, and much of it is online—on Facebook, Twitter, Tumblr, and other social media sites. Writing on social networking sites allows almost instant feedback; anticipating audience responses can make online writers very savvy about analyzing audiences and about using an appropriate style and tone for the occasion.

Student Stephanie Parker tweeted:

Rain's over, going to Trader Joe's for some healthy stuff to fight this cold . . . suggestions?

Student Erin McLaughlin posted on Facebook:

Help send one of my Ghanian friends to college. The smallest contribution helps! http://www.indiegogo.com/teachaman

In these two short messages, Stephanie and Erin show a keen awareness of audience and two common purposes for social writing—to ask for information (healthy food suggestions for Stephanie) and to give information (about a cause Erin supports). Erin is asking her audience to help a friend from Ghana go to college, and since most of her friends are also college students, she assures them that they don't need to have a lot of money to make a difference. The link goes to a site about a group effort to raise enough funds to send a young man, Jey, to the University of Ghana.

Like Stephanie and Erin, you are probably adept at informal social writing across a range of genres and media. You may not think very hard about your audience for a tweet or Facebook post, or about your purpose for writing in such spaces, but you are probably more skilled than you give yourself credit for when it comes to making appropriate choices for informal writing.

In the writing you do from now on, you'll need to be able to move back and forth between informal and formal situations. Look closely at your informal writing: What do you assume about your audience? What is your purpose? How do you represent yourself online? What do the photos you post and your likes and dislikes say about you? Do you achieve the self-representation you want? Why do you write the way you do in these situations? Analyzing the choices you make in an informal writing context will help you develop the ability to make good choices in other contexts as well.

1b Meeting expectations for academic writing

Expectations about academic writing vary considerably from field to field (see Chapter 5), but becoming familiar with widespread conventions will prepare you well for writing in most academic contexts.

Authority.   Most instructors expect you to begin to establish your own authority—to become a constructive critic who can analyze and interpret the works of others.

To establish authority, assume that your opinions count (as long as they are informed rather than tossed out with little thought) and

---

that your audience expects you to present them in a well-reasoned manner. Show your familiarity with the ideas and works of others, both from the assigned course reading and from good points your instructor and classmates have made.

Directness and clarity. Research for this book confirms that readers depend on writers to organize and present their material—using sections, paragraphs, sentences, arguments, details, and source citations—to aid understanding. Good academic writing prepares readers for what is coming next, provides definitions, and includes topic sentences.

To achieve directness in your writing, try the following strategies:

- State your main point early and clearly.

- Avoid overqualifying your statements. Instead of writing *I think the facts reveal*, come right out and say *The facts reveal*.

- Avoid digressions. If you use an anecdote or example from personal experience, be sure it relates directly to the point you are making.

▶ Checklist

U.S. Academic Style

▶ Consider your purpose and audience carefully, making sure that your topic is appropriate to both. (1c–e)

▶ State your **claim** or **thesis** explicitly, and support it with evidence and authorities of various kinds. (Chapter 3)

▶ Carefully document all of your sources, including visual ones. (Chapters 41–43)

▶ Make explicit links between ideas. (2e)

▶ Use the appropriate level of formality. (32a)

▶ Use conventional formats for academic genres. (1g)

▶ Use conventional grammar, spelling, punctuation, and mechanics. (Chapters 7–28)

▶ Use an easy-to-read type size and typeface and conventional margins. For print projects, double-space text. (2f)

- Use appropriate evidence, such as examples and concrete details, to support each point.
- Make obvious and clear transitions from point to point. The first sentence of a new paragraph should reach back to the paragraph before and then look forward to what comes next.
- Follow logical organizational patterns.
- Design and format the project appropriately for the audience and purpose you have in mind (2f).

1c Considering the assignment and purpose

For the writing you do that isn't connected to a class or work assignment, you may have a clear purpose in mind. Even so, analyzing exactly what you want to accomplish and why can help you communicate more effectively.

An academic assignment may explain why, for whom, and about what you are supposed to write, or it may seem to come out of the blue. Comprehending the assignment is crucial to your success, so make every effort to understand what your instructor expects.

- What is the primary purpose of your writing—to persuade? to explain? to entertain? something else?
- What purpose did the person who gave you the assignment want to achieve—to test your understanding? to evaluate your thinking and writing abilities? to encourage you to think outside the box?
- What, exactly, does the assignment ask you to do? Look for words such as *analyze*, *explain*, *prove*, and *survey*. Remember that these words may differ in meaning from discipline to discipline and from job to job.

1d Choosing a topic

Experienced writers say that the best way to choose a topic is to let it choose you. Look to topics that compel, puzzle, or pose a problem for you: these are likely to engage your interests and hence produce your best writing.

---

bedfordstmartins.com/easy
Video > Pay attention to what you're interested in

- Can you focus the topic enough to write about it effectively in the time and space available?
- What do you know about the topic? What else do you need to learn?
- What seems most important about it?
- What do you expect to conclude about the topic? (Remember, you may change your mind.)

For information on exploring a topic, see 2a.

1e Reaching appropriate audiences

Every communicator can benefit from thinking carefully about who the audience is, what the audience already knows or thinks, and what the audience needs and expects to find out. One of the characteristics of an effective communicator is the ability to write for a variety of audiences, using language, style, and evidence appropriate to particular readers, listeners, or viewers. Even if your text can theoretically reach people all over the world, focus your analysis on those you most want or need to reach and those who are likely to take an interest.

- What audience do you most want to reach—people who are already sympathetic to your views? people who disagree with you? members of a group you belong to? members of a group you don't belong to?
- In what ways are the members of your audience different from you? from one another?
- What assumptions can you legitimately make about your audience? What might they value—brevity, originality, deference, honesty, wit? How can you appeal to their values?
- What sorts of information and evidence will your audience find most compelling—quotations from experts? personal experiences? statistics? images?
- What responses do you want as a result of what you write? How can you make clear what you want to happen? (For more on audience, see 29c.)

1f Considering stance and tone

Knowing your own stance—where you are coming from—can help you think about ways to get your readers to understand and perhaps share your views. What is your overall attitude toward the topic—approval? disapproval? curiosity? What social, political, religious, or other factors account for your attitude? You should also be aware of any preconceptions about your topic that may affect your stance.

Your purpose, audience, and stance will help to determine the tone your writing should take. Should it be humorous? serious? impassioned? Think about ways to show that you are knowledgeable and trustworthy. Remember, too, that visual and audio elements can influence the tone of your writing as much as the words you choose.

1g Considering time, genre, medium, and format

Many other elements of your context for a particular writing project will shape the final outcome.

- How much time will you have for the project? Do you need to do research or learn unfamiliar technology? Allow time for revision and editing.

- What genre does your text call for—a report? a review? an argument essay? a lab report? a blog post? Study examples if you are unfamiliar with the conventions of the genre.

- In what medium will the text appear—on the open Internet? on a password-protected Web site? in a print essay? in a presentation? Will you use images, video, or audio?

- What kind of organization should you use?

- How will you document your sources? Will your audience expect a particular documentation style (see Chapters 41–43)? Should you embed links?

bedfordstmartins.com/easy
Video > Working with other people

1h   Planning timed writing

If you are writing a timed essay on a topic you can find out about in advance, do your homework on the subject. If you are not expected to know the topic beforehand, consider the following tips for writing an essay examination.

Analyzing the prompt. Before you begin writing, read the question several times, and analyze what it asks you to do. Most essay examination questions contain strategy terms (such as *analyze, describe,* and *explain*) that define your task and content terms that limit the scope of the topic. If the strategy terms are not explicitly stated in an essay question, you can probably infer a strategy from the content terms; for example, a question that mentions two groups working toward a goal may call for comparison and contrast.

Planning your response. You may be tempted to begin writing an essay at once, but spend some time (about 10 percent of the allotted time is a good rule of thumb) thinking through your answer. Decide what major points you need to make, and outline the order you want to follow. Jot down support for each point. Based on this outline, craft a clear, succinct **thesis** that satisfies the strategy term of the question (2b).

Drafting your essay. Follow your outline as closely as you can to keep your discussion on track. As a general rule, develop each major

⊕ For Multilingual Writers

Learning Idioms

Why does it mean one thing to *look over* an item, but something entirely different to *overlook* an item? Idioms are very difficult to master because the only solution is to learn them individually (see Chapter 36). But be aware that most instructors and test-scorers understand and forgive idiomatic errors, especially if the writer has mastered other aspects of the language.

point into at least one paragraph (2e). Make the connections among your points clear by using **transitions**.

In addition to referring to your outline, pause and reread what you have written before going on to a new point. Rereading will help you establish clear connections and may also remind you of other ideas while you still have time to include them. If you are writing on paper, leave space in margins or between lines for changes or additions, and write as legibly as you can.

Revising and editing.   Leave five to ten minutes to read your answer carefully. Consider the following questions:

- Is the thesis clearly stated? Does it answer the question?
- Are the major points adequately developed and supported?
- Is each sentence complete?
- Are spelling, punctuation, and syntax as correct as you can make them?

1i Writing application essays

Essays that accompany an application—for admission to college or for an internship or scholarship, for example—are frequently the only part of the application that the student creates in its entirety. Readers of such essays want to see what you say about yourself. In general, try to tell them who you are and what your values are—not just what you have done.

Topic.   If the application asks a question, be sure to answer it. Substituting an essay on a topic of your choice will not reflect well on you. Avoid overused topics—such as why you're a better person for your involvement in sports, why your parent or grandparent is your hero, and how you want to change the world—unless the application asks directly for one of them.

If the essay has no set topic, consider writing about how you faced a challenge and what resulted from the experience, or about how you became interested in your area of study and what your goals are for studying it. Make sure the essay is about you, rather than about an impersonal topic; note, for example, that admissions

▶ Checklist

Application Essays

▶ Go through the same process of exploring, drafting, revising, and editing for this essay that you do for your other writing (see Chapter 2).

▶ Provide a strong opening paragraph—you have only one chance to make a first impression! The overall structure should resemble any other formal essay (2d).

▶ Even though this is a personal essay, it is not an informal essay. Avoid overly casual writing that uses slang or texting abbreviations (32a).

▶ In general, don't try to be funny. If you see an appropriate opportunity to use humor effectively, keep it brief, mature, and understated.

▶ Be succinct. Admissions officers and application committee members read a lot of essays, and they will appreciate your making your points clearly and directly.

▶ Write in your own voice. The most frequently offered advice from admissions officers is simple: be sincere. Avoid the temptation to use the thesaurus to find "impressive" or unfamiliar words.

▶ Be creative, but not at the expense of substance.

officers are not looking for an essay on how many high-paying engineering jobs are available. As with any writing, try to choose a topic that you care about (1d).

Audience. As with any writing task, you should consider what your audience will find persuasive. Tailor your response to the specific school as much as possible by considering the following (1e):

• For a college application, be sure you are sending the materials to the right school. Admissions officers know that you are likely to apply to more than one school, but they will expect you to make sure that your papers are in order, so check and double-check.

- What do you want to do with your education and why? How can this college, internship, or scholarship help you achieve that goal?
- What can you learn about the school or program from Web sites, mission statements, and so on? Can you show in your essay that you and the college or program are a good fit?

A student's college application essay. In response to the question "Tell us something about yourself we wouldn't know from your transcript and test scores," student Melissa Freilich wrote the essay on the following pages.

STUDENT
WRITING

Freilich 1

APPLICATION ESSAY

The essay responds directly to the question

From reading my application, you can probably assume that I can conjugate a Latin verb, calculate an instantaneous velocity, and recite passages from Shakespeare or Virgil. You know what I can do. But to really know me, you must know what I can't do.

A strong opening paragraph captures the reader's attention

I can't do a handstand.

The summer after my freshman year was my sixth at Centauri Summer Arts Camp, my favorite place in the world. That summer, my stage combat teacher, watching me practice my shoulder roll, commented, "You know, you could do a handstand." I laughed off this bit of lunacy. A handstand? I am unathletic and uncoordinated. I have a chronic fear of falling. I can't even manage monkey bars!

The essay focuses on a specific challenge

But somehow, I couldn't let go of the idea. So I went back to my combat director and asked her to teach me.

I learned to kick my feet up and to roll out if I went too far over, working every day, sometimes several times a day. I got to the point where I could occasionally hold a handstand for one or two seconds. But even after two summers, I still wasn't completely successful.

I was immensely frustrated. Handstands weren't difficult for other people, but I struggled for days on end with no improvement. Many times I considered giving up. After all, I had accepted my lack of athleticism. I knew my strengths and weaknesses. Why bother beating my head against a wall?

But, for the first time in my life, I wouldn't accept that. Deep down, I'd always worried I was a quitter. Maybe I was simply focusing on my strengths. After all, I always approach academic challenges aiming for my absolute best. But when it came to anything to which I didn't have a natural inclination, I tended to avoid it, or quit. I feared that I would spend my whole life drifting along, dodging

Annotations indicate effective choices.

Freilich 2

whenever I was confronted with a true challenge. Now, at last, I was facing my doubts and fears head on. Handstands became everything I had ever failed at, everything that I had been too afraid to try.

My junior year, I decided I wouldn't wait for the next summer. That year I woke up forty-five minutes early every morning to use the school's gym mats. After a few months, I had made considerable progress. I had started to find my balance before rolling out of my handstand.

And then came a fateful day in February. Only a few minutes into my practice, I managed a good handstand and rolled. However, because I was balanced, instead of rolling with forward momentum, I came directly down onto the mat. My training enabled me to slow my fall. I wasn't injured, but the wind was knocked out of me.

Then I did the unthinkable. I got up, packed up the mats, and left early. For the first time in a year and half of work and hope, I didn't get back up, I didn't try once more, and I didn't give it my best. Instead, I ran away. For one awful day, I felt that I wasn't a real person, but simply a vessel for all the fears that dictated my life.

It was February 5, 2008—the worst birthday of my life.

But I am more mulishly persistent than even I knew. I didn't give up. The next morning, despite my trepidation, I went to the gym and faced down the mat. This time, when I fell, I didn't run away. And I've been working every day since then. Sometimes I fall, and sometimes I fail. I still can't do a handstand properly. Perhaps I'll never do a handstand.

But whether I succeed or not, I am not a coward, and I will keep working for as long as it takes.

The essay's narrative structure has a clear beginning, middle, and end

The essay uses a story to explore a personality trait that applies to her ability to succeed in college

The essay is a sincere response from the applicant. No one else could have written this essay for the student.

1j Collaborating

Writers often work together to come up with ideas, to respond to one another's drafts, or even to coauthor texts. Here are some strategies for working with others:

- Establish ground rules for the collaboration. Be sure every writer has an equal opportunity—and responsibility—to contribute.

- Exchange contact information, and plan face-to-face meetings (if any).

- Pay close attention to each writer's views. Expect disagreement, and remember that the goal is to argue through all possibilities.

- If you are preparing a collaborative document, divide up the drafting duties and set reasonable deadlines. Work together to iron out the final draft, aiming for consistency of tone. Proofread together, and have one person make corrections.

- Give credit where credit is due. In team projects, acknowledge all members' contributions as well as any help you receive from outsiders.

 Checklist

Guidelines for Group Projects

▶ Establish a regular meeting time and space (whether real or virtual), and exchange contact information.

▶ During your first meeting, discuss the overall project and establish ground rules. For example, you might agree that everyone has a responsibility to participate and to meet deadlines, and that all members will be respectful toward others in the group.

▶ Establish clear duties for each participant.

▶ With final deadlines in mind, create an overall agenda to organize the project. At each group meeting, take turns writing up notes on what was discussed and review them at the end of the meeting.

▶ Use group meetings to work together on difficult problems. If an assignment is complex, have each member explain one section to the others. Check with your instructor if part of the task is unclear or if members don't agree on what is required.

▶ Express opinions politely. If disagreements arise, try paraphrasing to see if everyone is hearing the same thing.

▶ Remember that the goal is not for everyone just to get along; constructive conflict is desirable. Get a spirited debate going, and discuss all the options.

▶ If your project requires a group-written document, assign one member to get the writing project started. Set deadlines for each part of the project. Come to an agreement about how you will edit and change each other's contributions to avoid offending any member of the group.

▶ Assess the group's effectiveness periodically. Should you make changes as you go forward? What has been accomplished? What has the group done best? What has it done less successfully? What has each member contributed? What have you learned about how to work with others on future projects?

2 Exploring, Planning, and Drafting

One student defines drafting as the time in a writing project "when the rubber meets the road." As you explore your topic, decide on a thesis, organize materials to support that central idea, and sketch out a plan, you have already begun the drafting process.

2a Exploring a topic

Among the most important parts of the writing process are choosing a topic (see 1d), exploring what you know about it, and determining what you need to find out. The following strategies can help you explore your topic:

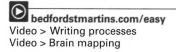

bedfordstmartins.com/easy
Video > Writing processes
Video > Brain mapping

- Brainstorm. Try out ideas, alone or with another person. Jot down key words and phrases about the topic, and see what they prompt you to think about next.

- Freewrite without stopping for ten minutes or so to see what insights or ideas you come up with.

- Draw or make word pictures about your topic.

- Try clustering—writing your topic on a sheet of paper, then writing related thoughts near the topic idea. Circle each idea or phrase, and draw lines to show how ideas are connected.

- Ask questions about the topic: *What is it? What caused it? What is it like or unlike? What larger system is the topic a part of? What do people say about it?* Or choose the journalist's questions: *Who? What? When? Where? Why? How?*

- Browse sources to find out what others say about the topic.

2b Developing a working thesis

Academic and professional writing in the United States often contains an explicit **thesis statement**. You should establish a working thesis early in your writing process. Your final thesis may be very different from the working thesis you begin with. Even so, a working thesis focuses your thinking and research, and helps keeps you on track.

A working thesis should have two parts: a topic, which indicates the subject matter the writing is about, and a comment, which makes an important point about the topic.

▶ In the graphic novel *Fun Home*, images and words combine to make meanings that are more subtle than either words alone or images alone could convey.

A successful working thesis has three characteristics:

1. It is potentially *interesting* to the intended audience.

2. It is as *specific* as possible.

3. It limits the topic enough to make it *manageable*.

🌐 For Multilingual Writers

Stating a Thesis

In some cultures, it is considered rude to state an opinion outright. In the United States, however, academic and business practices require writers to make key positions explicitly clear.

You can evaluate a working thesis by checking it against each of these characteristics, as in the following examples:

▶ **Graphic novels combine words and images.**

> **INTERESTING?**   The topic of graphic novels could be interesting, but this draft of a working thesis has no real comment attached to it—instead, it states a bare fact, and the only place to go from here is to more bare facts.

▶ **In graphic novels, words and images convey interesting meanings.**

> **SPECIFIC?**   This thesis is not specific. What are "interesting meanings," exactly? How are they conveyed?

▶ **Graphic novels have evolved in recent decades to become an important literary genre.**

> **MANAGEABLE?**   This thesis would not be manageable for a short-term project because it would require research on several decades of history and on hundreds of texts from all over the world.

2c Gathering evidence and doing research

What kinds of evidence will be most persuasive to your audience and most effective in the field you are working in—historical precedents? expert testimony? statistical data? experimental results? personal anecdotes? Knowing what kinds of evidence count most in a particular field or with particular audiences will help you make appropriate choices.

If the evidence you need calls for research, determine what research you need to do:

- Make a list of what you already know about your topic.
- Keep track of where information comes from so you can return to your sources later.
- What else do you need to know, and where are you likely to find good sources of information? Consider library resources, authoritative online sources, field research, and so on.

(For more on research, see Chapters 37–40.)

2d Planning and drafting

Sketch out a rough plan for organizing your writing. You can simply begin with your thesis; review your notes, research materials, and media; and list all the evidence you have to support the thesis. An informal way to organize your ideas is to figure out what belongs in your introduction, body paragraphs, and conclusion. You may also want—or be required—to make a formal outline, which can help you see exactly how the parts of your writing fit together.

Thesis statement
I. First main idea
   A. First subordinate idea
      1. First supporting detail or point
      2. Second supporting detail
      3. Third supporting detail
   B. Second subordinate idea
      1. First supporting detail
      2. Second supporting detail

II. Second main idea
   A. First subordinate idea
      1. First supporting detail
      2. Second supporting detail
   B. Second subordinate idea
      1. First supporting detail
      2. Second supporting detail
         a. First supporting detail
         b. Second supporting detail

The technique of storyboarding—working out a narrative or argument in visual form—can also be a good way to come up with an organizational plan. You can create your own storyboard by using note cards or sticky notes, taking advantage of different colors to keep track of threads of argument, subtopics, and so on. Move the cards and notes around, trying out different arrangements, until you find an organization that works well for your writing situation.

No matter how good your planning, investigating, and organizing have been, chances are you will need to do more work as you draft. The first principle of successful drafting is to be flexible. If you see that your plan is not working, don't hesitate to alter it. If some

> ## ▶ Checklist

Drafting

▶ **Set up a computer folder or file for your essay**. Give the file a clear and relevant name, and save to it often. Number your drafts. If you decide to try a new direction, save the file as a new draft—you can always pick up with a previous one if the new version doesn't work out.

▶ **Have all your information close at hand and arranged according to your organizational plan**. Stopping to search for a piece of information can break your concentration or distract you.

▶ **Try to write in stretches of at least thirty minutes**. Writing can provide momentum, and once you get going, the task becomes easier.

▶ **Don't let small questions bog you down**. Just make a note of them in brackets—or in all caps—or make a tentative decision and move on.

▶ **Remember that first drafts aren't perfect**. Concentrate on getting your ideas down, and don't worry about anything else.

▶ **Stop writing at a place where you know exactly what will come next**. Doing so will help you start easily when you return to the draft.

🔘 bedfordstmartins.com/easy
Video > You just have to start
Video > It's hard to delete things

information now seems irrelevant, leave it out. You may learn that you need to do more research, that your whole thesis must be reshaped, or that your topic is still too broad and should be narrowed further. Very often you will continue planning, investigating, and organizing throughout the writing process.

2e Developing paragraphs

The three qualities essential to most academic paragraphs are unity, development, and coherence.

Unity. An effective paragraph focuses on one main idea. You can achieve unity by stating the main idea clearly in one sentence—the **topic sentence**—and relating all other sentences in the paragraph to that idea. Like a thesis (see 2b), the topic sentence includes a topic and a comment on that topic. A topic sentence often begins a paragraph, but it may come at the end—or be implied rather than stated directly.

Development. In addition to being unified, a paragraph should hold readers' interest and explore its topic fully, using whatever details, evidence, and examples are necessary. Without such development, a paragraph may seem lifeless and abstract.

Most good academic writing backs up general ideas with specifics. Shifting between the general and the specific is especially important at the paragraph level. If a paragraph contains nothing but specific details, its meaning may not be clear—but if a paragraph makes only general statements, it may seem boring or unconvincing.

Coherence. A paragraph has coherence—or flows—if its details fit together in a way that readers can easily follow. The following methods can help you achieve paragraph coherence:

- A general-to-specific or specific-to-general *organization* helps readers move from one point to another.

- *Repetition* of key words or phrases links sentences and suggests that the words or phrases are important.

> ## ▶ Checklist

Strong Paragraphs

Most readers of English have certain expectations about how paragraphs work:

▶ Paragraphs begin and end with information that is important for the reader.

▶ The opening sentence is often the topic sentence that tells what the paragraph is about.

▶ The middle of the paragraph develops the idea.

▶ The end may sum up the paragraph's contents, closing the discussion of an idea and anticipating the paragraph that follows.

▶ A paragraph makes sense as a whole; the words and sentences are clearly related.

▶ A paragraph relates to other paragraphs around it.

- *Parallel structures* help make writing more coherent (see Chapter 17).

- **Transitions** such as *for example* and *however* help readers follow the progression of one idea to the next.

The same methods you use to create coherent paragraphs can be used to link paragraphs so that a whole piece of writing flows smoothly. You can create links to previous paragraphs by repeating or paraphrasing key words and phrases and by using parallelism and transitions.

The following sample paragraph from David Craig's research project (41e), which identifies a topic and a comment on the topic and then offers detailed evidence in support of the point, achieves coherence with a general-to-specific organization, repetition of key content related to digital communication and teenagers, and transitions that relate this paragraph to the preceding one and relate sentences to one another.

Transition from preceding paragraph —

Topic sentence —

Supporting evidence

STUDENT WRITING

Sentence-to-sentence transition

Based on the preceding statistics, parents and educators appear to be right about the decline in youth literacy, and this trend coincides with another phenomenon: digital communication is rising among the young. According to the Pew Internet & American Life Project, 85 percent of those aged 12–17 at least occasionally write text messages, instant messages, or comments on social networking sites (Lenhart, Arafeh, Smith, and Macgill). In 2001, the most conservative estimate based on Pew numbers showed that American youths spent at a minimum nearly three million hours per day on messaging services (Lenhart and Lewis 20). These numbers are now exploding thanks to texting, which was "the dominant daily mode of communication" for teens in 2012 (Lenhart), and messaging on popular social networking sites such as Facebook and Tumblr.

2f Designing texts

Because design elements help you get and keep the reader's attention and contribute to the tone of your text, they bring an important dimension to writing—what some call *visual rhetoric*.

Design principles. Designer Robin Williams, in her *Non-Designer's Design Book*, identifies four simple principles that are a good starting point for making any print or digital text more effective.

CONTRAST. Begin with a focal point—a dominant visual or text that readers should look at first—and structure the flow of other information from that point. Use color, boldface or large type, white space, and so on to set off the focal point.

ALIGNMENT. Horizontal or vertical alignment of words and visuals gives a text a cleaner, more organized look. In general, wherever you begin aligning elements—on the top or bottom, on the right or left, or in the center—stick with it throughout the text.

REPETITION. Readers are guided in large part by the repetition of key words or design elements. Use color, type, style, and other visual elements consistently throughout a document.

PROXIMITY. Parts of a text that are related should be physically close together (*proximate* to each other).

Appropriate formats.   Think about the most appropriate way to format a document to make it inviting and readable for your intended audience.

WHITE SPACE. Empty space, called "white space," guides the reader's eyes to parts of a page or screen. Consider white space at the page level (margins), paragraph level (spacing between paragraphs or sections), and sentence level (space between lines and between sentences). You can also use white space around particular content, such as a graphic or list, to make it stand out.

COLOR. Choose colors that relate to the purpose(s) of your text and its intended audience.

- Use color to draw attention to elements you want to emphasize—such as headings, bullets, boxes, or visuals—and be consistent in using color throughout your text.

- For academic work, keep the number of colors fairly small to avoid a jumbled or confused look.

- Make sure the colors you choose are readable in the format you're using. A color that looks clear onscreen may be less legible in print or projected on a screen.

PAPER. For print documents, choose paper that is an appropriate size and color for your purpose. A printed essay, poster, and brochure will probably call for different sizes and types of paper. For academic papers, put your last name and the page number in the upper-right-hand corner of each page unless your instructor requires a different formatting style.

TYPE. Choose an easy-to-read type size and typeface, and be consistent in the styles and sizes of type used throughout your project. For most college writing, 11- or 12-point type is standard. And although unusual fonts may seem attractive at first glance, readers may find them distracting and hard to read over long stretches of material.

SPACING. Final drafts of printed academic writing should be double-spaced, with the first line of paragraphs indented one-half inch. Other documents, such as memos, letters, and Web texts, are usually single-spaced, with a blank line between paragraphs and no paragraph indentation. Some kinds of documents, such as newsletters, may call for multiple columns of text.

HEADINGS. Consider organizing your text with headings that will aid comprehension. Some kinds of reports have standard headings (such as *Abstract*) that readers expect.

- Distinguish levels of headings using indents along with type. For example, you might center main headings and align lower-level headings at the left margin.

- Look for the most succinct and informative way to word your headings. You can state the topic in a single word (*Toxicity*); in a noun phrase (*Levels of Toxicity*) or gerund phrase (*Measuring Toxicity*); in a question to be answered in the text (*How Can Toxicity Be Measured?*); or in an imperative that tells readers what to do (*Measure the Toxicity*). Use the structure consistently for all headings of the same level.

Visuals.   Choose visuals that will help make a point more vividly and succinctly than words alone. In some cases, visuals may be your primary text. Consider carefully what you want visuals to do for your writing. What will your audience want or need you to show? Choose visuals that will enhance your credibility, allow you to make your points more emphatically, and clarify your overall text. (See the series of figures on p. 41 for advice on which visuals to use in particular situations.)

If you are using a visual created by someone else, be sure to give appropriate credit and to get permission before using any visual that will be posted online or otherwise made available to the public.

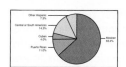

Use *pie charts* to compare parts to the whole.

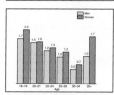

Use *bar graphs* and *line graphs* to compare one element with another, to compare elements over time, or to show correlations and frequency.

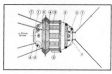

Use *tables* to draw attention to detailed numerical information.

Use *diagrams* to illustrate textual information or to point out details of objects or places described.

Use *maps* to show geographical locations and to emphasize spatial relationships.

Use *cartoons* to illustrate a point dramatically or comically.

Use *photographs* or *illustrations* to show particular people, places, objects, and situations described in the text or to help readers find or understand types of content.

POSITION AND IDENTIFICATION OF VISUALS. Position visuals alongside or after the text that refers to them. Number your visuals (number tables separately from other visuals), and give them informative titles. In some instances, you may need to provide captions to give readers additional data such as source information.

Fig. 1. College Enrollment for Men and Women by Age, 2007 (in millions)

Table 1. Word Choice by Race: *Seesaw* and *Teeter-totter*, Chicago, 1986

MANIPULATION OF VISUALS. Technical tools available today make it relatively easy to manipulate visuals. As you would with any source material, carefully assess any visuals you find for effectiveness, appropriateness, and validity.

 Checklist

Using Visuals Effectively

▶ Use visuals as a part of your text, not just as decoration.

▶ Tell the audience explicitly what the visual demonstrates, especially if it presents complex information. Do not assume readers will "read" the visual the way you do; your commentary on it is important.

▶ Number and title all visuals. Number tables and figures separately.

▶ Refer to each visual before it actually appears.

▶ Follow established conventions for documenting visual sources, and ask permission for use if someone else controls the rights. (See 39c.)

▶ Get responses to your visuals in an early draft. If readers can't follow them or are distracted by them, revise accordingly.

▶ If you crop, brighten, or otherwise alter a visual, be sure to do so ethically.

- Check the context in which the visual appears. Is it part of an official government, school, or library site?

- If the visual is a photograph, are the date, time, place, and setting shown or explained? Is the information about the photo believable?

- If the visual is a chart, graph, or diagram, are the numbers and labels explained? Are the sources of the data given? Will the visual representation help readers make sense of the information, or could it mislead them?

- Is biographical and contact information for the designer, artist, or photographer given?

At times, you may make certain changes to visuals that you use, such as cropping an image to show the most important detail or digitally brightening a dark image. To ensure that alterations to images are ethical, follow these guidelines:

- Do not attempt to mislead readers. Show things as accurately as possible.

- Tell your audience what changes you have made.

- Include all relevant information about the visual, including the source.

2g Reviewing

Ask classmates or your instructor to respond to your draft, answering questions like these:

- What do you see as the major point, claim, or thesis?

- How convincing is the evidence? What can I do to support my thesis more fully?

- What points are unclear? How can I clarify them?

- How easy is it to follow my organization? How can I improve?

- What can I do to make my draft more interesting?

bedfordstmartins.com/easy
Video > Lessons from being a peer reviewer
Video > Lessons from peer review
Analysis Activity > Practice peer review with Emily Lesk's draft

2h Revising

Revising means using others' comments along with your own analysis of the draft to make sure it is as complete, clear, and effective as possible. These questions can help you revise:

- How does the draft accomplish its purpose?
- Does the title tell what the draft is about?
- Is the thesis clearly stated, and does it contain a topic and a comment?
- How does the introduction catch readers' attention?
- Will the draft interest and appeal to its audience?
- How does the draft indicate your stance on the topic?
- What are the main points that illustrate or support the thesis? Are they clear? Do you need to add material to the points or add new points?
- Are the ideas presented in an order that will make sense to readers?
- Are the points clearly linked by logical transitions?
- Have you documented your research appropriately?
- How are visuals, media, and research sources (if any) integrated into your draft? Have you commented on their significance?
- How does the draft conclude? Is the conclusion memorable?

2i Editing

Once you are satisfied with your revised draft's big picture, edit your writing to make sure that every detail is as correct as you can make it.

- Read your draft aloud to make sure it flows smoothly and to find typos or other mistakes.
- Are your sentences varied in length and in pattern or type?
- Have you used active verbs and effective language?

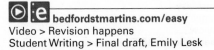
bedfordstmartins.com/easy
Video > Revision happens
Student Writing > Final draft, Emily Lesk

- Are all sentences complete and correct?
- Have you used the spell checker—and double-checked its recommendations?
- Have you chosen an effective design and used white space, headings, and color appropriately?
- Have you proofread one last time, going word for word?

(For more on troubleshooting your writing, see "The Top Twenty" on pp. 1–11.)

2j Reflecting

Thinking back on what you've learned helps make that learning stick. Whether or not your instructor requires you to write a formal reflection on a writing course or piece of writing, make time to think about what you have learned from the experience.

Your development as a writer. The following questions can help you think about your writing:

- What lessons have you learned from the writing? How will they help you with future writing projects?
- What aspects of your writing give you the most confidence? What needs additional work, and what can you do to improve?
- What confused you during this writing? How did you resolve your questions?
- How has this piece of writing helped you clarify your thinking or extend your understanding?
- Identify a favorite passage of your writing. What pleases you about it? Can you apply what you learn from this analysis to other writing situations?
- How would you describe your development as a writer?

Portfolios. You may want (or be required) to select samples of writing for inclusion in a portfolio.

- Consider your purpose and audience to make good choices about what to include and about whether the portfolio should be print or digital.

- Choose pieces that show your strengths as a writer, and decide how many to include.

- Consider organization. What arrangement will make most sense to readers?

- Think about what layout and design will present your work most effectively.

- Edit and proofread each piece, and get responses from peers or an instructor.

A student's portfolio cover letter. Go to the integrated media page at **bedfordstmartins.com/easy** to read a reflective statement written by student James Kung to accompany the portfolio for his first-year college composition course.

3   Critical Thinking and Argument

In one sense, all language has an argumentative edge: even when you greet friends, you want to convince them that you are genuinely glad to see them. In much academic and professional writing, however, **argument** is more narrowly defined as a text—verbal, visual, or both, in any medium—that makes a claim and supports it fully. Reading critically is essential to understanding such arguments.

3a   Reading critically

Reading critically means asking questions about the meaning of the text and how that meaning is presented, or about the author's purpose for creating the text. A critical reader does not simply accept what the author says; instead, a critical reader analyzes why the text is convincing (or not convincing).

e   bedfordstmartins.com/easy
Student Writing > Reflective cover letter, James Kung
Analysis Activity > Analyze formal reflection in James Kung's cover letter

Preview. Find out all you can about a text before beginning to look closely at it, considering its context, author, subject, genre, and design.

- Where have you encountered the work? Are you encountering it in its original context? What can you infer from the original or current context of the work about its intended audience and purpose?

- What information can you find about the author or creator of the text? What purpose, expertise, and possible agenda might you expect this person to have?

- What do you know about the subject of the text? What opinions do you have about it, and why?

- What does the title (or caption or other heading) indicate?

- What role does the medium play in achieving the purpose and connecting to the audience?

- What is the genre of the text—and what can it tell you about the intended audience or purpose?

- How is the text presented? What do you notice about its design and general appearance?

Annotation. As you read a text for the first time, mark it up or take notes. Consider the text's content, author, intended audience, and genre and design.

- What do you find confusing or unclear about the text? Where can you look for more information?

- What key terms and ideas—or key patterns—do you see? What key images stick in your mind?

- What sources or other works does this text refer to?

- Which points do you agree with? Which do you disagree with? Why?

- Do the authors or creators present themselves as you anticipated?

- For what audience was this text created? Are you part of its intended audience?

- What underlying assumptions can you identify in the text?

- Are the medium and genre appropriate for the topic, audience, and purpose?

- Is the design appropriate for the subject and genre?
- Does the composition serve a purpose—for instance, does the layout help you see what is more and less important in the text?
- How effectively do words, images, sound, and other media work together?
- How would you describe the style of the text? What contributes to this impression—word choice? references to research or popular culture? formatting? color? something else?

Summary.   Try to summarize the contents of the text in your own words. A summary *briefly* captures the main ideas of a text and omits information that is less important for the reader. Try to identify the key points in the text, find the essential evidence supporting those points, and then explain the contents concisely and fairly, so that a reader unfamiliar with the original text can make sense of it all. Deciding what to leave out can make summarizing a tricky task. To test your understanding—and to avoid unintentional plagiarism—it's wise to put the text aside while you write your summary.

Analysis.   You may want to begin the process of analysis by asking additional questions about the text.

- What are the main points in this text? Are they implied or explicitly stated?
- Which points do you agree with? Which do you disagree with? Why?
- Does anything in the text surprise you? Why, or why not?
- What kinds of examples does the text use? What other kinds of evidence does the text offer? What other examples or evidence should have been included?
- Are opposing viewpoints included and treated fairly?
- How trustworthy are the sources the text cites or refers to?
- What assumptions does the text make? Are those assumptions valid? Why, or why not?
- Do the authors or creators achieve their purpose? Why, or why not?

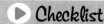 **Checklist**

Analyzing Verbal and Visual Arguments

▶ What cultural contexts—the time and place the argument was written; the economic, social, and political events surrounding the argument; and so on—inform the argument? What do they tell about where the writer or creator is coming from?

▶ What is the main issue of the argument?

▶ What emotional, ethical, or logical appeals is the argument making? Are the appeals reasonable and fair?

▶ How has the writer or creator established credibility?

▶ What sources does the argument rely on? How current and reliable are they? Are some perspectives left out, and if so, how does this exclusion affect the argument?

▶ What claim does the argument make, and how solid is the supporting evidence?

▶ How has the writer or creator used visuals and design to support the argument? How well do words and images work together to make a point?

▶ What overall impression does the argument create? Are you convinced?

• What intrigues, puzzles, or irritates you about the text? Why?

• What else would you like to know?

3b Identifying basic appeals in an argument

Emotional appeals. Emotional appeals stir our emotions and remind us of deeply held values. In analyzing any argument, look for what the writer or creator is doing to tug on the audience's emotions.

Ethical appeals. Ethical appeals support the credibility, moral character, and goodwill of the argument's creator. To find these appeals, ask yourself what the creator is doing to show that he or she has done homework on the subject and is knowledgeable and credible about it. What kind of character does he or she build, and how? Most important, ask if the creator of the argument seems trustworthy and has the best interests of the audience in mind.

Logical appeals. Logical appeals are often thought to be the most persuasive to Western audiences—as some say, "The facts don't lie" (although facts can certainly be manipulated). In addition to checking the facts of any argument, then, look for firsthand evidence drawn from observations, interviews, surveys or questionnaires, experiments, and personal experience, as well as secondhand evidence from authorities, precedents, the testimony of others, statistics, and other research sources. As you evaluate these sources, ask how trustworthy they are and whether all terms are clearly defined.

3c Analyzing the elements of an argument

Toulmin model. According to philosopher Stephen Toulmin's framework for analyzing arguments, most arguments contain common features: a **claim** (or claims); reasons for the claim; stated or unstated assumptions that underlie the argument (Toulmin calls these *warrants*); **evidence** such as facts, authoritative opinion, examples, and statistics; and qualifiers that limit the claim in some way.

Suppose you read a brief argument about providing sex education in schools. The diagram on p. 51 shows how you can use the elements of argument for analysis.

Inductive and deductive reasoning. Traditionally, logical arguments are classified as using either inductive or deductive reasoning, but in practice, the two types of reasoning usually appear together. Inductive reasoning is the process of making a generalization based on a number of specific instances. If you find you are ill on ten occasions after eating seafood, for example, you will likely draw the inductive generalization that seafood makes you ill. It may not be an absolute certainty that seafood was the culprit, but the probability lies in that direction.

Deductive reasoning, on the other hand, reaches a conclusion by assuming a general principle (known as a major premise) and then

Elements of a Toulmin Argument on Sex Education

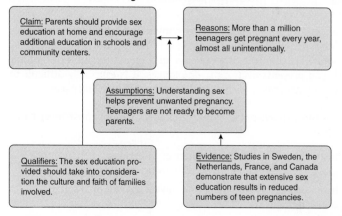

Claim: Parents should provide sex education at home and encourage additional education in schools and community centers.

Reasons: More than a million teenagers get pregnant every year, almost all unintentionally.

Assumptions: Understanding sex helps prevent unwanted pregnancy. Teenagers are not ready to become parents.

Qualifiers: The sex education provided should take into consideration the culture and faith of families involved.

Evidence: Studies in Sweden, the Netherlands, France, and Canada demonstrate that extensive sex education results in reduced numbers of teen pregnancies.

applying that principle to a specific case (the minor premise). In practice, this general principle is usually derived from induction. The inductive generalization *Seafood makes me ill*, for instance, could serve as the major premise for the deductive argument *Since all seafood makes me ill, the shrimp on this buffet is certain to make me ill.*

Deductive arguments have traditionally been analyzed as syllogisms—three-part statements containing a major premise, a minor premise, and a conclusion.

MAJOR PREMISE   All people die.

MINOR PREMISE   I am a person.

CONCLUSION   I will die.

Note that a deductive conclusion is only as strong as the premises on which it is based. The person who says *Don't bother to ask for Ramon's help with physics—he's a jock* is arguing deductively on the basis of an implied major premise: *Jocks don't know anything about physics.* In this case, careful listeners would demand proof of the unstated premise. Because bigoted or prejudiced statements often rest on this kind of reasoning—a type of fallacy (3e)—writers should be particularly alert to it.

3d Making an argument

Chances are you've been making convincing arguments since early childhood. But if family members and friends are not always easy to convince, then making effective arguments to those unfamiliar with you presents even more challenges. It is especially difficult to argue constructively with complete strangers in cyberspace.

Arguable statements. An arguable statement must meet three criteria:

1. It should seek to convince readers of something, to change their minds, or to urge them to do something.
2. It should address a problem that has no obvious or absolute solution or answer.
3. It should present a position that readers can have varying perspectives on.

ARGUABLE STATEMENT	Violent video games lead to violent behavior.
UNARGUABLE STATEMENT	Video games earn millions of dollars every year.

Argumentative thesis or claim. To move from an arguable statement to an argumentative thesis, begin with an arguable statement:

ARGUABLE STATEMENT	Pesticides should be banned.

Attach at least one good reason.

REASON	because they endanger the lives of farmworkers

You now have a working argumentative thesis.

ARGUMENTATIVE THESIS	Because they endanger the lives of farmworkers, pesticides should be banned.

Develop the underlying assumption that supports your argument.

ASSUMPTION	Farmworkers have a right to a safe working environment.

Identifying this assumption will help you gather evidence in support of your argument. Finally, consider whether you need to qualify your claim in any way.

Ethical appeals. To make any argument effective, you need to establish your credibility. Here are some good ways to do so:

- Demonstrate that you are knowledgeable about the issues and topic.

- Show that you respect the views of your audience and have their best interests at heart.

- Demonstrate that you are fair and evenhanded by showing that you understand opposing viewpoints and can make a reasonable counterargument.

Visuals can also make ethical appeals. Just as you consider the impression your Facebook profile photo makes on your audience, you should think about what kind of case you're making when you choose images and design elements for your argument

Logical appeals. Audiences almost always want proof—logical reasons that back up your argument. You can create good logical appeals in the following ways:

- Provide strong examples that are representative and that clearly support your point.

- Introduce precedents—particular examples from the past—that support your point.

- Use narratives or stories in support of your point.

- Cite authorities and their testimony, as long as each authority is timely and is genuinely qualified to speak on the topic.

- Establish that one event is the cause—or the effect—of another.

Visuals that make logical appeals can be useful in arguments, since they present factual information that can be taken in at a glance. Consider how long it would take to explain all the information in the following chart by using words alone.

A Visual That Makes a Logical Appeal

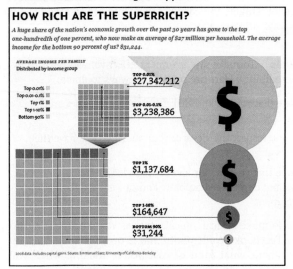

HOW RICH ARE THE SUPERRICH?

A huge share of the nation's economic growth over the past 30 years has gone to the top one-hundredth of one percent, who now make an average of $27 million per household. The average income for the bottom 90 percent of us? $31,244.

AVERAGE INCOME PER FAMILY
Distributed by income group

Top 0.01%
Top 0.01-0.1%
Top 1%
Top 1-10%
Bottom 90%

TOP 0.01%
$27,342,212

TOP 0.01-0.1%
$3,238,386

TOP 1%
$1,137,684

TOP 1-10%
$164,647

BOTTOM 90%
$31,244

2008 data. Includes capital gains. Source: Emmanuel Saez, University of California-Berkeley

Emotional appeals. Audiences can feel manipulated when an argument tries too hard to appeal to pity, anger, or fear. You can appeal to the hearts as well as to the minds of your audience with the ethical use of strong emotional appeals:

- Introduce a powerful text that supports your point.
- Use concrete language and details to make your points more vivid.
- Use figurative language—metaphors, similes, analogies, and so on—to make your point both lively and memorable.

Visuals that make emotional appeals can add substance to your argument as long as you test them with potential readers to check whether they interpret the visual the same way you do.

3e Identifying logical fallacies

Fallacies, which are often quite convincing at first glance, can create serious flaws in an argument. Learn to identify fallacies, but be cautious in jumping to quick conclusions about them: what looks like a fallacy in one argument may not be in another. Rather than thinking of them as errors you can use to discredit an arguer, you might think of them as barriers to common ground, honest debate, and understanding.

AD HOMINEM. Ad hominem charges make a personal attack rather than focusing on the issue at hand.

► Who cares what that fat loudmouth says about the health care system?

GUILT BY ASSOCIATION. Guilt by association attacks someone's credibility by linking that person with a person or an activity the audience considers bad, suspicious, or untrustworthy.

► She does not deserve reelection; her husband had a gambling addiction.

FALSE AUTHORITY. False authority is often used by advertisers who show famous actors or athletes testifying to the greatness of a product about which they may know very little.

► He's today's greatest NASCAR driver—and he banks at National Mutual!

BANDWAGON APPEAL. Bandwagon appeal suggests that a great movement is under way and the reader would be a fool or a traitor not to join it.

► This new phone is everyone's must-have item. Where's yours?

FLATTERY. Flattery tries to persuade readers by suggesting that they are thoughtful, intelligent, or perceptive enough to agree with the writer.

► You have the taste to recognize the superlative artistry of Bling diamond jewelry.

IN-CROWD APPEAL. In-crowd appeal, a special kind of flattery, invites readers to identify with an admired and select group.

► Want to know a secret that more and more of Middletown's successful young professionals are finding out about? It's Mountainbrook Manor condominiums.

VEILED THREAT. Veiled threats try to frighten readers into agreement by hinting that they will suffer adverse consequences if they don't agree.

▶ If Public Service Electric Company does not get an immediate 15 percent rate increase, its services to you may be seriously affected.

FALSE ANALOGY. False analogies make comparisons between two situations that are not alike in important respects.

▶ The volleyball team's sudden descent in the rankings resembled the sinking of the Titanic.

BEGGING THE QUESTION. Begging the question is a kind of circular argument that treats a debatable statement as if it had been proved true.

▶ Television news covered that story well; I learned all I know about it by watching TV.

POST HOC FALLACY. The post hoc fallacy (from the Latin *post hoc, ergo propter hoc,* which means "after this, therefore caused by this") assumes that just because B happened *after* A, it must have been *caused* by A.

▶ We should not rebuild the town docks because every time we do, a big hurricane comes along and damages them.

NON SEQUITUR. A non sequitur (Latin for "it does not follow") attempts to tie together two or more logically unrelated ideas as if they were related.

▶ If we can send a spaceship to Mars, then we can discover a cure for cancer.

EITHER-OR FALLACY. The either-or fallacy insists that a complex situation can have only two possible outcomes.

▶ If we do not build the new highway, businesses downtown will be forced to close.

HASTY GENERALIZATION. A hasty generalization bases a conclusion on too little evidence or on bad or misunderstood evidence.

▶ I couldn't understand the lecture today, so I'm sure this course will be impossible.

OVERSIMPLIFICATION. Oversimplification claims an overly direct relationship between a cause and an effect.

▶ If we prohibit the sale of alcohol, we will get rid of binge drinking.

STRAW MAN. A straw-man argument misrepresents the opposition by pretending that opponents agree with something that few reasonable people would support.

▶ My opponent believes that we should offer therapy to the terrorists. I disagree.

3f Organizing an argument

Although there is no universally "ideal" organizational framework for an argument, the following pattern (often referred to as the classical system) has been used throughout the history of the Western world:

INTRODUCTION

- Gets readers' attention and interest
- Establishes your qualifications to write about your topic
- Establishes common ground with readers
- Demonstrates fairness
- States or implies your argumentative thesis

BACKGROUND

- Presents any necessary background data or information, including pertinent personal narratives or stories

LINES OF ARGUMENT

- Present good reasons and evidence (including logical and emotional appeals) in support of your thesis, usually in order of importance
- Demonstrate ways your argument is in readers' best interest

CONSIDERATION OF ALTERNATIVE ARGUMENTS

- Examines alternative or opposing points of view
- Notes advantages and disadvantages of alternative views
- Explains why one view is better than other(s)

CONCLUSION

- May summarize the argument briefly
- Elaborates on the implication of your thesis
- Makes clear what you want readers to think and do
- Makes a strong ethical or emotional appeal in a memorable way

3g A student's argument essay

Go to the integrated media page at **bedfordstmartins.com/easy** to read an essay by Benjy Mercer-Golden, which argues that sustainability and capitalism can and must work together for an effective response to environmental degradation.

4 Multimodal and Digital Writing

Writing today occurs across a wide range of genres and media—your audience may encounter your work in print, online, as a presentation, or in some other way. But no matter what genre or medium you are writing for, you still need to consider your rhetorical situation—the audience, purpose, and complete context for your writing.

4a Planning online assignments

Writing assignments that your audiences will encounter online may repurpose your print-based work, or they may be entirely new, online-only texts that take advantage of the technology to include material that print texts can't offer, such as sound and video.

 bedfordstmartins.com/easy
Student Writing > Argument project, Benjy Mercer-Golden
Analysis Activity > Analyze evidence in Benjy Mercer-Golden's argument

Checklist

Guidelines for Creating an Online Text

▶ Consider purpose, audience, and message. How can your text appeal to the right readers? How will it accomplish its purpose? (Chapter 1)

▶ Be realistic about the time available for the project, and plan accordingly.

▶ Think about the various types of online texts you can create, and determine which suits your needs based on what you want or need to do and what your audience expects: text, images, audio, video, or a combination? the latest updates first, or an index page? the ability to collaborate or comment? Make appropriate choices for your project and skills.

▶ Create an appealing design, or choose a template that follows basic design principles. (2f)

▶ Pay attention to user feedback, and make appropriate adjustments.

Whether you are starting with work on a printed page or tackling an online assignment from scratch, think just as carefully about your online context as you would about any other writing situation.

Rhetorical considerations of online texts.   Early on, consider time and technical constraints carefully to make sure that your plan for an online text is manageable. But also remember to think about rhetorical concerns.

• Why are you creating this text? How do you want readers to use it? Considering purpose helps you determine what features to incorporate.

• What potential audience can you identify? If your intended audience is limited to people you know (such as a class wiki), you may be able to make assumptions about their background, knowledge, and likely responses to your text. Plan your text to appeal to the readers you expect—but remember that an online text may reach other, unanticipated audiences.

- What will you talk about? Your topic will also affect the content and design of your project.
- Will you present yourself as an expert, a fan, or a novice seeking input from others? What information will make you seem credible and persuasive to your audience?

Types of online texts.   Among the most common types of online texts are Web sites, blogs, wikis, and audio or video texts.

- Web sites and blogs usually include links to other parts of the site or to other sites. Both are relatively easy to update. Web sites are often organized as a cluster of associations. Readers expect blog content to be refreshed frequently, and the newest content appears first. Blogs usually invite readers to comment publicly on each post, while Web sites often have a single contact link.
- Wikis—collaborative online texts—create communities where all content is peer reviewed and evaluated by other members. They draw on the collective knowledge of many contributors.
- Audio and video content can vary widely. Writers who create podcasts and streaming media may produce episodic content with a common host or theme. Audio and video files can stand alone as online texts, but they can also be embedded on a Web page or blog or included in a presentation to add dimension to still images and written words.

Interactive digital communication.   Because digital communication is so common, it's easy to fall into the habit of writing very informally. If you forget to adjust style and voice for different occasions and readers, you may undermine your own intentions.

EMAIL. You will probably use email mainly for more formal purposes, particularly to communicate for work and for school. When writing most academic and professional messages, then, follow the conventions of standard academic English, and be careful not to offend or irritate your audience—remember that jokes may be read as insults and that ALL CAPS may look like shouting. Finally, proofread to make sure your message is clear and free of errors, and that it is addressed to your intended audience, before you hit SEND.

- Use a subject line that states your purpose clearly.
- Use a formal greeting and closing (*Dear Ms. Aulie* rather than *Hey*).
- Keep messages as concise as possible.
- Conclude your message with your name and email address.
- Consider your email messages permanent and always findable.
- Make sure that the username on the email account you use for formal messages does not present a poor impression. If your username is *Party2Nite*, consider changing it, or use your school account for academic and professional communication.

DISCUSSION FORUMS. Be polite and professional when posting to a course space or other public list.

- Avoid unnecessary criticism of others' spelling or language. If a message is unclear, ask politely for a clarification. If you disagree with an assertion, offer what you believe to be the correct information, but don't insult the writer.
- If you think you've been insulted, give the writer the benefit of the doubt. Replying with patience establishes your credibility and helps you appear mature and fair.
- For email discussion lists, decide whether to reply off-list to the sender of a message or to the whole group, and be careful to use REPLY or REPLY ALL accordingly to avoid potential embarrassment.
- Keep in mind that because many discussion forums and email lists are archived, more people than you think may be reading your messages.

INFORMAL SITUATIONS. Sometimes your audience will expect informality. When you write in certain situations—Twitter posts, for example, and most text messages—you can play with (or ignore) the conventions you would probably follow in formal writing. You may want to stick to a more formal method of contact if your employer or instructor has not explicitly invited you to send text messages—or texted you first.

Even when you think the situation calls for an informal tone, be attuned to your audience's needs and your purpose for writing. And when writing for any online writing space that allows users to comment freely on the postings of others, don't say anything you want to remain private, and avoid personal attacks.

4b Creating presentations

More and more students report that formal presentations are becoming part of their work both in and out of class.

Task, purpose, and audience.   Think about how much time you have to prepare; where the presentation will take place; how long the presentation is to be; whether you will use written-out text or note cards; whether visual aids, handouts, or other accompanying materials are called for; and what equipment you will need. If you are making a group presentation, you will need time to divide duties and to practice with your classmates.

Consider the purpose of your presentation. Are you to lead a discussion? teach a lesson? give a report? engage a group in an activity?

Consider your audience. What do they know about your topic, what opinions do they already hold about it, and what do they need to know to follow your presentation and perhaps accept your point of view?

Memorable introduction and conclusion.   Listeners tend to remember beginnings and endings most readily. Consider making yours memorable by using a startling statement, opinion, or question; a vivid anecdote; or a powerful quotation.

Explicit structure and signpost language.   Organize your presentation clearly and carefully, and give an overview of your main points at the outset. (You may wish to recall these points toward the end of the talk.) Then pause between major points, and use signpost language as you move from one idea to the next. Such signposts should be clear and concrete: *The second crisis point in the breakup of the Soviet Union* *occurred hard on the heels of the first* instead of *Another thing about the Soviet Union's problems.* . . . You can also offer signposts by repeating key words and ideas; avoiding long, complicated sentences; and using as many concrete verbs and nouns as possible. If you are talking about abstract ideas, try to provide concrete examples for each.

Prepared text for ease of presentation. If you decide to speak from a full text of your presentation, use fairly large double- or triple-spaced print that will be easy to read. End each page with the end of a sentence so that you won't have to pause while you turn a page. Whether you speak from a full text, a detailed outline, note cards, or points on flip charts or slides, mark the places where you want to pause, and highlight the words you want to emphasize. (If you are using presentation software, print out a paper version and mark it up.)

Visuals. Visuals carry a lot of the message the speaker wants to convey, so think of your visuals not as add-ons but as a major means of getting your points across. Many speakers use presentation software (such as PowerPoint or Prezi) to help keep themselves on track and to guide the audience. In addition, posters, flip charts, chalkboards, or interactive whiteboards can also help you make strong visual statements.

When you work with visuals for your own presentation, remember that they must be large enough to be easily seen and read. Be sure the information is simple, clear, and easy to understand. And remember *not* to read from your visuals or turn your back on your audience as you refer to them. Most important, make sure your visuals engage and help your listeners rather than distract them from your message. Try out each visual on your classmates, friends, or roommates: if they do not clearly grasp the meaning and purpose of the visual, scrap it and try again.

You may also want to prepare handouts for your audience: pertinent bibliographies, for example, or text too extensive to be presented otherwise. Unless the handouts include material you want your audience to use while you speak, distribute them at the end of the presentation.

▶ bedfordstmartins.com/easy
Video > You want them to hear you
Video > Presentation is performance

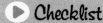 **Checklist**

Reviewing Your Presentation

Before your instructor or another audience evaluates your presentation, do a review for yourself:

▶ Does your presentation have a clear thesis, a compelling introduction and conclusion, and a simple, clear structure?

▶ Do you use sources to support your points and demonstrate your knowledge? Do you include a works-cited slide at the end of the presentation?

▶ Is your use of media (posters, slides, and so on) appropriate for your topic and thesis? If you are using slides, will they appeal to your audience and make your points effectively?

▶ Do you use clear signpost language and effective repetition?

▶ Are you satisfied with your delivery—your tone and projection of voice, pacing, and stance?

POWERPOINT SLIDES

• Don't put too much information on one slide. Just one word or picture may make your point. Use no more than five bullet points (or no more than fifty words)—and never read the bullet points. Instead, say something that will enhance the material on the slide.

• Use light backgrounds in a darkened room, dark backgrounds in a lighted one.

• If you include audio or video clips, make sure they are audible.

• Use only visuals that are large and sharp enough to be clearly visible to your audience.

Practice. Set aside enough time to practice your presentation—including the use of all visuals—at least twice. You might also record your rehearsals, or practice in front of a mirror or with friends who can comment on content and style.

Timing your run-throughs will tell you whether you need to cut (or expand) material to make the presentation an appropriate length.

---

bedfordstmartins.com/easy
Student Writing > Multimedia presentation, Shuqiao Song
Analysis Activity > Analyze Shuqiao Song's genre choices

The actual presentation. To calm your nerves and get off to a good start, know your material thoroughly and use the following strategies to good advantage before, during, and after your presentation:

- Visualize your presentation with the aim of feeling comfortable during it.

- Consider doing some deep-breathing exercises before the presentation, and concentrate on relaxing; avoid too much caffeine.

- If possible, stand up. Most speakers make a stronger impression standing rather than sitting.

- Face your audience, and make eye contact as much as possible.

- Allow time for questions.

- Thank the audience at the end of your presentation.

4c A student's presentation

For her presentation, "Words, Images, and the Mystical Way They Work Together in Alison Bechdel's *Fun Home*," Shuqiao Song developed a series of very simple slides aimed at underscoring her points and keeping her audience focused on them. Go to the integrated media page at **bedfordstmartins.com/easy** to see her presentation.

5 Writing in the Disciplines

Writing is important in almost every profession, but it works in different ways in different disciplines. You may begin to get a sense of such differences as you prepare assignments for courses in the humanities, social sciences, and natural sciences.

5a Writing in academic genres

There is no single "correct" style of communication in any country, including the United States. Effective oral styles differ from effective written styles (4b), and what is considered good writing in one field of study may not be appropriate in another. Even the variety of English often referred to as "standard" covers a wide range of styles (31a). New contexts require the use of different sets of conventions, strategies, and resources. Early in your writing process, you should consider the **genre** or kind of text the instructor expects you to write. If you are not sure what kind of text you are supposed to write, ask your instructor for clarification. (Examples may also be available at your school's writing center.) You may want to find multiple examples so that you can develop a sense of how different writers approach the same writing task.

5b Understanding disciplinary styles and evidence

You will need to become familiar with the vocabularies, styles, and methods of proof used in a discipline.

Vocabulary. A good way to enter into the conversation of a field or discipline is to study its vocabulary. Highlight key terms in your reading or notes to help you distinguish any specialized terms. If you find only a little specialized vocabulary, try to master the new terms quickly by reading your textbook carefully, asking your instructor questions, and looking up key words or phrases.

Style. Study writing in the field to identify its stylistic features.

- How would you describe the overall tone of the writing? Do writers in the field usually strive for an objective stance? (See 1f.)

- Do they use the first person (*I*) or prefer such terms as *one* or *the investigator*? What is the effect of this choice?

- In general, how long are the sentences and paragraphs?

- Are verbs generally active or passive—and why? (See 7e.)

- Does the writing integrate visual elements—graphs, tables, charts, photographs, or maps—or include video or sound?

- How is the writing organized? Does it typically include certain features, such as an abstract, a discussion of methods, headings, or other formatting elements?

Evidence. As you grow familiar with any area of study, you will develop a sense of what it takes to prove a point in that field. As you read assigned materials, consider the following questions about evidence:

- How do writers in the field use precedent and authority?
- What kinds of quantitative data (items that can be counted and measured) and qualitative data (items that can be systematically observed) are used—and why?
- How is logical reasoning used? How are definition, cause and effect, analogy, and example used in this discipline?
- What are the primary materials—the firsthand sources of information—in this field? What are the secondary materials—the sources of information derived from others? (See 38b.)
- How is research used and integrated into the text?
- What documentation style is typically used in this field? (See Chapters 41–43.)

EVIDENCE IN THE HUMANITIES. Evidence for assignments in the humanities may come from a primary source you are examining, such as a poem, a philosophical treatise, an artifact, or a painting. For certain assignments, secondary sources such as journal articles or reference works will also provide useful evidence. Ground your analysis of each source in key questions about the work you are examining that will lead you to a thesis.

EVIDENCE IN THE SOCIAL SCIENCES. You will need to understand both the quantitative and qualitative evidence used in your sources as well as other evidence you may create from research you conduct on your own. Summarizing and synthesizing information drawn from sources will be key to your success.

EVIDENCE IN THE NATURAL AND APPLIED SCIENCES. You will probably draw on two major sources of evidence: research—including studies, experiments, and analyses—conducted by reputable and credible scientists, and research you conduct by yourself or with others. Each source should provide a strong piece of evidence for your project.

6 Writing to Make Something Happen in the World

A large group of college students participating in a research study were asked, "What is good writing?" The students kept coming back to one central idea: good writing "makes something happen in the world." They felt particular pride in the writing they did for family, friends, and community groups—and for many extracurricular activities that were meaningful to them. At some point during your college years or soon after, you are highly likely to create writing that is not just something that you turn in for a grade but writing that you do because you want to make a difference. The writing that matters most to many students and citizens, then, is writing that gets up off the page or screen, puts on its working boots, and marches out to get something done!

6a Deciding what should happen

When you decide to write to make something happen, you'll generally have some idea of what effect you want that writing to have. Clarify what actions you want your readers to take in response to your writing, and then think about what people you most want to reach. Who will be interested in the topic you are writing about?

---

bedfordstmartins.com/easy
Video > Writing for the real world

Checklist

Characteristics of Writing That Makes Something Happen

▶ Public writing has a very clear *purpose*.

▶ It is intended for a specific *audience* and addresses those people directly.

▶ It uses the *genre* most suited to its purpose and audience (a poster, a newsletter, a brochure, a letter to the editor), and it appears in a *medium* (print, online, or both) where the intended audience will see it.

▶ It generally uses straightforward, everyday *language*.

6b Connecting with your audience

Once you have a target audience in mind, you'll need to think carefully about where and how you are likely to find them, how you can get their attention so they will read what you write, and what you can say to get them to achieve your purpose.

If you want to convince your neighbors to pool time, effort, and resources to build a local playground, then you have a head start: you already know something about what they value and about what appeals would get their attention and convince them to join in this project. If you want to create a flash mob to publicize ineffective security at chemical plants near your city, on the other hand, you will need to reach as many people as possible, most of whom you will not know.

Genre and media. Even if you know the members of your audience, you still need to think about the genre and medium that will be most likely to reach them. To get neighbors involved in the playground project previously mentioned, you might decide that a print flyer delivered door-to-door and posted at neighborhood gathering places would work best. For a flash mob, however, an easily forwarded message—text, tweet, or email—will probably work best.

Appropriate language. For all public writing, think carefully about the audience you want to reach—as well as *unintended* audiences your message might reach. Doing so can help you craft writing that will be persuasive without being offensive.

Timing. Making sure your text will appear in a timely manner is crucial to the success of your project. If you want people to plan to attend an event, present your text to them at least two weeks ahead of time. If you are issuing a newsletter or blog, make sure that you create posts or issues often enough to keep people interested (but not so often that readers can't or won't keep up). If you are reporting information based on something that has already happened, make it available as soon as possible so that your audience won't consider your report "old news."

6c Sample writing that makes something happen in the world

Look on the following pages and on the integrated media page at **bedfordstmartins.com/easy** for some examples of the forms public writing can take.

Poster

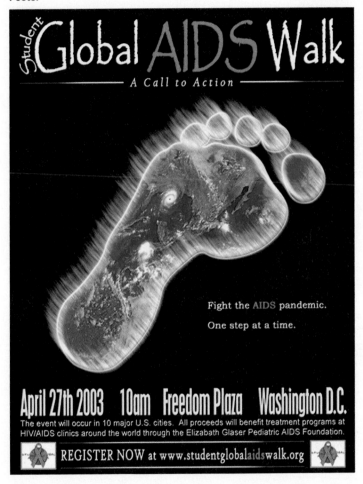

This poster, created by student Amrit Rao, has a very clear purpose: to attract student participants to a walk aimed at raising money in support of AIDS research. To reach as many students as possible, Amrit distributed the poster in both print and digital forms.

Flyer

El Boletin de Trabajadores Temporales

Local 715
ŠEIU

Volume 1: Issue 3

Servicios educativos para sus hijos:

Necesitan mas ayuda sus niños con la tarea? o Quieren hacer algo despues de la escuela para divertirse? Informece sobre los varios programas que ofrece Stanford para niños que viven en la area cercana. Hay programas para niños de todos años desde la escuela primaria hasta la preparatoria. Ofrecen apoyo academico como ayuca con la tarea y tambien actividades Los programes son durante y despues de la escuela. Para aprender como puede inscribir sus hijos en uno de estos programas, llame a Leticia Rodriguez en la oficina de SEIU Local 715 al (650) 723-3680.

Preocupado por dinero?

Esta endeudado con tarjetas de credito? Quiere saber como obtener su reporte de credito? Nosotros podemos ayudarle a crear un presupuesto mensual, mejorar su puntuacion en su reporte de credito, reducir los intereses que paga en tarjetas de credito, y ahorrar dinero. Para citas gratuitas comuniquese con Araceli Rodriguez o Nancy Villareal a la oficina de SEIU, Local 715 al (650) 723-3680.

OPORTUNIDADES PARA TRABAJOS PERMANENTES

Según el acuerdo en el nuevo contracto de la unión, Stanford va a crear 40 posiciones permanentes en los próximos 4 años. Adicionalmente, trabajadores temporales que han trabajado 20 horas por semana por más de cuatro

CUENTO PERSONAL

Student Anna Mumford created and posted copies of this flyer advocating for pay raises for campus workers. Her purpose is to raise awareness of what she views as inequitable salaries and working conditions for temporary workers. Her audience is primarily the temporary workers, but it also includes the students, faculty, and administrators on her campus. Anna was not certain that all of the temporary workers had access to computers, so she chose to produce a print flyer that would be easy to distribute across campus. She wrote in Spanish, the home language of most of the temporary workers, to reach her target audience more effectively.

Newsletter

As with the writers of the poster and flyer, yoga teacher Joelle Hann has a clear purpose in mind for her e-newsletter: to provide information to her audience—students and others interested in her yoga classes and developments in the yoga community. Emailing the newsletter to her subscribers allows Joelle to reach an interested audience quickly and to provide links to more of the content she's discussing, and it also means that she can include photos, illustrations, and color to enhance her document's design impact.

e bedfordstmartins.com/easy
Student Writing > Pitch package, Deborah Jane and Jamie Burke
Student Writing > Reflective blog post, Thanh Nguyen

Sentence Grammar

Writing

Sentence Grammar

Sentence Style

Punctuation/ Mechanics

Language

Multilingual Writers

Research

Documentation

7 Verbs

One famous restaurant in Boston offers to bake, broil, pan-fry, deep-fry, poach, sauté, fricassee, blacken, or scallop any of the fish entrées on its menu. To someone ordering—or cooking—at this restaurant, the important distinctions lie entirely in the **verbs**.

7a Using regular and irregular verb forms

The past **tense** and past **participle** of a **regular verb** are formed by adding -*ed* or -*d* to the **base form**.

BASE FORM	PAST TENSE	PAST PARTICIPLE
love	loved	loved
honor	honored	honored
obey	obeyed	obeyed

An **irregular verb** does not follow the -*ed* or -*d* pattern. If you are unsure about whether a verb is regular or irregular, or what the correct form is, consult the following list or a dictionary. Dictionaries list any irregular forms under the entry for the base form.

Some common irregular verbs

BASE FORM	PAST TENSE	PAST PARTICIPLE
arise	arose	arisen
be	was/were	been
beat	beat	beaten
become	became	become
begin	began	begun
bite	bit	bitten, bit
blow	blew	blown
break	broke	broken
bring	brought	brought
build	built	built
burn	burned, burnt	burned, burnt

BASE FORM	PAST TENSE	PAST PARTICIPLE
burst	burst	burst
buy	bought	bought
catch	caught	caught
choose	chose	chosen
come	came	come
cost	cost	cost
cut	cut	cut
dig	dug	dug
dive	dived, dove	dived
do	did	done
draw	drew	drawn
dream	dreamed, dreamt	dreamed, dreamt
drink	drank	drunk
drive	drove	driven
eat	ate	eaten
fall	fell	fallen
feel	felt	felt
fight	fought	fought
find	found	found
fly	flew	flown
forget	forgot	forgotten, forgot
freeze	froze	frozen
get	got	gotten, got
give	gave	given
go	went	gone
grow	grew	grown
hang (suspend)[1]	hung	hung
have	had	had
hear	heard	heard
hide	hid	hidden

[1]*Hang* meaning "execute by hanging" is regular: *hang, hanged, hanged.*

BASE FORM	PAST TENSE	PAST PARTICIPLE
hit	hit	hit
keep	kept	kept
know	knew	known
lay	laid	laid
lead	led	led
leave	left	left
lend	lent	lent
let	let	let
lie (recline)[2]	lay	lain
lose	lost	lost
make	made	made
mean	meant	meant
meet	met	met
pay	paid	paid
prove	proved	proved, proven
put	put	put
read	read	read
ride	rode	ridden
ring	rang	rung
rise	rose	risen
run	ran	run
say	said	said
see	saw	seen
send	sent	sent
set	set	set
shake	shook	shaken
shoot	shot	shot
show	showed	showed, shown
shrink	shrank	shrunk
sing	sang	sung

[2]*Lie* meaning "tell a falsehood" is regular: *lie, lied, lied.*

BASE FORM	PAST TENSE	PAST PARTICIPLE
sink	sank	sunk
sit	sat	sat
sleep	slept	slept
speak	spoke	spoken
spend	spent	spent
spread	spread	spread
spring	sprang, sprung	sprung
stand	stood	stood
steal	stole	stolen
strike	struck	struck, stricken
swim	swam	swum
swing	swung	swung
take	took	taken
teach	taught	taught
tear	tore	torn
tell	told	told
think	thought	thought
throw	threw	thrown
wake	woke, waked	waked, woken
wear	wore	worn
win	won	won
write	wrote	written

▶ Checklist

Editing the Verbs in Your Writing

- ▶ Check verb endings that cause you trouble. (7a)
- ▶ Double-check forms of *lie* and *lay, sit* and *set, rise* and *raise*. (7b)
- ▶ Refer to action in a literary work in the present tense. (7c)
- ▶ Check that verb tenses in your writing express meaning accurately. (7c and 7d)
- ▶ Use passive voice appropriately. (7e)

7b Using *lie* and *lay*, *sit* and *set*, *rise* and *raise*

These pairs of verbs cause confusion because both verbs in each pair have similar-sounding forms and somewhat related meanings. In each pair, one verb is transitive, meaning that it is followed by a direct **object** (*I lay the package on the counter*). The other is intransitive, meaning that it does not have an object (*He lies on the floor, unable to move*). The best way to avoid confusing these verbs is to memorize their forms and meanings.

BASE FORM	PAST TENSE	PAST PARTICIPLE	PRESENT PARTICIPLE	*-S* FORM
lie (recline)	lay	lain	lying	lies
lay (put)	laid	laid	laying	lays
sit (be seated)	sat	sat	sitting	sits
set (put)	set	set	setting	sets
rise (get up)	rose	risen	rising	rises
raise (lift)	raised	raised	raising	raises

▶ The doctor asked the patient to ~~lay~~ *lie* on his side.

▶ She ~~sat~~ *set* the vase on the table.

▶ He ~~rose~~ *raised* himself to a sitting position.

7c Using verb tenses

Tenses show when the verb's action takes place. The three **simple tenses** are the **present tense**, the **past tense**, and the **future tense**.

PRESENT TENSE	I ask, write
PAST TENSE	I asked, wrote
FUTURE TENSE	I will ask, will write

More complex aspects of time are expressed through **progressive**, **perfect**, and **perfect progressive** forms of the simple tenses.

PRESENT PROGRESSIVE	she is asking, is writing
PAST PROGRESSIVE	she was asking, was writing
FUTURE PROGRESSIVE	she will be asking, will be writing
PRESENT PERFECT	she has asked, has written
PAST PERFECT	she had asked, had written
FUTURE PERFECT	she will have asked, will have written
PRESENT PERFECT PROGRESSIVE	she has been asking, has been writing
PAST PERFECT PROGRESSIVE	she had been asking, had been writing
FUTURE PERFECT PROGRESSIVE	she will have been asking, will have been writing

The simple tenses locate an action only within the three basic time frames of present, past, and future. Progressive forms express continuing actions; perfect forms express completed actions; perfect progressive forms express actions that continue up to some point in the present, past, or future.

Special purposes of the present tense. When writing about action in literary works, use the present tense.

> ▶ Ishmael slowly ~~realized~~ realizes all that ~~was~~ is at stake in the search for the white whale.

General truths or scientific facts should be in the present tense, even when the **predicate** in the main **clause** is in the past tense.

> ▶ Pasteur demonstrated that his boiling process ~~made~~ makes milk safe to drink.

In general, when you are quoting, summarizing, or paraphrasing a work, use the present tense.

▶ Keith Walters ~~wrote~~ *writes* that the "reputed consequences and promised blessings of literacy are legion."

But when using APA (American Psychological Association) style, report the results of your experiments or another researcher's work in the past tense (*wrote, noted*) or the present perfect (*has discovered*). (For more on APA style, see Chapter 42.)

▶ Comer (1995) ~~notes~~ *noted* that protesters who deprive themselves of food are seen not as dysfunctional but rather as "caring, sacrificing, even heroic" (p. 5).

7d Sequencing verb tenses

Careful and accurate use of tenses is important for clear writing. When you use the appropriate tense for each action, readers can follow time changes easily.

▶ By the time he lent her the money, she *had* declared bankruptcy.

The revision makes clear that the bankruptcy occurred before the loan.

7e Using active and passive voice

Voice tells whether a **subject** is acting (*He questions us*) or being acted upon (*He is questioned*). When the subject is acting, the verb is in the **active voice**; when the subject is being acted upon, however, the verb is in the **passive voice**. Most contemporary writers use the active voice as much as possible because it makes their prose stronger and livelier. To shift a sentence from passive to active voice, make the performer of the action the subject of the sentence.

▶ ~~The~~ prizewinning photograph. ~~was taken by my sister.~~
  My sister took the
  ^   ^

Use the passive voice when you want to emphasize the recipient of an action rather than the performer of the action.

▶ Colonel Muammar el-Qaddafi was killed during an uprising in his hometown of Surt.

In scientific and technical writing, use the passive voice to focus attention on what is being studied.

▶ The volunteers' food intake was closely monitored.

7f Using mood appropriately

The **mood** of a verb indicates the writer's attitude toward what he or she is saying. The indicative mood states facts or opinions and asks questions: *I did the right thing.* The imperative mood gives commands and instructions: *Do the right thing.* The subjunctive mood (used primarily in **dependent clauses** beginning with *that* or *if*) expresses wishes and conditions that are contrary to fact: *If I were doing the right thing, I'd know it.*

The present subjunctive uses the base form of the verb with all subjects.

▶ It is important that children be ready for a new sibling.

The past subjunctive is the same as the simple past except for the verb *be*, which uses *were* for all subjects.

▶ He spent money as if he had infinite credit.
▶ If the store were better located, it would attract more customers.

Because the subjunctive creates a rather formal tone, many people today substitute the indicative mood in informal conversation.

INFORMAL

▶ If the store was better located, it would attract more customers.

For academic or professional writing, use the subjunctive in the following contexts:

CLAUSES EXPRESSING A WISH

▶ He wished that his brother ~~was~~ *were* still living nearby.

***THAT* CLAUSES EXPRESSING A REQUEST OR DEMAND**

▶ The plant inspector insists that a supervisor ~~is~~ *be* on site at

all times.

***IF* CLAUSES EXPRESSING A CONDITION THAT DOES NOT EXIST**

▶ If public transportion ~~was~~ *were* widely available, fewer Americans

would commute by car.

One common error is to use *would* in both clauses. Use the subjunctive in the *if* clause and *would* in the other clause.

▶ If I ~~would have~~ *had* played harder, I would have won.

8   Subject-Verb Agreement

In everyday terms, the word *agreement* refers to an accord of some sort: you reach an agreement with your boss about salary; friends agree to go to a movie; the members of a family agree to share household chores. This meaning covers grammatical **agreement** as well. Verbs must agree with their subjects in number (singular or plural) and in **person** (first, second, or third).

To make a verb in the **present tense** agree with a third-person singular subject, add *-s* or *-es* to the **base form**.

▶ A vegetarian diet lowers the risk of heart disease.

To make a verb in the present tense agree with any other subject, use the base form of the verb.

▶ I **miss** my family.

▶ They **live** in another state.

Have and *be* do not follow the *-s* or *-es* pattern with third-person singular subjects. *Have* changes to *has*; *be* has irregular forms in both the present tense and the **past tense**.

▶ War **is** hell.

▶ The soldier **was** brave beyond the call of duty.

8a Checking for words between subject and verb

Make sure the verb agrees with the **simple subject** and not with another **noun** that falls in between.

▶ Many books on the best-seller list ~~has~~ ^{have} little literary value.

The simple subject is *books*, not *list*.

Be careful when you use *as well as, along with, in addition to, together with,* and similar phrases. They do not make a singular subject plural.

▶ A passenger, as well as the driver, ~~were~~ ^{was} injured in the accident.

Though this sentence has a grammatically singular subject, it would be clearer with a compound subject: *The driver and a passenger were injured in the accident.*

8b Checking agreement with compound subjects

Compound **subjects** joined by *and* are generally plural.

▶ A backpack, a canteen, and a rifle ~~was~~ ^{were} issued to each recruit.

When subjects joined by *and* are considered a single unit or refer to the same person or thing, they take a singular verb form.

▸ The lead singer and chief songwriter *wants* to make the new

songs available online.

The singer and songwriter are the same person.

▸ Drinking and driving ~~remain~~ remains a major cause of highway accidents

and fatalities.

In this sentence, *drinking and driving* is considered a single activity, and a singular verb is used.

With subjects joined by *or* or *nor*, the verb agrees with the part closer to the verb.

▸ Neither my roommate nor my neighbors *like* my loud music.

▸ Either the witnesses or the defendant *is* lying.

If you find this sentence awkward, put the plural noun closer to the verb: *Either the defendant or the witnesses <u>are</u> lying.*

▶ Checklist

Editing for Subject-Verb Agreement

▸ Identify the subject that goes with each verb to check for agreement problems. (8a)

▸ Check compound subjects joined by *and, or,* and *nor.* (8b)

▸ Check collective-noun subjects to determine whether they refer to a group as a single unit or as multiple members. (8c)

▸ Check indefinite-pronoun subjects. Most take a plural verb. (8d)

8c Making verbs agree with collective nouns

Collective nouns—such as *family, team, audience, group, jury, crowd, band, class,* and *committee*—and fractions can take either singular or plural verbs, depending on whether they refer to the group as a single unit or to the multiple members of the group. The meaning of a sentence as a whole is your guide.

▶ After deliberating, the jury *reports* its verdict.

The jury acts as a single unit.

▶ The jury still *disagree* on a number of counts.

The members of the jury act as multiple individuals.

▶ Two-thirds of the park ~~have~~ has burned.

Two-thirds refers to the single portion of the park that burned.

▶ One-third of the student body ~~was~~ were commuters.

One-third here refers to the students who commuted as individuals.

Treat phrases starting with *the number of* as singular and with *a number of* as plural.

SINGULAR	The number of applicants for the internship *was* unbelievable.
PLURAL	A number of applicants *were* put on the waiting list.

8d Making verbs agree with indefinite pronouns

Indefinite pronouns do not refer to specific persons or things. Most take singular verb forms.

SOME COMMON INDEFINITE PRONOUNS

another	each	much	one
any	either	neither	other
anybody	everybody	nobody	somebody
anyone	everyone	no one	someone
anything	everything	nothing	something

▶ Of the two jobs, neither holds much appeal.

▶ Each of the plays ~~depict~~ *depicts* a hero undone by a tragic flaw.

Both, *few*, *many*, *others*, and *several* are plural.

▶ Though many apply, few are chosen.

All, *any*, *enough*, *more*, *most*, *none*, and *some* can be singular or plural, depending on the noun they refer to.

▶ All of the cake *was* eaten.

▶ All of the candidates *promise* to improve the schools.

8e Making verbs agree with *who*, *which*, and *that*

When the relative **pronouns** *who*, *which*, and *that* are used as subjects, the verb agrees with the **antecedent** of the pronoun (11b).

▶ Fear is an ingredient that goes into creating stereotypes.

▶ Guilt and fear are ingredients that go into creating stereotypes.

Problems often occur with the words *one of the*. In general, *one of the* takes a plural verb, while *the only one of the* takes a singular verb.

▶ Carla is one of the employees who always ~~works~~ work overtime.

Some employees always work overtime. Carla is among them. Thus *who* refers to *employees*, and the verb is plural.

▶ Ming is the only one of the employees who always ~~work~~ works overtime.

Only one employee, Ming, always works overtime. Thus *one* is the antecedent of *who*, and the verb form must be singular.

8f Making linking verbs agree with subjects

A **linking verb** should agree with its subject, which usually precedes the verb, not with the subject complement, which follows it.

▶ These three key treaties ~~is~~ are the topic of my talk.

The subject is *treaties*, not *topic*.

▶ Nero Wolfe's passion ~~were~~ was orchids.

The subject is *passion*, not *orchids*.

8g Making verbs agree with subjects that end in *-s*

Some words that end in *-s* seem to be plural but are singular in meaning and thus take singular verb forms.

▶ Measles still ~~strike~~ strikes many Americans.

Some nouns of this kind (such as *statistics* and *politics*) may be either singular or plural, depending on context.

| SINGULAR | Statistics *is* a course I really dread. |
| PLURAL | The statistics in that study *are* questionable. |

8h Checking for subjects that follow the verb

In English, verbs usually follow subjects. When this order is reversed, make the verb agree with the subject, not with a noun that happens to precede it.

▶ Beside the barn ~~stands~~ ^{stand} silos filled with grain.

The subject, *silos*, is plural, so the verb must be *stand*.

In sentences beginning with *there is* or *there are* (or *there was* or *there were*), *there* serves only as an introductory word; the subject follows the verb.

▶ There are five basic positions in classical ballet.

8i Making verbs agree with titles and words used as words

Titles and words used as words always take singular verb forms, even if their own forms are plural.

▶ *One Writer's Beginnings* ~~describe~~ ^{describes} Eudora Welty's child-

hood.

▶ *Steroids* ~~are~~ ^{is} a little word that packs a big punch in the

world of sports.

8j Considering spoken forms of *be*

Conventions for subject-verb agreement with *be* in spoken or vernacular varieties of English may differ from those of academic English. For instance, an Appalachian speaker might say "I been down" rather than "I have been down"; a speaker of African

American vernacular might say "He be at work" rather than "He is at work." You may want to quote such spoken phrases in your writing, but for most academic and professional writing, follow the conventions of academic English. (For information on using varieties of English appropriately, see Chapter 31.)

9 Adjectives and Adverbs

Adjectives and **adverbs** can add indispensable differences in meaning to the words they describe or modify. In basketball, for example, there is an important difference between a *flagrant* foul and a *technical* foul, a layup and a *reverse* layup, and an *angry* coach and an *abusively angry* coach. In each instance, the **modifiers** are crucial to accurate communication.

Adjectives modify **nouns** and **pronouns**; they answer the questions *which? how many?* and *what kind?* Adverbs modify **verbs**, adjectives, and other adverbs; they answer the questions *how? when? where?* and *to what extent?* Many adverbs are formed by adding *-ly* to adjectives (*slight, slightly*), but some are formed in other ways (*outdoors*) or have forms of their own (*very*).

9a Using adjectives after linking verbs

When adjectives come after **linking verbs** (such as *is*), they usually describe the **subject**: *I am <u>patient</u>*. Note that in specific sentences, certain verbs may or may not be linking verbs—*appear, become, feel, grow, look, make, prove, seem, smell, sound,* and *taste,* for instance. When a word following one of these verbs modifies the subject, use an adjective; when it modifies the verb, use an adverb.

ADJECTIVE	Fluffy looked angry.
ADVERB	Fluffy looked angrily at the poodle.

🌐 For Multilingual Writers

Using Adjectives with Plural Nouns

In Spanish, Russian, and many other languages, adjectives agree in number with the nouns they modify. In English, adjectives do not change number in this way: *the kittens are cute* (not *cutes*).

Linking verbs suggest a state of being, not an action. In the preceding examples, *looked angry* suggests the state of being angry; *looked angrily* suggests an angry action.

In everyday conversation, you will often hear (and perhaps use) adjectives in place of adverbs. For example, people often say *go quick* instead of *go quickly*. When you write in academic and professional English, however, use adverbs to modify verbs, adjectives, and other adverbs.

▶ You can feel the song's meter if you listen ~~careful.~~ *carefully.*

▶ The audience was ~~real~~ *really* disappointed by the show.

Good, well, bad, **and** *badly.*   The modifiers *good, well, bad*, and *badly* cause problems for many writers because the distinctions between *good* and *well* and between *bad* and *badly* are often not observed in conversation. Problems also arise because *well* can function as either an adjective or an adverb.

▶ I look ~~well~~ *good* in blue.

▶ Now that the fever has broken, I feel ~~good~~ *well* again.

▶ He plays the trumpet ~~good.~~ *well.*

▶ I feel ~~badly~~ *bad* for the Toronto fans.

▶ Their team played ~~bad.~~ *badly.*

9b Using comparatives and superlatives

Most adjectives and adverbs have three forms: positive, **comparative**, and **superlative**. You usually form the comparative and superlative of one- or two-syllable adjectives by adding *-er* and *-est*: *short, shorter, shortest*. With some two-syllable adjectives, longer adjectives, and most adverbs, use *more* and *most* (or *less* and *least*): *scientific, more scientific, most scientific; elegantly, more elegantly, most elegantly*. Some short adjectives and adverbs have irregular comparative and superlative forms: *good, better, best; badly, worse, worst*.

Comparatives versus superlatives. In academic writing, use the comparative to compare two things; use the superlative to compare three or more things.

▶ Rome is a much *older* city than New York.

▶ Damascus is one of the ~~older~~ cities in the world.
^oldest^

Double comparatives and superlatives. Double comparatives and superlatives are those that unnecessarily use both the *-er* or *-est* ending and *more* or *most*. Occasionally, these forms can add a special emphasis, as in the title of Spike Lee's movie *Mo' Better Blues*. In academic and professional writing, however, do not use *more* or *most* before adjectives or adverbs ending in *-er* or *-est*.

▶ Paris is the ~~most~~ loveliest city in the world.

Absolute concepts. Some readers consider modifiers such as *perfect* and *unique* to be absolute concepts; according to this view, a thing is either unique or it isn't, so modified forms of the concept don't make sense. However, many seemingly absolute words have multiple meanings, all of which are widely accepted as correct. For example, *unique* may mean *one of a kind* or *unequaled*, but it can also simply mean *distinctive* or *unusual*.

If you think your readers will object to a construction such as *more perfect* (which appears in the U.S. Constitution), then avoid such uses.

10 Modifier Placement

To be effective, **modifiers** should clearly refer to the words they modify and should be positioned close to those words. Consider this command:

DO NOT USE THE ELEVATORS IN CASE OF FIRE.

Should we avoid the elevators altogether, or only in case there is a fire? Repositioning the modifier *in case of fire* eliminates such confusion—and makes clear that we are to avoid the elevators only if there is a fire: IN CASE OF FIRE, DO NOT USE THE ELEVATORS.

10a Revising misplaced modifiers

Modifiers can cause confusion or ambiguity if they are not close enough to the words they modify or if they seem to modify more than one word in the sentence.

▶ She teaches a seminar this term ~~on voodoo~~ at Skyline College.

The voodoo is not at the college; the seminar is.

▶ ~~Billowing from the window,~~ He saw clouds of smoke, billowing from the window.

People cannot billow from windows.

▶ After he lost the 1962 race, Nixon told reporters that he planned to get out of politics. ~~after he lost the 1962 race.~~

Nixon did not predict that he would lose the race.

Limiting modifiers. Be especially careful with the placement of limiting modifiers such as *almost, even, just, merely,* and *only*. In general, these modifiers should be placed right before or after the words they modify. Putting them in other positions may produce not just ambiguity but a completely different meaning.

AMBIGUOUS	The court *only* hears civil cases on Tuesdays.
CLEAR	The court hears only civil cases on Tuesdays.
CLEAR	The court hears civil cases on Tuesdays only.

Squinting modifiers. If a modifier can refer either to the word before it or to the word after it, it is a squinting modifier. Put the modifier where it clearly relates to only a single word.

SQUINTING	Students who practice writing *often* will benefit.
REVISED	Students who often practice writing will benefit.
REVISED	Students who practice writing will often benefit.

10b Revising disruptive modifiers

Disruptive modifiers interrupt the connections between parts of a sentence, making it hard for readers to follow the progress of the thought.

If they are cooked too long, vegetables will

▶ ~~Vegetables will, if they are cooked too long,~~ lose most
   ^
   of their nutritional value.

Split infinitives. In general, do not place a modifier between the *to* and the **verb** of an **infinitive** (*to often complain*). Doing so makes it hard for readers to recognize that the two go together.

                              surrender
▶ Hitler expected the British to fairly quickly. ~~surrender.~~
                                ^   ^

In some sentences, however, a modifier sounds awkward if it does not split the infinitive. Most language experts consider split infinitives acceptable in such cases. Another option is to reword the sentence to eliminate the infinitive altogether.

| SPLIT | I hope *to* almost *equal* my last year's income. |
| REVISED | I hope that I will earn almost as much as I did last year. |

10c Revising dangling modifiers

Dangling modifiers are words or **phrases** that modify nothing in the rest of a sentence. They often *seem* to modify something that is implied but not actually present in the sentence. Dangling modifiers frequently appear at the beginnings or ends of sentences, as in the following example.

DANGLING   Exploding in rapid bursts of red, white, and blue, the picnickers cheered for the Fourth of July celebration.

REVISED   With fireworks exploding in rapid bursts of red, white, and blue, the picnickers cheered for the Fourth of July celebration.

To revise a dangling modifier, often you need to add a **subject** that the modifier clearly refers to; sometimes you have to turn the modifier into a phrase or a **clause**.

             our family gave
▶ Reluctantly, the hound ~~was given~~ to a neighbor.

In the original sentence, was the dog reluctant, or was someone else who is not mentioned reluctant?

     When he was
▶ As a young boy, his grandmother told stories of her years as a migrant worker.

His grandmother was never a young boy.

     My
▶ ~~Thumbing through the magazine, my~~ eyes automatically noticed
                       as I was thumbing through the magazine.
the perfume ads.

Eyes cannot thumb through a magazine.

11 Pronouns

As words that stand in for **nouns**, **pronouns** carry a lot of weight in our everyday discourse. The following directions show why it's important for a pronoun to refer clearly to a specific noun or pronoun **antecedent**:

▶ **When you see a dirt road on the left side of Winston Lane, follow it for two more miles.**

The word *it* could mean either the dirt road or Winston Lane.

11a Considering a pronoun's role in the sentence

Most speakers of English usually know intuitively when to use *I*, *me*, and *my*. The choices reflect differences in **case**, the form a pronoun takes to indicate its function in a sentence. Pronouns functioning as **subjects** or subject complements are in the subjective case (*I*); those functioning as **objects** are in the objective case (*me*); those functioning as possessives are in the possessive case (*my*).

SUBJECTIVE	OBJECTIVE	POSSESSIVE
I	me	my/mine
we	us	our/ours
you	you	your/yours
he/she/it	him/her/it	his/her/hers/its
they	them	their/theirs
who/whoever	whom/whomever	whose

Problems tend to occur in the following situations.

In subject complements.   Americans routinely use the objective case for subject complements in conversation: *Who's there? It's me.* If the subjective case for a subject complement sounds stilted or awkward (*It's I*), try rewriting the sentence using the pronoun as the subject (*I'm here*).

 bedfordstmartins.com/easy
LearningCurve > Pronouns

▶ Checklist

Editing Pronouns

▶ Make sure all pronouns in subject complements are in the subjective case. (11a)

▶ Check for correct use of *who, whom, whoever,* and *whomever.* (11a)

▶ In compound structures, check that pronouns are in the same case they would be in if used alone. (11a)

▶ When a pronoun follows *than* or *as,* complete the sentence mentally to determine whether the pronoun should be in the subjective or objective case. (11a)

▶ Check that pronouns agree with indefinite-pronoun antecedents, and revise sexist pronouns. (11b)

▶ Identify the antecedent that a pronoun refers to. Supply one if none appears in the sentence. If more than one possible antecedent is present, revise the sentence. (11c)

▶ ~~The~~ **She was the** first person to see Kishore after the awards. ~~was she.~~

Before gerunds. Pronouns before a **gerund** should be in the possessive case.

▶ The doctor argued for ~~him~~ **his** writing a living will.

With *who, whoever, whom,* and *whomever*. Today's speakers tend not to use *whom* and *whomever,* which can create a very formal tone. But for academic and professional writing in which formality is appropriate, remember that problems distinguishing between *who* and *whom* occur most often in two situations: when they begin a question, and when they introduce a **dependent clause** (13c). You can determine whether to use *who* or *whom* at the beginning of a question by answering the question using a personal pronoun. If the answer is in the subjective case, use *who*; if it is in the objective case, use *whom*.

> Whom
> ~~Who~~ did you visit?
> ^

I visited *them*. *Them* is objective, so *whom* is correct.

> Who
> ~~Whom~~ do you think wrote the story?
> ^

I think *she* wrote the story. *She* is subjective, so *who* is correct.

If the pronoun acts as a subject or subject complement in the clause, use *who* or *whoever*. If the pronoun acts as an object in the clause, use *whom* or *whomever*.

> who
> Anyone can hypnotize a person ~~whom~~ wants to be hypnotized.
> ^

The verb of the clause is *wants*, and its subject is *who*.

> Whomever
> ~~Whoever~~ the party suspected of disloyalty was executed.
> ^

Whomever is the object of *suspected* in the clause *whomever the party suspected of disloyalty*.

In compound structures. When a pronoun is part of a compound subject, complement, or object, put it in the same case you would use if the pronoun were alone.

> he
> When ~~him~~ and Zelda were first married, they lived in New York.
> ^

> her
> The boss invited ~~she~~ and her family to dinner.
> ^

> me.
> This morning saw yet another conflict between my sister and ~~I.~~
> ^

In elliptical constructions. Elliptical constructions are sentences in which some words are understood but left out. When an elliptical construction ends in a pronoun, put the pronoun in the case it would be in if the construction were complete.

> His sister has always been more athletic than *he* [is].

In some elliptical constructions, the case of the pronoun depends on the meaning intended.

▶ **Willie likes Lily more than** *she* **[likes Lily].**

She is the subject of the omitted verb *likes*.

▶ **Willie likes Lily more than [he likes]** *her*.

Her is the object of the omitted verb *likes*.

With *we* and *us* before a noun.   If you are unsure about whether to use *we* or *us* before a noun, use whichever pronoun would be correct if the noun were omitted.

    We
▶ ~~Us~~ fans never give up hope.
    ^

Without *fans*, *we* would be the subject.

             us
▶ **The Rangers depend on ~~we~~ fans.**
               ^

Without *fans*, *us* would be the object of the preposition *on*.

11b Making pronouns agree with antecedents

The **antecedent** of a pronoun is the word the pronoun refers to. Pronouns and antecedents are said to agree when they match up in **person**, number, and gender.

SINGULAR   The choirmaster raised his baton.

PLURAL   The boys picked up their music.

Compound antecedents.   Whenever a compound antecedent is joined by *or* or *nor*, the pronoun agrees with the nearer or nearest antecedent. If the parts of the antecedent are of different genders, however, this kind of sentence can be awkward and may need to be revised.

AWKWARD   Neither Annie nor Henry got *his* work done.

REVISED
Annie didn't get *her* work done, and neither did Henry.

When a compound antecedent contains both singular and plural parts, the sentence may sound awkward unless the plural part comes last.

► Neither the blog nor the newspapers would reveal their sources.

Collective-noun antecedents. A collective noun such as *herd*, *team*, or *audience* may refer to a group as a single unit. If so, use a singular pronoun.

► The *committee* presented *its* findings to the board.

When a collective noun refers to the members of the group as individuals, however, use a plural pronoun.

► The *herd* stamped *their* hooves and snorted nervously.

Indefinite-pronoun antecedents. **Indefinite pronouns** do not refer to specific persons or things. Most indefinite pronouns are always singular; a few are always plural. Some can be singular or plural depending on the context.

► One of the ballerinas lost her balance.

► Many in the audience jumped to their feet.

SINGULAR
Some of the furniture was showing *its* age.

PLURAL
Some of the farmers abandoned *their* land.

Sexist pronouns. Pronouns often refer to antecedents that may be either male or female. Writers used to use a masculine pronoun, known as the "generic *he*," to refer to such antecedents: *Everyone should know <u>his</u> legal rights.* However, such wording ignores or even excludes females—and thus should be revised: *Everyone should know <u>his</u> or <u>her</u> legal rights,* for example, or *People should know <u>their</u> legal rights.*

11c Making pronouns refer to clear antecedents

If a pronoun does not refer clearly to a specific antecedent, readers will have trouble making the connection between the two.

Ambiguous antecedents.   In cases where a pronoun could refer to more than one antecedent, revise the sentence to make the meaning clear.

▶ The car went over the bridge just before ~~it~~ _{the bridge} fell into the water.

What fell into the water—the car or the bridge? The revision makes the meaning clear.

▶ Kerry told Ellen, ^{"I} ~~that she~~ should be ready soon."

Reporting Kerry's words directly, in quotation marks, eliminates the ambiguity.

Vague use of *it, this, that,* and *which*.   The words *it, this, that,* and *which* often function as a shortcut for referring to something mentioned earlier. Like other pronouns, each must refer to a specific antecedent.

▶ When the senators realized the bill would be defeated, they tried to postpone the vote but failed. ~~It~~ _{The entire effort} was a fiasco.

▶ Nancy just found out that she won the lottery, ~~which~~ _{and her sudden wealth} explains her resignation.

Indefinite use of *you, it,* and *they*.   In conversation, we frequently use *you, it,* and *they* in an indefinite sense in such expressions as *you never know* and *on television, they said.* In academic and professional writing, however, use *you* only to mean "you, the reader," and *they* or *it* only to refer to a clear antecedent.

▶ Commercials try to make ~~you~~ buy without thinking.
   people

▶ ~~On the~~ Weather Channel, ~~it~~ reported a powerful earthquake
   The

in China.

▶ ~~In France, they~~ allow dogs. ~~in many restaurants.~~
   Many restaurants in France

Implied antecedents. A pronoun may suggest a noun antecedent that is implied but not present in the sentence.

▶ Detention centers routinely blocked efforts by ~~detainees'~~
   detainees.

families and lawyers to locate ~~them.~~

12 Comma Splices and Fused Sentences

A **comma splice** results from placing only a comma between **independent clauses**—groups of words that can stand alone as a sentence. We often see comma splices used to give slogans a catchy
rhythm.

▶ Dogs have owners, cats have staff.   —Bumper Sticker

A related construction is a **fused sentence**, or run-on, which results
from joining two independent clauses with no punctuation or connecting word between them. The bumper sticker as a fused sentence
would be "Dogs have owners cats have staff."

In academic and professional English, using comma splices or
fused sentences will almost always be identified as an error.

12a Separating the clauses into two sentences

The simplest way to revise comma splices or fused sentences is to
separate them into two sentences.

COMMA SPLICE   My mother spends long hours every spring

tilling the soil and moving manure⸝.
     T

ʈhis part of gardening is nauseating.

If the two clauses are very short, making them two sentences may sound abrupt and terse, so some other method of revision is probably preferable.

12b Linking the clauses with a comma and a coordinating conjunction

If the two clauses are closely related and equally important, join them with a comma and a **coordinating conjunction** (*and*, *but*, *or*, *nor*, *for*, *so*, or *yet*).

FUSED   Interest rates fell⸝ people began borrowing
SENTENCE   ^so

more money.

12c Linking the clauses with a semicolon

If the ideas in the two clauses are closely related and you want to give them equal emphasis, link them with a semicolon.

COMMA SPLICE   This photograph is not at all realistic⸝; it uses

dreamlike images to convey its message.

Be careful when you link clauses with a **conjunctive adverb** like *however* or *therefore* or with a **transition** like *in fact*. In such sentences, the two clauses must be separated by a semicolon or by a comma and a coordinating conjunction.

COMMA SPLICE   Many developing countries have high

birthrates⸝; therefore, most of their citizens
are young.

For Multilingual Writers

Judging Sentence Length

In U.S. academic contexts, readers sometimes find a series of short sentences "choppy" and undesirable. If you want to connect two independent clauses into one sentence, join them using one of the methods discussed in this chapter to avoid creating a comma splice or fused sentence. Another useful tip for writing in American English is to avoid writing several very long sentences in a row. If you find this pattern in your writing, try breaking it up by including a shorter sentence occasionally.

12d Rewriting the two clauses as one independent clause

Sometimes you can reduce two spliced or fused independent clauses to a single independent clause.

FUSED SENTENCE	A large part of my mail is advertisements most of the rest is bills.

(shown with handwritten edits: "Most" replacing "A large part", "and" inserted, "of the rest is" struck through)

12e Rewriting one independent clause as a dependent clause

When one independent clause is more important than the other, try converting the less important one to a **dependent clause** by adding an appropriate **subordinating conjunction**.

COMMA SPLICE	*Although* Zora Neale Hurston is regarded as one of America's major novelists, she died in obscurity.

In the revision, the writer emphasizes the second clause and makes the first one into a dependent clause by adding the subordinating conjunction *although*.

FUSED SENTENCE

, which reacted against mass production,

The arts and crafts movement called for hand-

made objects. ~~it reacted against mass production.~~

In the revision, the writer chooses to emphasize the first clause (the one describing what the movement advocated) and make the second clause into a dependent clause.

12f Linking the two clauses with a dash

In informal writing, you can use a dash to join the two clauses, especially when the second clause elaborates on the first clause.

COMMA SPLICE

Exercise trends come and go / this year yoga is hot.

13 Sentence Fragments

Sentence fragments are often used to make writing sound conversational, as in this Facebook status update:

Realizing that there are no edible bagels in this part of Oregon. Sigh.

Fragments—groups of words that are punctuated as sentences but are not sentences—are often seen in intentionally informal writing and in public writing, such as advertising, that aims to attract attention or give a phrase special emphasis. But you should think carefully before using fragments in academic or professional writing, where readers might regard them as errors.

13a Revising phrase fragments

A **phrase** is a group of words that lacks a **subject**, a **verb**, or both. When a phrase is punctuated like a sentence, it becomes a fragment.

To revise a phrase fragment, attach it to an independent clause, or make it a separate sentence.

▶ NBC is broadcasting the debates, ~~With~~ *with* discussions afterward.

With discussions afterward is a prepositional phrase, not a sentence. The editing combines the phrase with an independent clause.

▶ The town's growth is controlled by zoning laws, ~~A~~ *a* strict set of regulations for builders and corporations.

A strict set of regulations for builders and corporations is a phrase renaming *zoning laws*. The editing attaches the fragment to the sentence containing that noun.

▶ Kamika stayed out of school for three months after Linda was born. *She did so to* ~~To~~ recuperate and to take care of her baby.

The revision—adding a subject (*she*) and a verb (*did*)—turns the fragment into a separate sentence.

Fragments beginning with transitions. If you introduce an example or explanation with a transitional word or phrase like *also*, *for example*, *such as*, or *that*, be certain you write a sentence, not a fragment.

▶ Joan Didion has written on many subjects, ~~Such~~ *such* as the Hoover Dam and migraine headaches.

The second word group is a phrase, not a sentence. The editing combines it with an independent clause.

13b Revising compound-predicate fragments

A fragment occurs when one part of a compound **predicate** lacks a subject but is punctuated as a separate sentence. Such a fragment usually begins with *and*, *but*, or *or*. You can revise it by attaching it to the independent clause that contains the rest of the predicate.

▶ They sold their house. ~~And~~ ^and^ moved into an apartment.

13c Revising clause fragments

A **dependent clause** contains both a subject and a verb, but it cannot stand alone as a sentence; it depends on an independent clause to complete its meaning. A dependent clause usually begins with a **subordinating conjunction**, such as *after*, *because*, *before*, *if*, *since*, *that*, *though*, *unless*, *until*, *when*, *where*, *while*, *who*, or *which*. You can usually combine dependent-clause fragments with a nearby independent clause.

▶ When I decided to switch to part-time work ^,^ I gave up a lot of

   my earning potential.

If you cannot smoothly attach a clause to a nearby independent clause, try deleting the opening subordinating word and turning the dependent clause into a sentence.

▶ Most injuries in automobile accidents occur in two ways.
   ^An^
   ~~When an~~ occupant either is hurt by something inside the car

   or is thrown from the car.

Sentence Style

Writing

Sentence Grammar

Sentence Style

Punctuation/ Mechanics

Language

Multilingual Writers

Research

Documentation

14 Consistency and Completeness

If you listen carefully to the conversations around you, you will hear inconsistent and incomplete structures all the time. For instance, during an interview with journalist Bill Moyers, Jon Stewart discussed the supposed objectivity of news reporting:

> But news has never been objective. It's always . . . what does every newscast start with? "Our top stories tonight." That's a list. That's a subjective . . . some editor made a decision: "Here's our top stories. Number one: There's a fire in the Bronx."

Because Stewart is talking casually, some of his sentences begin one way but then move in another direction. The mixed structures pose no problem for the viewer, but sentences such as these can be confusing in writing.

14a Revising faulty sentence structure

Beginning a sentence with one grammatical pattern and then switching to another one confuses readers.

> MIXED   The fact that I get up at 5:00 AM, a wake-up time that explains why I'm always tired in the evening.

This sentence starts out with a **subject** (*The fact*) followed by a **dependent clause** (*that I get up at 5:00 AM*). The sentence needs a **predicate** to complete the **independent clause**, but instead it moves to another **phrase** followed by a dependent clause (*a wake-up time that explains why I'm always tired in the evening*), and a **fragment** results.

> REVISED   The fact that I get up at 5:00 AM explains why I'm always tired in the evening.

Deleting *a wake-up time that* changes the rest of the sentence into a predicate.

> REVISED   I get up at 5:00 AM, a wake-up time that explains why I'm always tired in the evening.

Deleting *The fact that* turns the beginning of the sentence into an independent clause.

14b Matching subjects and predicates

Another kind of mixed structure, called faulty predication, occurs when a subject and predicate do not fit together grammatically or simply do not make sense together.

▶ A characteristic that I admire is ~~a person who is generous.~~ *generosity.*

   A person is not a characteristic.

▶ The rules of the corporation ~~expect~~ *require that* employees ~~to~~ be on time.

   Rules cannot expect anything.

Is when, is where, the reason . . . is because. Although you will often hear these expressions in everyday use, such constructions are inappropriate in academic or professional writing.

▶ A stereotype is ~~when someone characterizes~~ *an unfair characterization of* a group. ~~unfairly.~~

▶ Spamming is ~~where companies send~~ *the practice of sending* electronic junk mail.

▶ ~~The reason~~ I like to play soccer ~~is~~ because it provides aerobic exercise.

14c Using consistent compound structures

Sometimes writers omit certain words in compound structures. If the omitted word does not fit grammatically with other parts of the compound, the omission can be inappropriate.

▶ His skills are weak, and his performance only *is* average.

   The omitted verb *is* does not match the verb in the other part of the compound (*are*), so the writer needs to include it.

14d Making complete comparisons

When you compare two or more things, the comparison must be complete and clear.

▶ I was often embarrassed because my parents were so
   ~~from my friends' parents.~~
   different/
         ^
Adding *from my friends' parents* completes the comparison.

UNCLEAR	Aneil always felt more affection for his brother than his sister.
CLEAR	Aneil always felt more affection for his brother than his sister did.
CLEAR	Aneil always felt more affection for his brother than he did for his sister.

15 Coordination and Subordination

You may notice a difference between your spoken and your written language. In speech, people tend to use *and* and *so* as all-purpose connectors.

He enjoys psychology, and he has to study hard.

The meaning of this sentence may be perfectly clear in speech, which provides clues with voice, facial expressions, and gestures. But in writing, the sentence could have more than one meaning.

Although he enjoys psychology, he has to study hard.

He enjoys psychology although he has to study hard.

The first sentence links two ideas with a **coordinating conjunction**, *and*; the other two sentences link ideas with a **subordinating conjunction**, *although*. A coordinating conjunction gives the ideas equal emphasis, and a subordinating conjunction emphasizes one idea more than another.

15a Relating equal ideas

When you want to give equal emphasis to different ideas in a sentence, link them with a coordinating conjunction (*and*, *but*, *for*, *nor*, *or*, *so*, *yet*) or a semicolon.

▶ They acquired horses, **and** their ancient nomadic spirit was suddenly free of the ground.

▶ There is perfect freedom in the mountains, **but** it belongs to the eagle and the elk, the badger and the bear.
    —N. Scott Momaday, *The Way to Rainy Mountain*

Coordination can help make explicit the relationship between two separate ideas.

▶ My son watches *The Simpsons* religiously/; ~~Forced~~ *forced* to choose, he

would probably take Homer Simpson over his sister.

Connecting these two sentences with a semicolon strengthens the connection between two closely related ideas.

When you connect ideas in a sentence, make sure that the relationship between the ideas is clear.

▶ Surfing the Internet is a common way to spend leisure time,
~~and~~ *but* it should not replace human contact.

What does being a common form of leisure have to do with replacing human contact? Changing *and* to *but* better relates the two ideas.

15b Distinguishing main ideas

Subordination allows you to distinguish major points from minor points or to bring supporting details into a sentence. If, for instance, you put your main idea in an **independent clause**, you might then put any less significant ideas in **dependent clauses**, **phrases**, or even single words. The following sentence highlights the subordinated point:

▶ **Mrs. Viola Cullinan was a plump woman who lived in a three-bedroom house somewhere behind the post office.**
—Maya Angelou, "My Name Is Margaret"

The dependent clause adds important information about Mrs. Cullinan, but it is subordinate to the independent clause.

Notice that the choice of what to subordinate rests with the writer and depends on the intended meaning. Angelou might have given the same basic information differently:

▶ **Mrs. Viola Cullinan, a plump woman, lived in a three-bedroom house somewhere behind the post office.**

Subordinating the information about Mrs. Cullinan's size to that about her house would suggest a slightly different meaning, of course. As a writer, you must think carefully about what you want to emphasize and must subordinate information accordingly.

Subordination also establishes logical relationships among different ideas. These relationships are often specified by subordinating conjunctions.

SOME COMMON SUBORDINATING CONJUNCTIONS

after	if	though
although	in order that	unless
as	once	until
as if	since	when
because	so that	where
before	than	while
even though	that	

The following sentence highlights the subordinate clause and italicizes the subordinating word:

▶ **She usually rested her smile until late afternoon *when* her women friends dropped in and Miss Glory, the cook, served them cold drinks on the closed-in porch.**
—Maya Angelou, "My Name Is Margaret"

Using too many coordinate structures can be monotonous and can make it hard for readers to recognize the most important ideas. Subordinating lesser ideas can help highlight the main ideas.

▶ Many people check email in the evening, and so they turn on

the computer. ~~They~~ *Though they* may intend to respond only to urgent

messages, ~~and~~ a friend sends a link to a blog post, *which* and they decide

to read ~~it~~ for just a short while~~.~~/ *Eventually,* ~~and~~ they get engrossed in

Facebook, and they end up spending the whole evening in front

of the screen.

Determining what to subordinate

▶ *Although our* ~~Our~~ new boss can be difficult, ~~although~~ she has revived and

maybe even saved the division.

The editing puts the more important information—that the new boss has saved part of the company—in an independent clause and subordinates the rest.

Avoiding excessive subordination

When too many subordinate clauses are strung together, readers may have trouble keeping track of the main idea expressed in the independent clause.

TOO MUCH SUBORDINATION

▶ Philip II sent the Spanish Armada to conquer England, which was ruled by Elizabeth, who had executed Mary because she was plotting to overthrow Elizabeth, who was a Protestant, whereas Mary and Philip were Roman Catholics.

REVISED

▶ Philip II sent the Spanish Armada to conquer England, which was ruled by Elizabeth, a Protestant. She had executed Mary, a Roman Catholic like Philip, because Mary was plotting to overthrow her.

Putting the facts about Elizabeth executing Mary into an independent clause makes key information easier to recognize.

16 Conciseness

If you have a Twitter account, you know a lot about being concise—that is, about getting messages across in no more than 140 characters. Recently, *New York Times* editor Bill Keller tweeted, "Twitter makes you stupid. Discuss." That little comment drew a large number of responses, including one from his wife that read, "I don't know if Twitter makes you stupid, but it's making you late for dinner. Come home."

No matter how you feel about the effects of Twitter on the brain (or stomach!), you can make any writing more effective by choosing words that convey exactly what you mean to say.

16a Eliminating redundant words

Sometimes writers add words for emphasis, saying that something is large *in size* or red *in color* or that two ingredients should be combined *together*. The italicized words are redundant (unnecessary for meaning), as are the deleted words in the following examples.

▶ ~~Compulsory~~ ^A^ attendance at assemblies is required.

▶ The auction featured ~~contemporary~~ "antiques" made recently.

▶ Many different forms of hazing occur, such as physical ~~abuse~~ and mental abuse.

16b Eliminating empty words

Words that contribute little or no meaning to a sentence include vague **nouns** like *area*, *kind*, *situation*, and *thing* as well as vague **modifiers** like *definitely*, *major*, *really*, and *very*. Delete such words, or find a more specific way to say what you mean.

▶ ~~The~~ housing ~~situation~~ can ~~have a really significant impact~~ *strongly influence* ~~on the social aspect of~~ a student's life. *social*

16c Replacing wordy phrases

Many common **phrases** can be reduced to a word or two with no loss in meaning.

WORDY	CONCISE
at all times	always
at that point in time	then
at the present time	now/today
due to the fact that	because
for the purpose of	for
in order to	to
in spite of the fact that	although
in the event that	if

16d Simplifying sentence structure

Using the simplest grammatical structures can tighten and strengthen your sentences considerably.

▶ Hurricane Katrina, ~~which was certainly~~ one of the most powerful storms ever to hit the Gulf Coast, caused damage *widespread* ~~to a very wide area.~~

Strong verbs. *Be* **verbs** (*is, are, was, were, been*) often result in wordiness.

> ▸ A high-fat, high-cholesterol diet ~~is bad for~~ your heart.
> _harms_

Expletives. Sometimes expletive constructions such as *there is*, *there are*, and *it is* introduce a topic effectively; often, however, your writing will be better without them.

> ▸ ~~There are~~ many people ~~who~~ fear success because they
> _M_
>
> believe they do not deserve it.

> ▸ ~~It is necessary for~~ presidential candidates to perform well
> _P_   _need_
>
> on television.

Active voice. Some writing situations call for the passive **voice**, but it is always wordier than the active—and often makes for dull or even difficult reading (see 7e).

> ▸ ~~In Gower's research, it was~~ found that pythons often dwell
> _Gower_
>
> in trees.

17 Parallelism

If you look and listen, you will see parallel grammatical structures in everyday use. Bumper stickers often use parallelism to make their messages memorable (*Minds are like parachutes; both work best when open*), as do song lyrics and jump-rope rhymes. In addition to creating pleasing rhythmic effects, parallelism helps clarify meaning.

17a Making items in a series or list parallel

All items in a series should be in parallel form—all **nouns**, all **verbs**, all prepositional **phrases**, and so on. Parallelism makes a series both graceful and easy to follow.

▶ In the eighteenth century, armed forces could fight in open fields and on the high seas. Today, they can clash on the ground anywhere, on the sea, under the sea, and in the air.

—Donald Snow and Eugene Brown, *The Contours of Power*

The parallel structure of the phrases (highlighted here), and of the sentences themselves, highlights the contrast between the eighteenth century and today.

▶ The quarter horse skipped, pranced, and ~~was sashaying~~ *sashayed* onto the track.

▶ The children ran down the hill, skipped over the lawn, and *jumped* into the swimming pool.

▶ The duties of the job include baby-sitting, housecleaning, and *preparing* ~~preparation of~~ meals.

Items that are in a list, in a formal outline, and in headings should be parallel.

▶ Kitchen rules: (1) Coffee to be made only by library staff.

(2) Coffee service to be closed at 4:00 AM. (3) Doughnuts to be kept in cabinet. (4) ~~No faculty members should handle~~ *Coffee materials not to be handled* ~~coffee materials.~~ *by faculty.*

17b Making paired ideas parallel

Parallel structures can help you pair two ideas effectively. The more nearly parallel the two structures are, the stronger the connection between the ideas will be.

▶ I type in one place, but I write all over the house.

—Toni Morrison

▶ Writers are often more interesting on the page than they
      the flesh.
are in ~~person.~~
     ^

In these examples, the parallel structures help readers see an important contrast between two ideas or acts.

With conjunctions. When you link ideas with *and, but, or, nor, for, so,* or *yet,* try to make the ideas parallel in structure. Always use the same structure after both parts of a **correlative conjunction**: *either . . . or, both . . . and, neither . . . nor, not . . . but, not only . . . but also, just as . . . so,* and *whether . . . or.*

        who is
▶ Consult a friend in your class or who is good at math.
         ^

▶ The wise politician promises the possible and ~~should~~
   accepts
~~accept~~ the inevitable.
  ^

                             live in
▶ I wanted not only to go away to school but also to New
                                           ^

England.

17c Using words necessary for clarity

In addition to making parallel elements grammatically similar, be sure to include any words—**prepositions**, articles, verb forms, and so on—that are necessary for clarity.

► We'll move to a city in the Southwest or *in* Mexico.

To a city in Mexico or to Mexico in general? The editing clarifies this.

18 Shifts

A shift in writing is an abrupt change that results in inconsistency. Sometimes a writer or speaker will shift deliberately, as Geneva Smitherman does in this passage from *Word from the Mother*:

> There are days when I optimistically predict that Hip Hop will survive—and thrive. . . . In the larger realm of Hip Hop culture, there is cause for optimism as we witness Hip Hop younguns tryna git they political activist game togetha.

Smitherman's shift from formal academic language to vernacular speech calls out for and holds our attention. Although writers make shifts for good rhetorical reasons, unintentional shifts can be confusing to readers.

18a Revising shifts in tense

If **verbs** in a passage refer to actions occurring at different times, they may require different **tenses**. Be careful, however, not to change tenses without a good reason.

► A few countries produce almost all of the world's illegal drugs,

but addiction ~~affected~~ *affects* many countries.

18b Revising shifts in voice

Do not shift between the **active voice** (she *sold* it) and the **passive voice** (it *was sold*) without a reason. Sometimes a shift in voice is justified, but often it only confuses readers.

e✓ bedfordstmartins.com/easy
Exercise > Verb tense shifts
LearningCurve > Active and passive voice

> Two youths approached ~~me, and I was~~ asked for my wallet. *(me inserted above)*

The original sentence shifts from active to passive voice, so it is unclear who asked for the wallet.

18c Revising shifts in point of view

Unnecessary shifts in point of view between first person (*I* or *we*), second person (*you*), and third person (*he, she, it, one,* or *they*), or between singular and plural subjects, can be very confusing to readers.

> ~~One~~ can do well on this job if you budget your time. *(You inserted above)*

Is the writer making a general statement or giving advice to someone? Revising the shift eliminates this confusion.

18d Revising shifts between direct and indirect discourse

When you quote someone's exact words, you are using direct discourse: *She said, "I'm an editor."* When you report what someone says without repeating the exact words, you are using indirect discourse: *She said she was an editor.* Shifting between direct and indirect discourse in the same sentence can cause problems, especially with questions.

> Bob asked what could ~~he~~ do to help~~?~~. *(he inserted above)*

The editing eliminates an awkward shift by reporting Bob's question indirectly. It could also be edited to quote Bob directly: *Bob asked, "What can I do to help?"*

18e Revising shifts in tone and diction

Watch out for shifts in your tone (overall attitude toward a topic or audience) and word choice. These shifts can confuse readers and leave them wondering what your real attitude is.

INCONSISTENT TONE

The question of child care forces a society to make profound decisions about its values. If some conservatives had their way, June Cleaver would still be in the kitchen baking cookies for Wally and the Beaver and waiting for Ward to bring home the bacon, but with only one income, the Cleavers would be lucky to afford hot dogs.

REVISED

The question of child care forces a society to make profound decisions about its values. Some conservatives believe that women with young children should not work outside the home, but many mothers are forced to do so for financial reasons.

The shift in diction from formal to informal makes readers wonder whether the writer is presenting a serious analysis or a humorous satire. As revised, the passage makes more sense because the words are consistently formal.

Punctuation/
Mechanics

Writing

Sentence
Grammar

Sentence
Style

**Punctuation/
Mechanics**

Language

Multilingual
Writers

Research

Documentation

19 Commas

It's hard to go through a day without encountering directions of some kind, and commas often play a crucial role in how you interpret instructions. See how important the comma is in the following directions for making hot cereal:

> Add Cream of Wheat slowly, stirring constantly.

That sentence tells the cook to *add the cereal slowly*. If the comma came before the word *slowly*, however, the cook might add all of the cereal at once and *stir slowly*.

19a Setting off introductory elements

In general, use a comma after any word, **phrase**, or **clause** that precedes the **subject** of the sentence.

- ▶ However, health care costs keep rising.

- ▶ Wearing new running shoes, Julie prepared for the race.

- ▶ To win the game, players need both skill and luck.

- ▶ Fingers on the keyboard, Maya waited for the test to begin.

- ▶ While her friends watched, Lila practiced her gymnastics routine.

Some writers omit the comma after a short introductory element that does not seem to require a pause after it. However, you will never be wrong if you use a comma.

19b Separating clauses in compound sentences

A comma usually precedes a **coordinating conjunction** (*and, but, or, nor, for, so,* or *yet*) that joins two **independent clauses** in a compound sentence.

▶ The climbers must reach the summit today‸ or they will

have to turn back.

With very short clauses, you can sometimes omit the comma (*She saw her chance and she took it*). But always use the comma if there is a chance the sentence will be misread without it.

▶ I opened the junk drawer‸ and the cabinet door jammed.

▶ Checklist

Editing for Commas

Research for this book shows that five of the most common errors in college writing involve commas.

▶ Check that a comma separates an introductory word, phrase, or clause from the main part of the sentence. (19a)

▶ Look at every sentence that contains a coordinating conjunction (*and, but, for, nor, or, so,* or *yet*). If the groups of words before and after this conjunction both function as complete sentences, use a comma before the conjunction. (19b)

▶ Look at each adjective clause beginning with *which, who, whom, whose, when,* or *where* and at each phrase and appositive. If the rest of the sentence would have a different meaning without the clause, phrase, or appositive, do not set off the element with commas. (19c)

▶ Make sure that adjective clauses beginning with *that* are not set off with commas. Do not use commas between subjects and verbs, verbs and objects or complements, or prepositions and objects; to separate parts of compound constructions other than compound sentences; to set off restrictive clauses; or before the first or after the last item in a series. (19i)

▶ Do not use a comma alone to separate sentences. (See Chapter 12.)

Use a semicolon rather than a comma when the clauses are long and complex or contain their own commas.

▶ When these early migrations took place, the ice was still confined to the lands in the far north; but eight hundred thousand years ago, when man was already established in the temperate latitudes, the ice moved southward until it covered large parts of Europe and Asia.

—Robert Jastrow, *Until the Sun Dies*

19c Setting off nonrestrictive elements

Nonrestrictive elements are word groups that do not limit, or restrict, the meaning of the noun or pronoun they modify. Setting nonrestrictive elements off with commas shows your readers that the information is not essential to the meaning of the sentence. **Restrictive elements**, on the other hand, *are* essential to meaning and should *not* be set off with commas. The same sentence may mean different things with and without the commas:

▶ The bus drivers rejecting the management offer remained on strike.

▶ The bus drivers, rejecting the management offer, remained on strike.

The first sentence says that only *some* bus drivers, the ones rejecting the offer, remained on strike. The second says that *all* the drivers did.

Since the decision to include or omit commas influences how readers will interpret your sentence, you should think especially carefully about what you mean and use commas (or omit them) accordingly.

| RESTRICTIVE | Drivers *who have been convicted of drunken driving* should lose their licenses. |

In the preceding sentence, the clause *who have been convicted of drunken driving* is essential because it explains that only drivers who have been convicted of drunken driving should lose their licenses. Therefore, it is *not* set off with commas.

NONRESTRICTIVE	The two drivers involved in the accident, *who have been convicted of drunken driving*, should lose their licenses.

In this sentence, however, the clause *who have been convicted of drunken driving* is not essential to the meaning because it does not limit what it modifies, *The two drivers involved in the accident*, but merely provides additional information about these drivers. Therefore, the clause *is* set off with commas.

To decide whether an element is restrictive or nonrestrictive, mentally delete the element, and see if the deletion changes the meaning of the rest of the sentence. If the deletion *does* change the meaning, you should probably not set the element off with commas. If it *does not* change the meaning, the element probably requires commas.

Adjective and adverb clauses. An adjective clause that begins with *that* is always restrictive; do not set it off with commas. An adjective clause beginning with *which* may be either restrictive or nonrestrictive; however, some writers prefer to use *which* only for nonrestrictive clauses, which they set off with commas.

RESTRICTIVE CLAUSES

▶ The claim *that men like seriously to battle one another to some sort of finish* is a myth.

> —John McMurtry, "Kill 'Em! Crush 'Em! Eat 'Em Raw!"

The adjective clause is necessary to the meaning because it explains which claim is a myth; therefore, the clause is not set off with commas.

▶ The man / who rescued Jana's puppy / won her eternal gratitude.

The adjective clause is necessary to the meaning because it identifies the man, so it takes no commas.

NONRESTRICTIVE CLAUSES

▶ I borrowed books from the rental library of Shakespeare and Company, *which was the library and bookstore of Sylvia Beach at 12 rue de l'Odeon.* —Ernest Hemingway, *A Moveable Feast*

The adjective clause is not necessary to the meaning of the independent clause and therefore is set off with a comma.

An adverb clause that follows a main clause does *not* usually require a comma to set it off unless the adverb clause expresses contrast.

▶ The park became a popular gathering place, although nearby

residents complained about the noise.

The adverb clause expresses contrast; therefore, it is set off with a comma.

Phrases. Participial **phrases** may be restrictive or nonrestrictive. Prepositional phrases are usually restrictive, but sometimes they are not essential to the meaning of a sentence and thus are set off with commas.

NONRESTRICTIVE PHRASES

▶ The singer's children, refusing to be ignored, interrupted the

recital.

Using commas around the participial phrase makes it nonrestrictive, telling us that all of the singer's children interrupted.

Appositives. An **appositive** is a **noun** or noun phrase that re-names a nearby noun. When an appositive is not essential to iden-tify what it renames, it is set off with commas.

NONRESTRICTIVE APPOSITIVES

▶ Savion Glover, the award-winning dancer, taps like poetry in

motion.

Savion Glover's name identifies him; the appositive *the award-winning dancer* provides extra information.

RESTRICTIVE APPOSITIVES

▶ Mozart's opera/ *The Marriage of Figaro*/ was considered

revolutionary.

The phrase is restrictive because Mozart wrote more than one opera. Therefore, it is *not* set off with commas.

19d   Separating items in a series

▶ He has plundered our seas, ravaged our coasts, burnt our towns, and destroyed the lives of our people.

—Declaration of Independence

You may see a series with no comma after the next-to-last item, particularly in newspaper writing. Occasionally, however, omitting the comma can cause confusion.

▶ All the cafeteria's vegetables—broccoli, green beans, peas

and carrots—were cooked to a gray mush.

> Without the comma after *peas*, you wouldn't know if there were three choices (the third being a *mixture* of peas and carrots) or four.

Coordinate adjectives—two or more adjectives that relate equally to the noun they modify—should be separated by commas.

▶ The long, twisting, muddy road led to a shack in the woods.

In a sentence like *The cracked bathroom mirror reflected his face*, however, *cracked* and *bathroom* are not coordinate because *bathroom mirror* is the equivalent of a single word, which is modified by *cracked*. Hence they are *not* separated by commas.

You can usually determine whether adjectives are coordinate by inserting *and* between them. If the sentence makes sense with the *and* added, the adjectives are coordinate and should be separated by commas.

▶ They are sincere *and* talented *and* inquisitive researchers.

> The sentence makes sense with the *and*s, so the adjectives should be separated by commas: *They are sincere, talented, inquisitive researchers.*

▶ Byron carried an elegant ~~and~~ pocket watch.

> The sentence does not make sense with *and*, so the adjectives *elegant* and *pocket* should not be separated by commas: *Byron carried an elegant pocket watch.*

19e Setting off parenthetical and transitional expressions

Parenthetical expressions add comments or information. Because they often interrupt the flow of a sentence, they are usually set off with commas.

▶ Some studies have shown that chocolate, of all things, helps

prevent tooth decay.

Transitions (such as *as a result*), **conjunctive adverbs** (such as *however*), and other expressions used to connect parts of sentences are usually set off with commas.

▶ Ozone is a by-product of dry cleaning, for example.

19f Setting off contrasting elements, interjections, direct address, and tag questions

▶ I asked you, *not your brother*, to sweep the porch.
▶ *Holy cow*, did you see that?
▶ Remember, *sir*, that you are under oath.
▶ The governor did not veto the bill, *did she*?

19g Setting off parts of dates and addresses

Dates. Use a comma between the day of the week and the month, between the day of the month and the year, and between the year and the rest of the sentence, if any.

▶ On Wednesday, November 26, 2008, gunmen arrived in Mumbai

by boat.

Do not use commas with dates in inverted order or with dates consisting of only the month and the year.

▶ She dated the letter 5 August 2013.
▶ Thousands of Germans swarmed over the wall in November 1989.

Addresses and place names. Use a comma after each part of an address or a place name, including the state if there is no ZIP code. Do not precede a ZIP code with a comma.

▶ Forward my mail to the Department of English, The Ohio State

University, Columbus, Ohio 43210.

▶ Portland, Oregon, is much larger than Portland, Maine.

19h Setting off quotations

Commas set off a quotation from words used to introduce or identify the source of the quotation. A comma following a quotation goes *inside* the closing quotation mark.

▶ A German proverb warns, "Go to law for a sheep, and lose

your cow."

▶ "All I know about grammar," said Joan Didion, "is its infinite

power."

Do not use a comma following a question mark or an exclamation point.

▶ "Out, damned spot!/" cries Lady Macbeth.

Do not use a comma to introduce a quotation with *that* or when you do not quote a speaker's exact words.

▶ The writer of Ecclesiastes concludes that/ "all is vanity."

▶ Patrick Henry declared/ that he wanted either liberty or death.

19i Avoiding unnecessary commas

Excessive use of commas can spoil an otherwise fine sentence.

Around restrictive elements. Do not use commas to set off restrictive elements—elements that limit, or define, the meaning of the words they modify or refer to (19c).

▶ I don't let my children watch movies/ that are violent.

▶ The actor/ Joaquin Phoenix/ might win the award.

Between subjects and verbs, verbs and objects or comple-ments, and prepositions and objects. Do not use a comma between a subject and its **verb**, a verb and its **object** or complement, or a **preposition** and its object.

▶ Watching movies late at night/ allows me to relax.

▶ Parents must decide/ what time their children should go

to bed.

▶ The winner of/ the prize for community service stepped

forward.

In compound constructions. In compound constructions other than compound sentences, do not use a comma before or after a coordinating conjunction that joins the two parts (19b).

▶ Improved health care/ and more free trade were two of the

administration's goals.

The *and* joins parts of a compound subject, which should not be separated by a comma.

▶ Mark Twain trained as a printer/ and worked as a steamboat

pilot.

The *and* joins parts of a compound predicate, which should not be separated by a comma.

In a series. Do not use a comma before the first or after the last item in a series.

▶ The auction included/ furniture, paintings, and china.

▶ The swimmer took slow, elegant, powerful/ strokes.

20 Semicolons

The following public-service announcement, posted in New York City subway cars, reminded commuters what to do with a used newspaper at the end of the ride:

> Please put it in a trash can; that's good news for everyone.

The semicolon in the subway announcement separates two clauses that could have been written as separate sentences. Semicolons, which create a pause stronger than that of a comma but not as strong as the full pause of a period, show close connections between related ideas.

20a Linking independent clauses

Although a comma and a **coordinating conjunction** often join **independent clauses** (19b), semicolons provide writers with subtler ways of signaling closely related clauses. The clause following a semicolon often restates an idea expressed in the first clause; it sometimes expands on or presents a contrast to the first.

▶ **Immigration acts were passed; newcomers had to prove, besides moral correctness and financial solvency, their ability to read.**
> —Mary Gordon, "More Than Just a Shrine"

The semicolon gives the sentence an abrupt rhythm that suits the topic: laws that imposed strict requirements.

If two independent clauses joined by a coordinating conjunction contain commas, you may use a semicolon instead of a comma before the conjunction to make the sentence easier to read.

▶ **Every year, whether the Republican or the Democratic party is in office, more and more power drains away from the individual to feed vast reservoirs in far-off places; and we have less and less say about the shape of events which shape our future.**
> —William F. Buckley Jr., "Why Don't We Complain?"

A semicolon should link independent clauses joined by a **conjunctive adverb** such as *however* or *therefore* or a **transition** such as *as a result* or *for example*.

▶ The circus comes as close to being the world in microcosm as anything I know; in a way, it puts all the rest of show business in the shade. —E. B. White, "The Ring of Time"

20b Separating items in a series containing other punctuation

Ordinarily, commas separate items in a series (19d). But when the items themselves contain commas or other punctuation, semicolons make the sentence clearer.

▶ Anthropology encompasses archaeology, the study of ancient

civilizations through artifacts/; linguistics, the study of

the structure and development of language/; and cultural

anthropology, the study of language, customs, and behavior.

20c Avoiding misused semicolons

Use a comma, not a semicolon, to separate an independent clause from a **dependent clause** or **phrase**.

▶ The police found fingerprints/, which they used to identify the thief.

▶ The new system would encourage students to register for courses

online/, thus streamlining registration.

Use a colon, not a semicolon, to introduce a series or list.

▶ The reunion tour includes the following bands/: Urban Waste,

Murphy's Law, Rapid Deployment, and Ism.

21 End Punctuation

Periods, question marks, and exclamation points often appear in advertising to create special effects:

You have a choice to make.
Where can you turn for advice?
Ask our experts today!

End punctuation tells us how to read each sentence—as a matter-of-fact statement, a question for the reader, or an enthusiastic exclamation.

21a Using periods

Use a period to close sentences that make statements or give mild commands.

▶ **All books are either dreams or swords.**   —Amy Lowell
▶ **Don't use a fancy word if a simpler word will do.**
                    —George Orwell, "Politics and the English Language"

A period also closes indirect questions, which report rather than ask questions.

▶ **I asked how old the child was.**

In American English, periods are used with most abbreviations. However, more and more abbreviations are now appearing without periods.

Mr.	MD	BCE *or* B.C.E.
Ms.	PhD	AD *or* A.D.
Sen.	Jr.	PM *or* p.m.

Some abbreviations rarely if ever appear with periods. These include the postal abbreviations of state names, such as *FL* and *TN*, and most groups of initials (*GE, CIA, AIDS, YMCA, UNICEF*). If you are not sure whether a particular abbreviation should include periods, check a dictionary or follow the style guidelines you are using for a research paper. (For more about abbreviations, see Chapter 26.)

Do not use an additional period when a sentence ends with an abbreviation that has its own period.

▶ **The social worker referred me to John Pintz Jr./**

21b Using question marks

Use question marks to close sentences that ask direct questions.

▶ **How is the human mind like a computer, and how is it different?**
—Kathleen Stassen Berger and Ross A. Thompson,
The Developing Person through Childhood and Adolescence

Question marks do not close indirect questions, which report rather than ask questions.

▶ **She asked whether I opposed his nomination?.**

21c Using exclamation points

Use an exclamation point to show surprise or strong emotion. Use these marks sparingly because they can distract your readers or suggest that you are exaggerating.

▶ **In those few moments of geologic time will be the story of all that has happened since we became a nation. And what a story it will be!**
—James Rettie, "But a Watch in the Night"

22 Apostrophes

The little apostrophe can make a big difference in meaning. The following sign at a neighborhood swimming pool, for instance, says something different from what the writer probably intended:

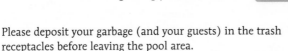

Please deposit your garbage (and your guests) in the trash
receptacles before leaving the pool area.

The sign indicates that guests, not their garbage, should be deposited in trash receptacles. Adding a single apostrophe would offer a more neighborly statement: *Please deposit your garbage (and your guests') in the trash receptacles before leaving the pool area.*

22a Signaling possessive case

The possessive case denotes ownership or possession. Add an apostrophe and *-s* to form the possessive of most singular **nouns**, including those that end in *-s*, and of **indefinite pronouns** (8d). The possessive forms of personal **pronouns** do not take apostrophes: *yours, his, hers, its, ours, theirs.*

▸ The **bus's** fumes overpowered her.

▸ George **Lucas's** movies have been wildly popular.

▸ **Anyone's** guess is as good as mine.

Plural nouns. To form the possessive case of plural nouns not ending in *-s*, add an apostrophe and *-s*. For plural nouns ending in *-s*, add only the apostrophe.

▸ The **men's** department sells business attire.

▸ The **clowns'** costumes were bright green and orange.

Compound nouns. For compound nouns, make the last word in the group possessive.

▸ Both her **daughters-in-law's** birthdays fall in July.

Two or more nouns. To signal individual possession by two or more owners, make each noun possessive.

▸ Great differences exist between **Jerry Bruckheimer's** and **Ridley Scott's** films.

    Bruckheimer and Scott produce different films.

To signal joint possession, make only the last noun possessive.

▶ **Wallace and Gromit's** creator is Nick Park.

Wallace and Gromit have the same creator.

22b Signaling contractions

Contractions are two-word combinations formed by leaving out certain letters, which are replaced by an apostrophe (*it is, it has/it's; will not/won't*).

Contractions are common in conversation and informal writing. Academic and professional work, however, often calls for greater formality.

Distinguishing *its* and *it's*. *Its* is a possessive **pronoun**—the possessive form of *it*. *It's* is a contraction for *it is* or *it has*.

▶ This disease is unusual; **its** symptoms vary from person to person.

▶ **It's** a difficult disease to diagnose.

22c Understanding apostrophes and plural forms

Many style guides now advise against using apostrophes for any plurals.

▶ The gymnasts need marks of **8s** and **9s** in order to qualify for the finals.

Other guidelines call for an apostrophe and -s to form the plural of numbers, letters, and words referred to as terms.

▶ The five **Shakespeare's** in the essay were spelled five different ways.

Check your instructor's preference.

23 Quotation Marks

"Hilarious!" "A great family movie!" "A must see!" The quotation marks are a key component of statements like these from movie ads; they make the praise more believable by indicating that it comes from people other than the movie promoter. Quotation marks identify a speaker's exact words or the titles of short works.

23a Signaling direct quotation

▶ The crowd chanted "Yes, we can" as they waited for the speech to begin.

▶ She smiled and said, "Son, this is one incident that I will never forget."

Use quotation marks to enclose the words of each speaker within running dialogue. Mark each shift in speaker with a new paragraph.

> "I want no proof of their affection," said Elinor; "but of their engagement I do."
> "I am perfectly satisfied of both."
> "Yet not a syllable has been said to you on the subject, by either of them." —Jane Austen, *Sense and Sensibility*

Single quotation marks. Single quotation marks enclose a quotation within a quotation. Open and close the quoted passage with double quotation marks, and change any quotation marks that appear *within* the quotation to single quotation marks.

▶ Baldwin says, "The title 'The Uses of the Blues' does not refer to music; I don't know anything about music."

Long quotations. To quote a passage that is more than four typed lines, set the quotation off by starting it on a new line and indenting it one inch from the left margin. This format, known as block quotation, does not require quotation marks.

In "Suspended," Joy Harjo tells of her first awareness of jazz as a child:

> My rite of passage into the world of humanity occurred then,
> via jazz. The music made a startling bridge between the
> familiar and strange lands, an appropriate vehicle, for . . . we
> were there when jazz was born. I recognized it, that humid
> afternoon in my formative years, as a way to speak beyond
> the confines of ordinary language. I still hear it. (84)

This block quotation, including the ellipsis dots and the page number in parentheses at the end, follows the style of the Modern Language Association, or MLA (see Chapter 41). The American Psychological Association, or APA, has different guidelines for setting off block quotations (see Chapter 42).

Poetry. When quoting poetry, if the quotation is brief (fewer than four lines), include it within your text. Separate the lines of the poem with slashes, each preceded and followed by a space, in order to tell the reader where one line of the poem ends and the next begins.

> In one of his best-known poems, Robert Frost remarks, "Two roads
> diverged in a yellow wood, and I — / I took the one less traveled by / And
> that has made all the difference."

To quote more than three lines of poetry, indent the block one inch from the left margin. Do not use quotation marks. Take care to follow the spacing, capitalization, punctuation, and other features of the original poem.

> The duke in Robert Browning's poem "My Last Duchess" is clearly
> a jealous, vain person, whose arrogance is illustrated through this
> statement:
>
>> She thanked men — good! but thanked
>> Somehow — I know not how — as if she ranked
>> My gift of a nine-hundred-years-old name
>> With anybody's gift. (lines 31–34)

23b Identifying titles of short works and definitions

Use quotation marks to enclose the titles of short poems, short stories, articles, essays, songs, sections of books, and episodes of television and radio programs. Quotation marks also enclose definitions.

▶ The essay "Big and Bad" analyzes some reasons for the popularity of SUVs.

▶ In social science, the term *sample size* means "the number of individuals being studied in a research project."
—Kathleen Stassen Berger and Ross A. Thompson,
The Developing Person through Childhood and Adolescence

23c Using quotation marks with other punctuation

Periods and commas go *inside* closing quotation marks.

▶ "Don't compromise yourself," said Janis Joplin. "You are all you've got."

Colons, semicolons, and footnote numbers go *outside* closing quotation marks.

▶ I felt one emotion after finishing "Eveline": sorrow.

▶ Tragedy is defined by Aristotle as "an imitation of an action that is serious and of a certain magnitude."[1]

Question marks, exclamation points, and dashes go *inside* if they are part of the quoted material, *outside* if they are not.

PART OF THE QUOTATION

▶ The cashier asked, "Would you like to super-size that?"

NOT PART OF THE QUOTATION

▶ What is the theme of "The Birth-Mark"?

⊕ For Multilingual Writers

Quoting in American English

Remember that the way you mark quotations in American English (" ") may not be the same as in other languages. In French, for example, quotations are marked with *guillemets* (« »), while in German, quotations take split-level marks (‚‚ "). American English and British English offer opposite conventions for double and single quotation marks. If you are writing for an American audience, be careful to follow the U.S. conventions governing quotation marks.

23d Avoiding misused quotation marks

Do not use quotation marks for indirect quotations—those that do not use someone's exact words.

▸ Mother smiled and said that /"she was sure she would

never forget the incident./"

Do not use quotation marks merely to add emphasis to particular words or phrases.

▸ The hikers were startled by the appearance of a /"gigantic/"

grizzly bear.

Do not use quotation marks around slang or colloquial language; they create the impression that you are apologizing for using those words. If you have a good reason to use slang or a colloquial term, use it without quotation marks.

▸ After our twenty-mile hike, we were completely exhausted and

ready to /"turn in./"

24 Other Punctuation

Parentheses, brackets, dashes, colons, slashes, and ellipses are everywhere. Every URL includes colons and slashes, many sites use brackets or parentheses to identify updates and embedded media, and dashes and ellipses are increasingly common in writing that expresses conversational informality.

You can also use these punctuation marks for more formal purposes: to signal relationships among parts of sentences, to create particular rhythms, and to help readers follow your thoughts.

24a Using parentheses

Use parentheses to enclose material that is of minor or secondary importance in a sentence—material that supplements, clarifies, comments on, or illustrates what precedes or follows it.

▶ Inventors and men of genius have almost always been regarded as fools at the beginning **(and very often at the end)** of their careers.
—Fyodor Dostoyevsky

▶ During my research, I found problems with the flat-rate income tax **(a single-rate tax with no deductions)**.

Parentheses are also used to enclose textual citations and numbers or letters in a list.

▶ Freud and his followers have had a most significant impact on the ways abnormal functioning is understood and treated **(Joseph, 1991)**. —Ronald J. Comer, *Abnormal Psychology*

The in-text citation in this sentence shows the style of the American Psychological Association (APA).

▶ Five distinct styles can be distinguished: **(1)** Old New England, **(2)** Deep South, **(3)** Middle American, **(4)** Wild West, and **(5)** Far West or Californian. —Alison Lurie, *The Language of Clothes*

With other punctuation.   A period may be placed either inside or outside a closing parenthesis, depending on whether the parenthetical text is part of a larger sentence. A comma, if needed, is always placed *outside* a closing parenthesis (and never before an opening one).

▶ Gene Tunney's single defeat in an eleven-year career was to a flamboyant and dangerous fighter named Harry Greb ("The Human Windmill"), who seems to have been, judging from boxing literature, the dirtiest fighter in history.

—Joyce Carol Oates, "On Boxing"

24b Using brackets

Use brackets to enclose any parenthetical elements in material that is itself within parentheses. Brackets should also be used to enclose any explanatory words or comments that you are inserting into a quotation.

▶ Eventually, the investigation had to examine the major agencies (including the National Security Agency [NSA]) that were conducting covert operations.

▶ Massing notes that "on average, it [Fox News] attracts more than eight million people daily—more than double the number who watch CNN."

The bracketed words *Fox News* clarify the meaning of *it* in the original quotation.

In the quotation in the following sentence, the artist Gauguin's name is misspelled. The bracketed word *sic*, which means "so," tells readers that the person being quoted—not the writer who has picked up the quotation—made the mistake.

▶ One admirer wrote, "She was the most striking woman I'd ever seen—a sort of wonderful combination of Mia Farrow and one of Gaugin's [*sic*] Polynesian nymphs."

24c Using dashes

Use dashes to insert a comment or to highlight material in a sentence.

▶ The pleasures of reading itself—who doesn't remember?—were like those of Christmas cake, a sweet devouring.
—Eudora Welty, "A Sweet Devouring"

A single dash can be used to emphasize material at the end of a sentence, to mark a sudden change in tone, to indicate hesitation in speech, or to introduce a summary or an explanation.

▶ In the twentieth century it has become almost impossible to moralize about epidemics—except those which are transmitted sexually.
—Susan Sontag, *AIDS and Its Metaphors*

▶ In walking, the average adult person employs a motor mechanism that weighs about eighty pounds—sixty pounds of muscle and twenty pounds of bone.
—Edwin Way Teale

Dashes give more emphasis than parentheses to the material they enclose or set off. Many word-processing programs automatically convert two typed hyphens with no spaces before or after into a solid dash.

24d Using colons

Use a colon to introduce an explanation, an example, an appositive, a series, a list, or a quotation.

▶ At the baby's one-month birthday party, Ah Po gave him the Four Valuable Things: ink, inkslab, paper, and brush.
—Maxine Hong Kingston, *China Men*

Use a colon rather than a comma to introduce a quotation when the lead-in is a complete sentence on its own.

▶ The 2013 State of the Union address ended with a bold challenge: "Well into our third century as a nation, it remains the task of us all . . . to be the authors of the next great chapter in our American story."

Colons are also used after salutations in letters; with numbers indicating hours, minutes, and seconds; with ratios; with biblical chapters and verses; with titles and subtitles; and in bibliographic entries.

▶ Dear Dr. Chapman:

▶ 4:59 PM

▶ a ratio of 5:1

▶ Ecclesiastes 3:1

▶ *The Joy of Insight: Passions of a Physicist*

▶ Boston: Bedford/St. Martin's, 2013

Misused colons. Do not put a colon between a **verb** and its **object** or complement (unless the object is a quotation), between a **preposition** and its object, or after such expressions as *such as*, *especially*, and *including*.

▶ Some natural fibers are: cotton, wool, silk, and linen.

▶ In poetry, additional power may come from devices such as:

simile, metaphor, and alliteration.

24e Using slashes

Use a slash to separate alternatives.

▶ Then there was Daryl, the cabdriver/bartender.
                    —John L'Heureux, *The Handmaid of Desire*

Use a slash, preceded and followed by a space, to divide lines of poetry quoted within running text.

▶ The speaker of Sonnet 130 says of his mistress, "I love to hear her speak, yet well I know / That music hath a far more pleasing sound."

Slashes also separate parts of fractions and Internet addresses.

24f Using ellipses

An ellipsis is three equally spaced dots that indicate that something has been omitted from a quoted passage. Just as you should carefully use quotation marks around any material that you are quoting directly from a source, so you should carefully use an ellipsis to indicate that you have left out part of a quotation that otherwise appears to be a complete sentence. Ellipses have been used in the following example to indicate two omissions—one in the middle of the first sentence and one at the end of the second sentence.

ORIGINAL TEXT

▶ The quasi-official division of the population into three economic classes called high-, middle-, and low-income groups rather misses the point, because as a class indicator the amount of money is not as important as the source.

—Paul Fussell, "Notes on Class"

WITH ELLIPSES

▶ As Paul Fussell argues, "The quasi-official division of the population into three economic classes . . . rather misses the point. . . ."

When you omit the last part of a quoted sentence, add a period before the ellipsis—for a total of four dots. Be sure a complete sentence comes before the four dots. If your shortened quotation ends with a source citation (such as a page number, a name, or a title), place the documentation source in parentheses after the three ellipsis points and the closing quotation mark but before the period.

▶ Packer argues, "The Administration is right to reconsider its strategy . . ." (34).

You can also use an ellipsis to indicate a pause or a hesitation in speech in the same way that you can use a dash for that purpose.

▶ **Then the voice, husky and familiar, came to wash over us—"The winnah, and still heavyweight champeen of the world . . . Joe Louis."**
—Maya Angelou, *I Know Why the Caged Bird Sings*

25 Capital Letters

Capital letters are a key signal in everyday life. Look around any store to see their importance: you can shop for Levi's or *any* blue jeans, for Pepsi or *any* cola, for Kleenex or *any* tissue. In each of these instances, the capital letter indicates the name of a particular brand.

25a Capitalizing the first word of a sentence

With very few exceptions, capitalize the first word of a sentence. If you are quoting a full sentence, capitalize its first word.

▶ **Kennedy said, "Let us never negotiate out of fear."**

Capitalization of a nonquoted sentence following a colon is optional.

▶ **Gould cites the work of Darwin: The [*or* the] theory of natural selection incorporates the principle of evolutionary ties among all animals.**

Capitalize a sentence within parentheses unless the parenthetical sentence is inserted into another sentence.

▶ **Gould cites the work of Darwin. (Other researchers cite more recent evolutionary theorists.)**

▶ **Gould cites the work of Darwin (see p. 150).**

When citing poetry, follow the capitalization of the original poem. Though most poets capitalize the first word of each line in a poem, some do not.

▶ Morning sun heats up the young beech tree
  leaves and almost lights them into fireflies

—June Jordan, "Aftermath"

25b Capitalizing proper nouns and proper adjectives

Capitalize proper **nouns** (those naming specific persons, places, and things) and most **adjectives** formed from proper nouns. All other nouns are common nouns and are not capitalized unless they are used as part of a proper noun: *a street,* but *Elm Street.*

Capitalized nouns and adjectives include personal names; nations, nationalities, and languages; months, days of the week, and holidays (but not seasons of the year); geographical names; structures and monuments; ships, trains, aircraft, and spacecraft; organizations, businesses, and government institutions; academic institutions and courses; historical events and eras; and religions, with their deities, followers, and sacred writings. For trade names, follow the capitalization you see in company advertising or on the product itself.

PROPER	COMMON
Alfred Hitchcock, Hitchcockian	a director
Brazil, Brazilian	a nation, a language
Pacific Ocean	an ocean
Challenger	a spaceship
Library of Congress	a federal agency
Political Science 102	a political science course
the Qur'an	a holy book
Catholicism, Catholics	a religion
Cheerios, iPhone	cereal, a smartphone
Halloween	a holiday in the fall

25c   Capitalizing titles before proper names

When used alone or following a proper name, most titles are not capitalized. One common exception is the word *president*, which many writers capitalize whenever it refers to the President of the United States.

Professor Lisa Ede   my history professor

Dr. Teresa Ramirez   Teresa Ramirez, our doctor

25d   Capitalizing titles of works

Capitalize most words in titles of books, articles, speeches, stories, essays, plays, poems, documents, films, paintings, and musical compositions. Do not capitalize articles (*a, an, the*), **prepositions**, **conjunctions**, and the *to* in an **infinitive** unless they are the first or last words in a title or subtitle.

Walt Whitman: A Life   Declaration of Independence

"As Time Goes By"   *The Producers*

"Crazy in Love"   *The Living Dead*

25e   Revising unnecessary capitalization

Capitalize compass directions only if the word designates a specific geographical region.

▶ John Muir headed west, motivated by the desire to explore.

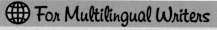

🌐 For Multilingual Writers

Learning English Capitalization

Capitalization systems vary considerably. Arabic, Chinese, Hebrew, and Hindi, for example, do not use capital letters at all. English may be the only language to capitalize the first-person singular pronoun (*I*), but Dutch and German capitalize some forms of the second-person pronoun (*you*)—and German also capitalizes all nouns.

▶ Water rights are an increasingly contentious issue in the West.

Capitalize family relationships only if the word is used as part of a name or as a substitute for the name.

▶ When she was a child, my mother shared a room with my aunt.

▶ I could always tell when Mother was annoyed with Aunt Rose.

26 Abbreviations and Numbers

Anytime you look up an address, you see an abundance of abbreviations and numbers, as in the following listing from a Google map:

Tarrytown Music Hall   13 Main St   Tarrytown, NY

Abbreviations and numbers allow writers to present detailed information in a small amount of space.

26a Using abbreviations

Certain titles are normally abbreviated.

Ms. Susanna Moller   Henry Louis Gates Jr.

Mr. Mark Otuteye   Karen Lancry, MD

Religious, academic, and government titles should be spelled out in academic writing but can be abbreviated in other writing when they appear before a full name.

Rev. Fleming Rutledge   Reverend Rutledge

Prof. Jaime Mejía   Professor Mejía

Sen. Christopher Dodd   Senator Dodd

Business, government, and science terms.   As long as you can be sure your readers will understand them, use common abbreviations such as *PBS*, *NASA*, and *DNA*. If an abbreviation may be unfamiliar, spell out the full term the first time you use it, and give the abbreviation in parentheses; after that, you can use the abbreviation by itself. Use abbreviations such as *Co.*, *Inc.*, *Corp.*, and *&* only if they are part of a company's official name.

▶ The Comprehensive Test Ban **(CTB)** Treaty was first proposed in the 1950s. For those nations signing it, the CTB would bring to a halt all nuclear weapons testing.

▶ Sears, Roebuck & Co. was the only large ~~corp.~~ *corporation* in town.

With numbers. The following abbreviations are acceptable with specific years and times.

399 BCE ("before the common era") *or* 399 BC ("before Christ")
49 CE ("common era") *or* AD 49 (*anno Domini*, Latin for "year of our Lord")
11:15 AM (*or* a.m.)
9:00 PM (*or* p.m.)

Symbols such as *%* and *$* are acceptable with figures (*$11*) but not with words (*eleven dollars*). Units of measurement can be abbreviated in charts and graphs (*4 in.*) but not in the body of a paper (*four inches*).

In notes and source citations. Certain Latin abbreviations required in notes and in source citations are not appropriate in the body of a paper.

cf.	compare (*confer*)
e.g.	for example (*exempli gratia*)
et al.	and others (*et alia*)
etc.	and so forth (*et cetera*)
i.e.	that is (*id est*)
N.B.	note well (*nota bene*)

In addition, except in notes and source citations, do not abbreviate such terms as *chapter*, *page*, and *volume* or the names of months, states, cities, or countries. Two exceptions are *Washington, D.C.*, and *U.S.* The latter abbreviation is acceptable as an **adjective** but not as a **noun**: *U.S. borders* but *in the United States*.

26b Using numbers

If you can write out a number in one or two words, do so. Use figures for longer numbers.

> ► Her screams were ignored by ~~38~~ people.
> *thirty-eight*

> ► A baseball is held together by ~~two hundred sixteen~~ red stitches.
> *216*

If one of several numbers *of the same kind* in the same sentence requires a figure, you should use figures for all the numbers in that sentence.

> ► An audio system can range in cost from ~~one hundred dollars~~
> *$100*
>
>   to $2,599.

When a sentence begins with a number, either spell out the number or rewrite the sentence.

> ► 119 years of CIA labor. ~~cost taxpayers sixteen million dollars.~~
> *Taxpayers spent sixteen million dollars for*

In general, use figures for the following:

ADDRESSES	23 Main Street; 175 Fifth Avenue
DATES	September 17, 1951; 6 June 1983; 4 BCE; the 1860s
DECIMALS AND FRACTIONS	65.34; 8½
EXACT AMOUNTS OF MONEY	$7,348; $1.46 trillion; $2.50; thirty-five (*or* 35) cents
PERCENTAGES	77 percent (*or* 77%)
SCORES AND STATISTICS	an 8–3 Red Sox victory; an average age of 22
TIME OF DAY	6:00 AM (*or* a.m.)

27 Italics

The slanted type known as *italics* is more than just a pretty typeface. Indeed, italics give words special meaning or emphasis. In the sentence "Many people read *People* on the subway every day," the italics (and the capital letter) tell us that *People* is a publication. You may use your computer to produce italic type; if not, underline words that you would otherwise italicize.

27a Italicizing titles

In general, use italics for titles and subtitles of long works; use quotation marks for shorter works (23b).

BOOKS	*Fun Home: A Family Tragicomic*
CHOREOGRAPHIC WORKS	Agnes de Mille's *Rodeo*
FILMS AND VIDEOS	*Star Wars*
LONG MUSICAL WORKS	*The Magic Flute*
LONG POEMS	*Bhagavad Gita*
MAGAZINES AND JOURNALS	*Ebony*; the *New England Journal of Medicine*
NEWSPAPERS	the Cleveland *Plain Dealer*
PAINTINGS AND SCULPTURE	Georgia O'Keeffe's *Black Iris*
PAMPHLETS	Thomas Paine's *Common Sense*
PLAYS	*Les Misérables*
RADIO SERIES	*All Things Considered*
RECORDINGS	*The Ramones Leave Home*
SOFTWARE	*Quicken*
TELEVISION SERIES	*Breaking Bad*
WEB SITES	*Salon*

Do not italicize titles of sacred books, such as the Bible and the Qur'an; public documents, such as the Constitution and the Magna Carta; or your own papers.

27b Italicizing words, letters, and numbers used as terms

▶ On the back of his jersey was the famous *24*.

▶ One characteristic of some New York speech is the absence of postvocalic *r*—for example, pronouncing the word *four* as "fouh."

27c Italicizing non-English words

Italicize words from other languages unless they have become part of English—like the French "bourgeois" or the Italian "pasta," for example. If a word is in an English dictionary, it does not need italics.

▶ At last one of the phantom sleighs gliding along the street would come to a stop, and with gawky haste Mr. Burness in his fox-furred *shapka* would make for our door.

—Vladimir Nabokov, *Speak, Memory*

27d Italicizing names of aircraft, ships, and trains

Spirit of St. Louis   Amtrak's *Silver Star*   U.S.S. *Iowa*

27e Using italics for emphasis

Italics can help create emphasis in writing, but use them sparingly for this purpose. It is usually better to create emphasis with sentence structure and word choice.

▶ Great literature and a class of literate readers are nothing new in India. What is new is the emergence of a gifted generation of Indian writers *working in English*.   —Salman Rushdie

28 Hyphens

Hyphens are undoubtedly confusing to many people—hyphen problems are now one of the twenty most common surface errors in student writing (see p. 10). The confusion is understandable. Over time, the conventions for hyphen use in a given word can change (*tomorrow* was once spelled *to-morrow*). New words, even compounds such as *firewall*, generally don't use hyphens, but controversy continues to rage over whether to hyphenate *email* (or is it *e-mail?*). And some words are hyphenated when they serve one kind of purpose in a sentence and not when they serve another.

28a Using hyphens with compound words

Compound nouns.   Some are one word (*rowboat*), some are separate words (*hard drive*), and some require hyphens (*sister-in-law*). You should consult a dictionary to be sure.

Compound adjectives.   Hyphenate most compound **adjectives** that precede a noun, but not those that follow a noun.

a *well-liked* boss	My boss is *well liked*.
a *six-foot* plank	The plank is *six feet long*.

In general, the reason for hyphenating compound adjectives is to make meaning clear.

▶ Designers often use potted plants as living‑room dividers.

  Without the hyphen, *living* may seem to modify *room dividers*.

Never hyphenate an *-ly* adverb and an adjective.

▶ They used a widely‑distributed mailing list.

Fractions and compound numbers.   Use a hyphen to write out fractions and to spell out compound numbers from twenty-one to ninety-nine.

one-seventh   fifty-four thousand

28b Using hyphens with prefixes and suffixes

The majority of words containing prefixes or suffixes are written without hyphens: *antiwar*, *Romanesque*. Following are some exceptions:

BEFORE CAPITALIZED BASE WORDS	un-American, non-Catholic
WITH FIGURES	pre-1960, post-1945
WITH CERTAIN PREFIXES AND SUFFIXES	all-state, ex-partner, self-possessed, quasi-legislative, mayor-elect, fifty-odd
WITH COMPOUND BASE WORDS	pre-high school, post-cold war
FOR CLARITY OR EASE OF READING	re-cover, anti-inflation, troll-like

Re-cover means "cover again"; the hyphen distinguishes it from *recover*, meaning "get well." In *anti-inflation* and *troll-like*, the hyphens separate confusing clusters of vowels and consonants.

Checklist

Editing for Hyphens

▶ Double-check compound words to be sure they are properly closed up, separated, or hyphenated. If in doubt, consult a dictionary. (28a)

▶ Check all terms that have prefixes or suffixes to see whether you need hyphens. (28b)

▶ Do not hyphenate two-word verbs or word groups that serve as subject complements. (28c)

28c Avoiding unnecessary hyphens

Unnecessary hyphens are at least as common a problem as omitted ones. Do not hyphenate the parts of a two-word verb such as *depend on*, *turn off*, or *tune out* (36b).

▶ Each player must pick/up a medical form before football

tryouts.

The words *pick up* act as a verb and should not be hyphenated.

However, be careful to check that two words do indeed function as a verb in the sentence; if they function as an adjective, a hyphen may be needed.

▶ Let's sign up for the early class.

The verb *sign up* should not have a hyphen.

▶ Where is the sign-up sheet?

The adjective *sign-up*, which modifies the noun *sheet*, needs a hyphen.

Do not hyphenate a subject complement—a word group that follows a linking verb (such as a form of *be* or *seem*) and describes the subject.

▶ Audrey is almost three/years/old.

Language

Writing

Sentence
Grammar

Sentence
Style

Punctuation/
Mechanics

Language

Multilingual
Writers

Research

Documentation

29 Writing to the World

People today often communicate instantaneously across vast distances and cultures. Businesspeople complete multinational transactions, students take online classes at distant universities, and Internet conversations circle the globe. You may even find yourself writing to (or with) people from other cultures, language groups, and countries. In this era of rapid global communication, you must know how to write effectively to the world.

29a Thinking about what seems "normal"

More than likely, your judgments about what is "normal" are based on assumptions that you are not aware of. Most of us tend to see our own way as the "normal" or right way to do things. If your ways seem inherently right, then perhaps you assume that other ways are somehow less than right. To communicate effectively with people across cultures, recognize the norms that guide your own behavior and how those norms differ from those of other people.

- Know that most ways of communicating are influenced by cultural contexts and differ from one culture to the next.
- Notice the ways that people from cultures other than your own communicate, and be flexible.
- Respect the differences among individuals within a culture. Don't assume that all members of a community behave in the same way or value the same things.

29b Clarifying meaning

All writers face challenges in trying to communicate across space, languages, and cultures. You can address these challenges by working to be sure that you understand what others say—and that they understand you. In such situations, take care to be explicit about the meanings of the words you use. In addition, don't hesitate to ask people to explain a point if you're not absolutely sure you understand, and invite responses by asking whether you're making yourself clear or what you could do to be *more* clear.

29c Meeting audience expectations

When you do your best to meet an audience's expectations about how a text should work, your writing is more likely to have the desired effect. In practice, figuring out what audiences want, need, or expect can be difficult—especially when you are writing in public spaces online and your audiences can be composed of anyone, anywhere. If you know little about your potential audiences, carefully examine your assumptions about your readers.

Expectations about your authority as a writer. Writers communicating across cultures often encounter audiences who have differing attitudes about authority and about the relationship between the writer and the people being addressed. In the United States, students are frequently asked to establish authority in their writing—by drawing on personal experience, by reporting on research, or by taking a position for which they can offer strong evidence and support. But some cultures position student writers as novices, whose job is to learn from others who have greater authority. When you write, think carefully about your audience's expectations and attitudes toward authority.

- What is your relationship to those you are addressing?
- What knowledge are you expected to have? Is it appropriate for you to demonstrate that knowledge—and if so, how?
- What is your goal—to answer a question? to make a point? to agree? something else?
- What tone is appropriate? If in doubt, show respect: politeness is rarely if ever inappropriate.

Expectations about persuasive evidence. You should think carefully about how to use evidence in writing, and pay attention to what counts as evidence to members of groups you are trying to persuade. Are facts, concrete examples, or firsthand experience convincing to the intended audience? Does the testimony of experts count heavily as evidence? What people are considered trustworthy experts, and why? Will the audience value citations from religious or philosophical texts, proverbs, or everyday wisdom? Are there other sources that would be considered strong evidence? If analogies are used as support, which kinds are most powerful?

Once you determine what counts as evidence in your own thinking and writing, consider where you learned to use and value this kind of evidence. You can ask these same questions about the use of evidence by members of other cultures.

Expectations about organization. The organizational patterns that you find pleasing are likely to be deeply embedded in your own culture. Many U.S. readers expect a well-organized piece of writing to use the following structure: introduction and thesis, necessary background, overview of the parts, systematic presentation of evidence, consideration of other viewpoints, and conclusion.

However, in cultures that value indirection, subtlety, or repetition, writers tend to prefer different organizational patterns. When writing for world audiences, think about how you can organize material to get your message across effectively. Consider where to state your thesis or main point (at the beginning, at the end, somewhere else, or not at all) and whether to use a straightforward organization or to employ digressions to good effect.

Expectations about style. Effective style varies broadly across cultures and depends on the rhetorical situation—purpose, audience, and so on. Even so, there is one important style question to consider when writing across cultures: what level of formality is most appropriate? In most writing to a general audience in the United States, a fairly informal style is often acceptable, even appreciated. Many cultures, however, tend to value a more formal approach. When in doubt, err on the side of formality in writing to people from other cultures, especially to your elders or to those in authority. Use appropriate titles (*Dr. Moss, Professor Mejía*); avoid slang and informal structures, such as **sentence fragments**; use complete words and sentences (even in email); and use first names only if invited to do so.

30 Language That Builds Common Ground

The supervisor who refers to her staff as "team members" (rather than as "my staff" or as "subordinates") has chosen language intended to establish common ground with people who are important to her. Your own language can work to build common ground if you carefully consider the sensitivities and preferences of others and if you watch for words that betray your assumptions, even though you have not directly stated them.

30a Examining assumptions and avoiding stereotypes

Unstated assumptions that enter into thinking and writing can destroy common ground by ignoring important differences. For example, a student in a religion seminar who uses *we* to refer to Christians and *they* to refer to members of other religions had better be sure that everyone in the class identifies as Christian, or some may feel left out of the discussion.

At the same time, don't overgeneralize about or stereotype a group of people. Because stereotypes are often based on half-truths, misunderstandings, and hand-me-down prejudices, they can lead to intolerance, bias, and bigotry.

Sometimes stereotypes and assumptions lead writers to call special attention to a group affiliation when it is not relevant to the point, as in *a woman plumber* or *a white basketball player*. Careful writers make sure that their language doesn't stereotype any group or individual.

30b Examining assumptions about gender

Powerful gender-related words can subtly affect our thinking and our behavior. For instance, at one time speakers commonly referred to hypothetical doctors or engineers as *he* (and then labeled a woman who worked as a doctor *a woman doctor*, as if to say, "She's an exception; doctors are normally men"). Similarly, a label like *male nurse* reflects stereotyped assumptions about proper roles for men. Equally problematic is the traditional use of *man* and *mankind* to refer to people of both sexes and the use of *he* and *him* to refer generally to any human being. Because such usage ignores half of the people on earth, it hardly helps a writer build common ground.

Sexist language, those words and phrases that stereotype or ignore members of either sex or that unnecessarily call attention to gender, can usually be revised fairly easily. There are several alternatives to using masculine **pronouns** to refer to persons whose gender is unknown:

▶ ~~A lawyer~~ Lawyers must pass the bar exam before he can practice. they
    ^   ^

▶ A lawyer must pass the bar exam before he can practice. or she
                                              ^

▶ A lawyer must pass the bar exam before ~~he can practice.~~ practicing.
                                            ^

Try to eliminate common sexist **nouns** from your writing.

INSTEAD OF	TRY USING
anchorman, anchorwoman	anchor
businessman	businessperson, business executive
congressman	member of Congress, representative
fireman	firefighter
male nurse	nurse
man, mankind	humans, human beings, humanity, the human race, humankind
policeman, policewoman	police officer
woman engineer	engineer

30c Examining assumptions about race and ethnicity

In building common ground, watch for any words that ignore differences not only among individual members of a race or ethnic group but also among subgroups. Be aware, for instance, of the many nations to which American Indians belong and of the diverse places from which Americans of Spanish-speaking ancestry come.

Preferred terms. Identifying preferred terms is sometimes not an easy task, for they can change often and vary widely.

- The word *colored* was once widely used in the United States to refer to Americans of African ancestry. By the 1950s, the preferred term had become *Negro*; in the 1960s, *black* came to be preferred by most, though certainly not all, members of that community. Then, in the late 1980s, some leaders of the community urged that *black* be replaced by *African American*.

- The word *Oriental*, once used to refer to people of East Asian descent, is now considered offensive.

- Once widely preferred, the term *Native American* is challenged by those who argue that the most appropriate way to refer to indigenous peoples is by the specific name such as *Chippewa*, *Tlingit*, or *Hopi*. It has also become common for tribal groups to refer to themselves as *Indians* or *Indian tribes*.

- Among Americans of Spanish-speaking descent, the preferred terms of reference are many: *Chicano/Chicana*, *Hispanic*, *Latin American*, *Latino/Latina*, *Mexican American*, *Dominican*, and *Puerto Rican*, to name but a few.

Clearly, then, ethnic terminology changes often enough to challenge even the most careful writers—including writers who belong to the groups they are writing about. The best advice may be to consider your words carefully, to listen for the way members of a group refer to themselves (or ask about preferences), and to check in a current dictionary for any term you're unsure of.

30d Considering other kinds of difference

Remember that your audiences may include people from many areas of the United States as well as from other countries, of many different ages and socioeconomic backgrounds, of many different abilities, of differing religious views, and of different sexual orientations. In short, you can almost never assume that audiences are just like you or that they share your background and experiences. Keeping this range of differences in mind can help you avoid overgeneralizing or stereotyping audiences—and thus help you to build common ground.

31 Varieties of Language

Comedian Dave Chappelle has said, "Every black American is bilingual. We speak street vernacular, and we speak job interview." As Chappelle understands, English comes in many varieties that differ from one another in pronunciation, vocabulary, usage, and grammar. You probably already adjust the variety of language you use depending on how well—and how formally—you know the audience you are addressing. Language variety can improve your communication with your audience if you think carefully about the effect you want to achieve.

31a Using standard varieties of English appropriately

The key to shifting among varieties of English and among languages is appropriateness: you need to consider when such shifts will help your audience appreciate your message and when shifts may be a mistake. Used appropriately and wisely, *any* variety of English can serve a good purpose.

One variety of English, often referred to as the "standard" or "standard academic," is that taught prescriptively in schools, represented in

🌐 For Multilingual Writers

Recognizing Global Varieties of English

Like other world languages, English is used in many countries, so it has many global varieties. For example, British English differs somewhat from U.S. English in certain vocabulary (*bonnet* for *hood* of a car), syntax (*to hospital* rather than *to the hospital*), spelling (*centre* rather than *center*), and pronunciation. If you have learned a non-American variety of English, you will want to recognize, and to appreciate, the ways in which it differs from the variety widely used in U.S. academic settings.

this and most other textbooks, used in the national media, and written and spoken widely by those wielding social and economic power. As the language used in business and most public institutions, standard English is a variety you will want to be completely familiar with. Standard English, however, is only one of many effective varieties of English and itself varies according to purpose and audience, from the more formal style used in academic writing to the informal style characteristic of casual conversation.

31b Using varieties of English to evoke a place or community

Weaving together regionalisms and standard English can be effective in creating a sense of place. Here, an anthropologist writing about one Carolina community takes care to let the residents speak their minds — and in their own words:

> For Roadville, schooling is something most folks have not gotten enough of, but everybody believes will do something toward helping an individual "get on." In the words of one oldtime resident, "Folks that ain't got no schooling don't get to be nobody nowadays."
> — Shirley Brice Heath, *Ways with Words*

Varieties of language, including slang and colloquial expressions, can also help writers evoke other kinds of communities. (See also 32a.)

31c Using varieties of English to build credibility with a community

Whether you are American Indian or trace your ancestry to Europe, Asia, Latin America, Africa, or elsewhere, your heritage lives on in the diversity of the English language. See how one Hawaiian writer uses a local variety of English to paint a picture of young teens hearing a "chicken skin" story from their grandmother.

> "—So, rather dan being rid of da shark, da people were stuck with many little ones, for dere mistake."
>
> Then Grandma Wong wen' pause, for dramatic effect, I guess, and she wen' add, "Dis is one of dose times. . . . Da time of da sharks."
>
> Those words ended another of Grandma's chicken skin stories. The stories she told us had been passed on to her by her grandmother, who had heard them from her grandmother. Always skipping a generation.
>
> —Rodney Morales, "When the Shark Bites"

Notice how the narrator of the story uses both standard and nonstandard varieties of English—presenting information necessary to the story line mostly in standard English and using a local, ethnic variety to represent spoken language. One important reason for the shift from standard English is to demonstrate that the writer is a member of the community whose language he is representing and thus to build credibility with others in the community. Take care, however, in using the language of communities other than your own. When used inappropriately, such language can have an opposite effect, perhaps destroying credibility and alienating your audience.

32 Word Choice

Deciding which word is the right word can be a challenge. It's not unusual to find many words that have similar but subtly different meanings, and each makes a different impression on your audience. For instance, the "pasta with marinara sauce" presented in a restaurant may look and taste much like the "macaroni and gravy" served at an Italian family dinner, but the choice of one label rather than the other tells us not only about the food but also about the people serving it and the people they expect to serve it to.

32a Using appropriate formality

In an email or letter to a friend or close associate, informal language is often appropriate. For most academic and professional writing, however, more formal language is appropriate, since you are addressing people you do not know well.

EMAIL TO SOMEONE YOU KNOW WELL

▶ Myisha is great—hire her if you can!

LETTER OF RECOMMENDATION TO SOMEONE YOU DO NOT KNOW

▶ I am pleased to recommend Myisha Fisher. She will bring good ideas and extraordinary energy to your organization.

Slang and colloquial language. Slang, or extremely informal language, is often confined to a relatively small group and changes very quickly, though some slang gains wide use (*yuppie*, *zine*). Colloquial language, such as *a lot*, *in a bind*, or *snooze*, is less informal, more widely used, and longer lasting than most slang.

Writers who use slang and colloquial language run the risk of not being understood or of not being taken seriously. If you are writing for a general audience about gun-control legislation and you use the term *gat*, some readers may not know what you mean, and others may be irritated by what they see as a frivolous reference to a deadly serious subject.

Jargon. Jargon is the special vocabulary of a trade or profession, enabling members to speak and write concisely to one another. Reserve jargon for an audience that will understand your terms. The example that follows, from a blog about fonts and typefaces, uses jargon appropriately for an interested and knowledgeable audience.

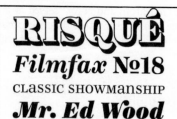

The Modern typeface classification is usually associated with Didones and display faces that often have too much contrast for text use. The Ingeborg family was designed with the intent of producing a Modern face that was readable at any size. Its roots might well be historic, but its approach is very contemporary. The three text weights (Regular, Bold, and Heavy) are functional and discreet while the Display weights (Fat and Block) catch the reader's eye with a dynamic form and a whole lot of ink on the paper. The family includes a boatload of extras like unicase alternates, swash caps, and a lined fill.

— fontshop.com blog

Jargon can be irritating and incomprehensible — or extremely helpful. Before you use technical jargon, remember your readers: if they will not understand the terms, or if you don't know them well enough to judge, then say whatever you need to say in everyday language.

Pompous language, euphemisms, and doublespeak. Stuffy or pompous language is unnecessarily formal for the purpose, audience, or topic. It often gives writing an insincere or unintentionally humorous tone, making a writer's ideas seem insignificant or even unbelievable.

POMPOUS

▸ Pursuant to the August 9 memorandum regarding unit costs of automotive fuels, it is incumbent upon us to endeavor to make maximal utilization of telephonic and digital communication in lieu of personal visitation.

For Multilingual Writers

Avoiding Fancy Language

In writing standard academic English, which is fairly formal, students are often tempted to use many "big words" instead of simple language. Although learning impressive words can be a good way to expand your vocabulary, it is usually best to avoid flowery or fancy language in college writing. Academic writing at U.S. universities tends to value clear, concise prose.

REVISED

▶ As of August 9, gas prices require us to telephone or email whenever possible rather than make personal visits.

As these examples illustrate, some writers use words in an attempt to sound expert or important, and these puffed-up words can easily backfire.

INSTEAD OF	TRY USING
ascertain	find out
commence	begin
finalize	finish or complete
functionality	function
impact (as a verb)	affect
methodology	method
operationalize	start; put into operation
optimal	best
parameters	boundaries
peruse	look at
ramp up	increase
utilize	use

Euphemisms are words and **phrases** that make unpleasant ideas seem less harsh. *Your position is being eliminated* seeks to soften the blow of being fired or laid off. Although euphemisms can sometimes appeal to an audience by showing that you are considerate of people's feelings, they can also sound insincere or evasive.

Doublespeak is language used to hide or distort the truth. During massive layoffs in the business world, companies may describe a job-cutting policy as *employee repositioning*, *deverticalization*, or *rightsizing*. The public—and particularly those who lose their jobs—recognize such terms as doublespeak.

32b Considering denotation and connotation

The words *enthusiasm*, *passion*, and *obsession* all carry roughly the same denotation, or dictionary meaning. But the connotations, or associations, are quite different: an *enthusiasm* is a pleasurable and absorbing interest; a *passion* has a strong emotional component and may affect someone positively or negatively; an *obsession* is an unhealthy attachment that excludes other interests.

Note the differences in connotation among the following three statements:

▶ Students Against Racism (SAR) erected a temporary barrier on the campus oval, saying the structure symbolized "the many barriers to those discriminated against by university policies."

▶ Left-wing agitators threw up an eyesore right on the oval to try to stampede the university into giving in to their demands.

▶ Supporters of human rights for all students challenged the university's investment in racism by erecting a protest barrier on campus.

The first statement is the most neutral, merely stating facts (and quoting the assertion about university policy to represent it as someone's opinion); the second, by using words with negative connotations (*agitators*, *eyesore*, *stampede*), is strongly critical; the third, by using words with positive connotations (*supporters of human rights*) and presenting assertions as facts (*the university's investment in racism*), gives a favorable slant to the protest.

32c Using general and specific language effectively

Effective writers balance general words (those that name groups or classes) with specific words (those that identify individual and particular things). Abstractions, which are types of general words, refer to things we cannot perceive through our five senses. Specific words are often concrete, naming things we can see, hear, touch, taste, or smell.

GENERAL	LESS GENERAL	SPECIFIC	MORE SPECIFIC
book	dictionary	abridged dictionary	the fourth edition of the *American Heritage College Dictionary*

ABSTRACT	LESS ABSTRACT	CONCRETE	MORE CONCRETE
culture	visual art	painting	van Gogh's *Starry Night*

32d Using figurative language effectively

Figurative language, or figures of speech, paints pictures in readers' minds, allowing readers to "see" a point readily and clearly. Far from being a frill, such language is crucial to understanding.

Similes, metaphors, and analogies.   Similes use *like*, *as*, *as if*, or *as though* to make explicit the comparison between two seemingly different things.

▶ The comb felt as if it was raking my skin off.
—Malcolm X, "My First Conk"

Metaphors are implicit comparisons, omitting the *like*, *as*, *as if*, or *as though* of similes.

▶ The Internet is the new town square.   —Jeb Hensarling

Analogies compare similar features of two dissimilar things; they explain something unfamiliar by relating it to something more familiar.

▶ The mouse genome . . . [is] the Rosetta Stone for understanding the language of life. —Tom Friend

Clichés and mixed metaphors. A cliché is an overused figure of speech, such as *busy as a bee.* By definition, we use clichés all the time, especially in speech, and many serve usefully as shorthand for familiar ideas. But if you use clichés to excess in your writing, readers may conclude that what you are saying is not very new or is even insincere.

Mixed metaphors make comparisons that are inconsistent.

▶ The lectures were like brilliant comets streaking through the
night sky, ~~showering~~ listeners with ~~a torrential rain~~ of insight.

(dazzling) *(flashes)*

The images of streaking light and heavy precipitation are inconsistent; in the revised sentence, all of the images relate to light.

32e Making spell checkers work for you

Research conducted for this book shows that spelling errors have changed dramatically in the past twenty years, thanks to spell checkers. Although these programs have weeded out many once-common misspellings, they are not foolproof. Look out for these typical errors allowed by spell checkers:

- **Homonyms.** Spell checkers cannot distinguish between words such as *affect* and *effect* that sound alike but are spelled differently.

- **Proper nouns.** A spell checker cannot tell you when you misspell a name.

- **Compound words written as two words.** Spell checkers will not see a problem if you write *nowhere* incorrectly as *no where.*

- **Typos.** The spell checker will not flag *heat* even if you meant to write *heart.*

Spell checkers and wrong words.   Wrong-word errors are the most common surface error in college writing today (see pp. 2–3), and spell checkers are partly to blame. Spell checkers may suggest bizarre substitutions for proper names and specialized terms, and if you accept the suggestions automatically, you may introduce wrong-word errors. A student who typed *fantic* instead of *frantic* found that the spell checker had substituted *fanatic*, a replacement that made no sense. Be careful not to take a spell checker's recommendation without paying careful attention to the replacement word.

Adapting spell checkers to your needs.   Always proofread carefully, even after running the spell checker. The following tips can help you:

- Check a dictionary if a spell checker highlights or suggests a word you are not sure of.
- If you can enter new words in your spell checker's dictionary, include names, non-English terms, or other specialized words that you use regularly. Be careful to enter the correct spelling!
- After you run the spell checker, look again for homonyms that you mix up regularly.
- Remember that spell checkers are not sensitive to capitalization.

32f   Improving spelling

Words work best for you, of course, when they are spelled correctly.

Spelling and pronunciation.   Pronunciation often leads spellers astray. Not only do people who live in different regions pronounce words differently, but speakers also tend to blur letters or syllables. To link spelling and pronunciation, try to pronounce words mentally the way they look, including every letter and syllable (so that, for example, you hear the *b* at the end of *crumb*). Doing so will help you "see" words with unpronounced letters or syllables, such as

Checklist

The Most Troublesome Homonyms

accept (to take or receive)

except (to leave out)

affect (an emotion; to have an influence)

effect (a result; to cause to happen)

its (possessive form of *it*)

it's (contraction of *it is* or *it has*)

their (possessive form of *they*)

there (in that place)

they're (contraction of *they are*)

to (in the direction of)

too (in addition; excessive)

two (number between *one* and *three*)

weather (climatic conditions)

whether (if)

who's (contraction of *who is* or *who has*)

whose (possessive form of *who*)

your (possessive form of *you*)

you're (contraction of *you are*)

those listed here. The frequently unpronounced letters or syllables are italicized.

can*d*idate	fore*i*gn	proba*b*ly
condem*n*	govern*m*ent	quan*t*ity
differ*e*nt	int*e*rest	rest*au*rant
drastica*l*ly	lib*r*ary	separate (adjective)
environ*m*ent	marri*a*ge	surprise
Febr*u*ary	mus*c*le	We*d*nesday

You can also use memory cues, or mnemonic devices, to master words that tend to trip you up. Here are two memory cues one student made up:

WORD	MISSPELLING	CUE
government	goverment	Government should serve those it *governs.*
separate	seperate	*Separate* rates two *a*'s.

For Multilingual Writers

Understanding American Spellings

You have likely noticed that different varieties of English often use different spelling conventions. If you have learned a British form of English, for example, you will want to be aware of some of the more common spelling differences in American English. For example, words ending in *-yse* or *-ise* in British English (*analyse, criticise*) usually end in *-yze* or *-ize* in American English (*analyze, criticize*); words ending in *-our* in British English (*colour, labour*) usually end in *-or* in American English (*color, labor*); and words ending in *-re* in British English (*theatre, centre*) usually end in *-er* in American English (*theater, center*).

i **before** *e.* Here is a slightly expanded version of the "*i* before *e*" rule:

> *i* before *e* except after *c* or when pronounced "ay" as in *neighbor* and *weigh*, or in weird exceptions like *either* and *species*

I BEFORE *E*	achieve, brief, field, friend
EXCEPT AFTER *C*	ceiling, conceivable, deceit, receive
OR WHEN PRONOUNCED "AY"	eighth, neighbor, reign, weigh
OR IN WEIRD EXCEPTIONS	ancient, foreign, height, leisure, neither, seize

Suffixes. A suffix, added to the end of a word (32g), may change the spelling of the word it is added to.

WORDS ENDING IN A SILENT *E.* In general, drop the final silent *e* on a word when you add a suffix that starts with a vowel. Keep the final silent *e* if the suffix starts with a consonant.

exercise, exercising	force, forceful
imagine, imaginable	state, stately
SOME EXCEPTIONS	argument, changeable, courageous, judgment, ninth, noticeable, truly

WORDS ENDING IN *Y*. In general, when you add a suffix to words ending in *y*, change the *y* to *i* if the *y* is preceded by a consonant. Keep the *y* if it is preceded by a vowel, if the suffix begins with *i*, or if the *y* is part of a proper name.

bounty, bountiful	busy, busily	try, tried	fry, fries
employ, employed	Kennedy, Kennedyesque	dry, drying	

WORDS ENDING IN A CONSONANT. When a word ends in a consonant preceded by a single vowel, adding a suffix beginning with a vowel requires you to double the final consonant if the word contains only one syllable or ends in an accented syllable.

stop, stopping   occur, occurrence

Do not double the consonant if the accent shifts from the last to a previous syllable when the suffix is added (*prefer, preference*).

Plurals.   For most words, simply add *-s* to form a plural. For singular nouns ending in *s*, *ch*, *sh*, *x*, or *z*, add *-es*.

book, books	ibis, ibises	fox, foxes	flash, flashes
bus, buses	church, churches	buzz, buzzes	

WORDS ENDING IN *O*. In general, add *-es* if the *o* is preceded by a consonant. Add *-s* if the *o* is preceded by a vowel.

potato, potatoes	hero, heroes	veto, vetoes
rodeo, rodeos	patio, patios	zoo, zoos

EXCEPTIONS

memo, memos	piano, pianos	solo, solos

WORDS ENDING IN *Y*. For words ending in *y*, change *y* to *i* and add *-es* if the *y* is preceded by a consonant. (Do not change a *y* at the end of a proper name.)

theory, theories	bay, bays	O'Malley, O'Malleys

COMPOUND WORDS. For compound nouns written as one word, make the last part of the compound plural (*briefcases, mailboxes*). For compound nouns written as separate or hyphenated words, make the most important part plural.

brothers-in-law   lieutenant governors

Checklist

Building Your Vocabulary

► Keep a list of new words. Each time you come across a new word in a text, try to come up with a definition, and then check the dictionary to see how close you came. Copy the word's definition next to the word on your list.

► Practice naming the opposites of some words. If you see *abbreviation*, for example, can you think of *enlargement* or *elaboration*?

► As you read, try to come up with better words than the authors have.

► While reading a work by a writer you admire, identify several words you like but do not yet use. Check the meanings of these words, and then try using them in your speech or writing.

32g Building vocabulary

In addition to using prefixes and suffixes, you can increase your vocabulary by analyzing contexts and reading actively.

If a word is at first unfamiliar to you, look carefully at its context, paying attention to all the clues the context provides; often, you will be able to deduce the meaning. For instance, if the word *accoutrements* is unfamiliar in the sentence *We stopped at a camping-supply store to pick up last-minute accoutrements*, the context—*a camping-supply store* and *last-minute*—suggests strongly that *equipment* or some similar word fits the bill. And that is what *accoutrements* means.

Word roots. As its name suggests, a root is a word from which other words grow, usually through the addition of prefixes or suffixes. From the Latin root *-dic-* or *-dict-* ("speak"), for instance, grows a whole range of words in English: *contradict, dictate,*

dictator, *diction*, *dictionary*, *predict*, and others. Here are some other Latin (L) and Greek (G) roots and examples of words derived from them.

ROOT	MEANING	EXAMPLES
-audi- (L)	to hear	audience, audio
-bene- (L)	good, well	benevolent, benefit
-bio- (G)	life	biography, biosphere
-duc(t)- (L)	to lead or to make	ductile, reproduce
-gen- (G)	race, kind	genealogy, gene
-geo- (G)	earth	geography, geometry
-graph- (G)	to write	graphic, photography
-jur-, -jus- (L)	law	justice, jurisdiction
-log(o)- (G)	word, thought	biology, logical
-luc- (L)	light	lucid, translucent
-manu- (L)	hand	manufacture, manual
-mit-, -mis- (L)	to send	permit, transmission
-path- (G)	feel, suffer	empathy, pathetic
-phil- (G)	love	philosopher, bibliophile
-photo- (G)	light	photography, telephoto
-port- (L)	to carry	transport, portable
-psych- (G)	soul	psychology, psychopath
-scrib-, -script- (L)	to write	scribble, manuscript
-sent-, -sens- (L)	to feel	sensation, resent
-tele- (G)	far away	telegraph, telepathy
-tend- (L)	to stretch	extend, tendency
-terr- (L)	earth	inter, territorial
-vac- (L)	empty	vacant, evacuation
-vid-, -vis- (L)	to see	video, envision, visit

Prefixes. Recognizing common prefixes can help you decipher the meaning of unfamiliar words.

PREFIXES OF NEGATION OR OPPOSITION

PREFIX	MEANING	EXAMPLES
a-, an-	without, not	amoral, anemia
anti-	against	antibody, antiphonal
contra-	against	contravene, contradict
de-	from, take away from	demerit, declaw
dis-	apart, away	disappear, discharge
il-, im-, in-, ir-	not	illegal, immature, indistinct, irreverent

PREFIX	MEANING	EXAMPLES
mal-	wrong	malevolent, malpractice
mis-	wrong, bad	misapply, misanthrope
non-	not	nonentity, nonsense
un-	not	unbreakable, unable

PREFIXES OF QUANTITY

PREFIX	MEANING	EXAMPLES
bi-	two	bipolar, bilateral
milli-	thousand	millimeter, milligram
mono-	one, single	monotone, monologue
omni-	all	omniscient, omnipotent
semi-	half	semicolon, semiconductor
tri-	three	tripod, trimester
uni-	one	unitary, univocal

PREFIXES OF TIME AND SPACE

PREFIX	MEANING	EXAMPLES
ante-	before	antedate, antebellum
circum-	around	circumlocution, circumnavigate

co-, col-, com-, con-, cor-	with	coequal, collaborate, commiserate, contact, correspond
e-, ex-	out of	emit, extort, expunge
hyper-	over, more than	hypersonic, hypersensitive
hypo-	under, less than	hypodermic, hypoglycemia
inter-	between	intervene, international
mega-	enlarge, large	megalomania, megaphone
micro-	tiny	micrometer, microscopic
neo-	recent	neologism, neophyte
post-	after	postwar, postscript
pre-	before	previous, prepublication
pro-	before, onward	project, propel
re-	again, back	review, re-create
sub-	under, beneath	subhuman, submarine
super-	over, above	supercargo, superimpose
syn-	at the same time	synonym, synchronize
trans-	across, over	transport, transition

Suffixes. Suffixes, which are attached to the end of words or roots, often alter the grammatical function or part of speech of the original word — for example, turning the verb *create* into a noun, an adjective, or an adverb.

VERB	create
NOUNS	creator/creation/creativity/creature
ADJECTIVE	creative
ADVERB	creatively

NOUN SUFFIXES

SUFFIX	MEANING	EXAMPLES
-acy	state or quality	democracy, privacy
-al	act of	dismissal, refusal

-ance, -ence	state or quality of	maintenance, eminence
-dom	place or state of being	freedom, kingdom
-er, -or	one who	trainer, investor
-ism	doctrine or belief characteristic of	liberalism, Taoism
-ist	one who	organist, physicist
-ity	quality of	veracity, opacity
-ment	condition of	payment, argument
-ness	state of being	watchfulness, cleanliness
-ship	position held	professorship, fellowship
-sion, -tion	state of being or action	digression, transition

VERB SUFFIXES

SUFFIX	MEANING	EXAMPLES
-ate	cause to be	concentrate, regulate
-en	cause to be or become	enliven, blacken
-ify, -fy	make or cause to be	unify, terrify, amplify
-ize	cause to become	magnetize, civilize

ADJECTIVE SUFFIXES

SUFFIX	MEANING	EXAMPLES
-able, -ible	capable of being	readable, edible
-al	pertaining to	regional, political
-esque	reminiscent of	picturesque, statuesque
-ful	having much of a quality	colorful, sorrowful
-ic	pertaining to	poetic, mythic
-ious, -ous	of or characterized by	famous, nutritious
-ish	having the quality of	prudish, clownish
-ive	having the nature of	festive, creative, massive
-less	without	endless, senseless

Multilingual
Writers

Writing

Sentence
Grammar

Sentence
Style

Punctuation/
Mechanics

Language

**Multilingual
Writers**

Research

Documentation

33 Sentence Structure

Short phrases, or sound bites, are everywhere—from the Dairy Council's "Got Milk?" to Volkswagen's "Drivers Wanted." These short, simple slogans may be memorable, but they don't say very much. In writing, you usually need more complex **sentences** to convey meaning. English sentences are put together in ways that may differ from sentence patterns in other languages.

33a Using explicit subjects and objects

English sentences consist of a **subject** and a **predicate**. While many languages can omit a sentence subject, English very rarely allows this. Though you might write *Responsible for analyzing data* on a résumé, in most varieties of spoken and written English you must explicitly state the subject.

▶ They took the Acela Express to Boston because ^it^ was fast.

English even requires a kind of "dummy" subject to fill the subject position in certain kinds of sentences.

▶ It is raining.
▶ There is a strong wind.

Transitive verbs typically require that **objects**—and sometimes other information—also be explicitly stated. For example, it is not enough to tell someone *Give!* even if it is clear what is to be given to whom. You must say, for example, *Give it to me* or *Give her the passport*.

33b Following English word order

In general, subjects, **verbs**, and objects must be placed in specific positions within a sentence.

SUBJECT   VERB   OBJECT   ADVERB

▶ **Francesca left Venice reluctantly.**

The only word in this sentence that can be moved to different locations is the **adverb** *reluctantly* (*Francesca reluctantly left Venice* or *Reluctantly, Francesca left Venice*). The three key elements of subject, verb, and object are moved out of their normal order only to create special effects.

33c Adapting structures from genres

If English is not your strongest language, you may find it useful to borrow and adapt transitional devices and pieces of sentence structure from other writing in the genre you are working in. You should not copy the whole structure, however, or your borrowed sentences may seem plagiarized (Chapter 39). Find sample sentence structures from similar genres but on different topics so that you borrow a typical structure (which does not belong to anyone) rather than the idea or the particular phrasing. Write your own sentences first, and look at other people's sentences just to guide your revision.

ABSTRACT FROM A SOCIAL SCIENCE PAPER

Using the interpersonal communications research of J. K. Brilhart and G. J. Galanes, along with T. Hartman's personality assessment, I observed and analyzed the group dynamics of my project collaborators in a communications course. Based on results of the Hartman personality assessment, I predicted that a single leader would emerge. However, complementary individual strengths and gender differences encouraged a distributed leadership style.

EFFECTIVE BORROWING OF STRUCTURES

Drawing on the research of Deborah Tannen on conversational styles, I analyzed the conversational styles of six first-year students at DePaul University. Based on Tannen's research, I expected that the three men I observed would use features typical of male conversational style and the three women would use features typical of female conversational style. In general, these predictions were accurate; however, some exceptions were also apparent.

33d Checking usage with search engines

To multilingual writers, search engines such as Google can provide a useful way of checking sentence structure and word usage. For example, if you are not sure whether you should use an **infinitive** form (*to* + verb) or a **gerund** (*-ing*) for the verb *confirm* after the main verb *expect* (35b), you can search for both "*expected confirming*" and "*expected to confirm*" to see which search term yields more results. A search for "*expected to confirm*" yields many more hits than a search for "*expected confirming*." These results indicate that *expected to confirm* is the more commonly used expression. Be sure to click through a few pages of the search engine's results to make sure that most results come from ordinary sentences rather than from headlines or phrases that may be constructed differently from standard English.

34 Nouns and Noun Phrases

Everyday life is filled with **nouns**: orange *juice*, the morning *news*, a *bus* to *work*, *meetings*, *pizza*, *email*, *Diet Coke*, *errands*, *dinner* with *friends*, a *chapter* in a good *book*. No matter what your first language is, it includes nouns. In English, articles (*a* book, *an* email, *the* news) often accompany nouns.

34a Understanding count and noncount nouns

Nouns in English can be either **count nouns** or **noncount nouns**. Count nouns refer to distinct individuals or things that can be directly counted: *a doctor, an egg, a child*; *doctors, eggs, children*. Noncount nouns refer to masses, collections, or ideas without distinct parts: *milk, rice, courage*. You cannot count noncount nouns except with a preceding **phrase**: *a glass of milk, three grains of rice, a little courage*.

Count nouns usually have singular and plural forms: *tree, trees*. Noncount nouns usually have only a singular form: *grass*.

COUNT	NONCOUNT
people (plural of *person*)	humanity
tables, chairs, beds	furniture
letters	mail
pebbles	gravel
suggestions	advice

Some nouns can be either count or noncount, depending on their meaning.

COUNT	Before video games, children played with marbles.
NONCOUNT	The palace floor was made of marble.

When you learn a noun in English, you need to learn whether it is count, noncount, or both. Many dictionaries provide this information.

34b Using determiners

Determiners are words that identify or quantify a noun, such as *this* study, *all* people, *his* suggestions.

COMMON DETERMINERS

- the articles *a, an, the*
- *this, these, that, those*
- *my, our, your, his, her, its, their*
- possessive nouns and noun phrases (*Sheila's paper, my friend's book*)
- *whose, which, what*
- *all, both, each, every, some, any, either, no, neither, many, much, (a) few, (a) little, several, enough*
- the numerals *one, two*, etc.

These determiners . . .	. . . can precede these noun types	Examples
a, an, each, every	singular count nouns	a book an American each word every Buddhist
this, that	singular count nouns noncount nouns	this book that milk
(*a*) *little, much*	noncount nouns	a little milk much affection
some, enough	noncount nouns plural count nouns	some milk enough trouble some books enough problems
the	singular count nouns plural count nouns noncount nouns	the doctor the doctors the information
these, those, (*a*) *few, many,* *both, several*	plural count nouns	these books those plans a few ideas many students both hands several trees

Determiners with singular count nouns. Every singular count noun must be preceded by a determiner. Place any adjectives between the determiner and the noun.

▶ sister

▶ the
  growing population
  ^

▶ that
  old neighborhood
  ^

Determiners with plural nouns or noncount nouns. Noncount and plural nouns sometimes have determiners and sometimes do not. For example, *This research is important* and *Research is important* are both acceptable but have different meanings.

34c Using articles

Articles (*a, an,* and *the*) are a type of determiner. In English, choosing which article to use—or whether to use an article at all—can be challenging. Although there are exceptions, the following general guidelines can help.

Using *a* or *an*. Use *a* and *an* indefinite articles with singular count nouns. Use *a* before a consonant sound (*a car*) and *an* before a vowel sound (*an uncle*). Consider sound rather than spelling: *a house, an hour*.

A or *an* tells readers they do not have enough information to identify specifically what the noun refers to. Compare these sentences:

▶ I need a new coat for the winter.

▶ I saw a coat that I liked at Dayton's, but it wasn't heavy enough.

The coat in the first sentence is hypothetical rather than actual. Since it is indefinite to the writer and the reader, it is used with *a*, not *the*. The second sentence refers to an actual coat, but since the writer cannot expect the reader to know which one, it is used with *a* rather than *the*.

If you want to speak of an indefinite quantity rather than just one indefinite thing, use *some* or *any* with a noncount noun or a plural count noun. Use *any* in negative sentences and questions.

▶ This stew needs some more salt.

▶ I saw some plates that I liked at Gump's.

▶ This stew doesn't need any more salt.

Using *the*. Use the definite article *the* with both count and noncount nouns whose identity is known or is about to be made known to readers. The necessary information for identification can come from the noun phrase itself, from elsewhere in the text, from context, from general knowledge, or from a **superlative**.

▶ Let's meet at *the* fountain in front of Dwinelle Hall.

> The phrase *in front of Dwinelle Hall* identifies the specific fountain.

▶ Last Saturday, a fire that started in a restaurant spread to a nearby clothing store. ~~Store~~ *The store* was saved, although it suffered water damage.

> The word *store* is preceded by *the*, which directs our attention to the information in the previous sentence, where the store is first identified.

▶ She asked him to shut *the* door when he left her office.

> The context shows that she is referring to her office door.

▶ ~~Pope~~ *The pope* is expected to visit Africa in October.

> There is only one living pope.

▶ Bill is now *the* best singer in the choir.

> The superlative *best* identifies the noun *singer*.

No article.   Noncount and plural count nouns can be used without an article to make generalizations:

▶ In this world nothing is certain but death and taxes.

> —Benjamin Franklin

Franklin refers not to a particular death or specific taxes but to death and taxes in general, so no article is used with *death* or with *taxes*.

English differs from many other languages that use the definite article to make generalizations. In English, a sentence like *The ants live in colonies* can refer only to particular, identifiable ants, not to ants in general.

35 Verbs and Verb Phrases

When we must act, **verbs** tell us what to do—from the street signs that say *stop* or *yield* to email commands such as *send* or *delete*. With a few stylistic exceptions, all written English sentences must include a verb.

35a Building verb phrases

Verb phrases can be built up out of a main **verb** and one or more **helping** (auxiliary) **verbs**.

▶ Immigration figures are rising every year.

▶ Immigration figures have risen every year.

Verb phrases have strict rules of order. If you try to rearrange the words in either of these sentences, you will find that most alternatives are impossible. You cannot say *Immigration figures rising are every year.*

Putting auxiliary verbs in order. In the sentence *Immigration figures may have been rising*, the main verb *rising* follows three auxiliaries: *may*, *have*, and *been*. Together these auxiliaries and the main verb make up a verb phrase.

- *May* is a modal that indicates possibility; it is followed by the base form of a verb.

- *Have* is an auxiliary verb that in this case indicates the perfect tense; it must be followed by a past participle (*been*).

- Any form of *be*, when it is followed by a present participle ending in *-ing* (such as *rising*), indicates the progressive tense.

- *Be* followed by a past participle, as in *New immigration policies have been passed in recent years*, indicates the passive voice (7e).

As shown in the following chart, when two or more auxiliaries appear in a verb phrase, they must follow a particular order based on the type of auxiliary: (1) modal, (2) a form of *have* used to indicate a perfect tense, (3) a form of *be* used to indicate a progressive tense,

	Modal	Perfect *Have*	Progressive *Be*	Passive *Be*	Main Verb	
Sonia	—	has	—	been	invited	to visit a family in Prague.
She	should	—	—	be	finished	with school soon.
The invitation	must	have	—	been	sent	in the spring.
She	—	has	been	—	studying	Czech.
She	may	—	be	—	feeling	nervous.
She	might	have	been	—	expecting	to travel elsewhere.
The trip	will	have	been	—	planned	for a month by the time she leaves.

and (4) a form of *be* used to indicate the passive voice. (Very few sentences include all four kinds of auxiliaries.)

Only one modal is permitted in a verb phrase.

> ▶ She will ~~can~~ speak Czech much better soon.
> ^ *be able to*

Forming auxiliary verbs. Whenever you use an auxiliary, check the form of the word that follows.

MODAL + BASE FORM. Use the base form of a verb after *can, could, will, would, shall, should, may, might,* and *must: Alice can read Latin.* In many other languages, modals like *can* or *must* are followed by the **infinitive** (*to* + base form). Do not substitute an infinitive for the base form in English.

> ▶ Alice can ~~to~~ read Latin.

PERFECT *HAVE, HAS,* OR *HAD* + PAST PARTICIPLE. To form the perfect tenses, use *have, has,* or *had* with a past participle: *Everyone has gone home. They have been working all day.*

PROGRESSIVE *BE* + PRESENT PARTICIPLE. A progressive form of the verb is signaled by two elements, a form of the auxiliary *be* (*am, is, are, was, were, be,* or *been*) and the *-ing* form of the next word: *The children are studying.* Be sure to include both elements.

▶ The children studying science.
   <small>*are*</small> ^

▶ The children are ~~study~~ science.
   <small>*studying*</small> ^

Some verbs are rarely used in progressive forms. These are verbs that express unchanging conditions or mental states rather than deliberate actions: *believe, belong, hate, know, like, love, need, own, resemble, understand.*

PASSIVE *BE* + PAST PARTICIPLE. Use *am, is, are, was, were, being, be,* or *been* with a past participle to form the passive voice.

▶ Tagalog is spoken in the Philippines.

Notice that the word following the progressive *be* (the present participle) ends in *-ing,* but the word following the passive *be* (the past participle) never ends in *-ing.*

PROGRESSIVE   Meredith is studying music.

PASSIVE   Natasha was taught by a famous violinist.

If the first auxiliary in a verb phrase is a form of *be* or *have,* it must show either present or past tense and must agree with the subject: *Meredith has played in an orchestra.*

35b Using infinitives and gerunds

Knowing whether to use an **infinitive** (*to read*) or a **gerund** (*reading*) in a sentence may be a challenge.

INFINITIVE

▶ My adviser urged me to apply to several colleges.

GERUND

▶ Applying took a great deal of time.

In general, infinitives tend to represent intentions, desires, or expectations, while gerunds tend to represent facts. The infinitive in the first sentence conveys the message that the act of applying was desired but not yet accomplished, while the gerund in the second sentence calls attention to the fact that the application process was actually carried out.

The association of intention with infinitives and facts with gerunds can often help you decide whether to use an infinitive or a gerund when another verb immediately precedes it.

INFINITIVES

▶ Kumar expected to get a good job after graduation.

▶ Last year, Fatima decided to become a math major.

▶ The strikers have agreed to go back to work.

GERUNDS

▶ Jerzy enjoys going to the theater.

▶ We resumed working after our coffee break.

▶ Kim appreciated getting candy from Sean.

A few verbs can be followed by either an infinitive or a gerund. With some, such as *begin* and *continue*, the choice makes little difference in meaning. With others, however, the difference in meaning is striking.

▶ Carlos was working as a medical technician, but he stopped to study English.

   The infinitive indicates that Carlos left his job because he intended to study English.

▶ Carlos stopped studying English when he left the United States.

   The gerund indicates that Carlos actually studied English but then stopped.

The distinction between fact and intention is a tendency, not a rule, and other rules may override it. Always use a gerund—not an infinitive—directly following a **preposition**.

▶ This fruit is safe for ~~to eat.~~
eating.
∧

You can also remove the preposition and keep the infinitive.

▶ This fruit is safe ~~for~~ to eat.

35c Using conditional sentences appropriately

English distinguishes among many different types of conditional sentences: sentences that focus on questions and that are introduced by *if* or its equivalent. Each of the following examples makes different assumptions about the likelihood that what is stated in the *if* **clause** is true.

▶ If you *practice* (or *have practiced*) writing often, you *learn* (or *have learned*) what your main problems are.

This sentence assumes that what is stated in the *if* clause may be true; any verb tense that is appropriate in a simple sentence may be used in both the *if* clause and the main clause.

▶ If you *practice* writing for the rest of this term, you *will* (or *may*) *understand* the process better.

This sentence makes a prediction and again assumes that what is stated may turn out to be true. Only the main clause uses the future tense (*will understand*) or a modal that can indicate future time (*may understand*). The *if* clause must use the present tense.

▶ If you *practiced* (or *were to practice*) writing every day, it *would* eventually *seem* easier.

This sentence indicates doubt that what is stated will happen. In the *if* clause, the verb is either past—actually, past subjunctive (7f)—or *were to* + the base form, though it refers to future time. The main clause contains *would* + the base form of the main verb.

▶ If you *practiced* writing on Mars, *you would find* no one to read your work.

This sentence imagines an impossible situation. Again, the past subjunctive is used in the *if* clause, although past time is not being referred to, and *would* + the base form is used in the main clause.

▶ If you *had practiced* writing in ancient Egypt, you *would have used* hieroglyphics.

This sentence shifts the impossibility back to the past; obviously you won't find yourself in ancient Egypt. But a past impossibility demands a form that is "more past": the past perfect in the *if* clause and *would* + the present perfect form of the main verb in the main clause.

36 Prepositions and Prepositional Phrases

Words such as *to* and *from*, which show the relations between other words, are **prepositions**. They are one of the more challenging elements of English writing.

36a Choosing the right preposition

Even if you usually know where to use prepositions, you may have difficulty knowing which preposition to use. Each of the most common prepositions has a wide range of different applications, and this range never coincides exactly from one language to another. See, for example, how *in* and *on* are used in English.

▶ The peaches are in the refrigerator.

▶ The peaches are on the table.

▶ Is that a diamond ring on your finger?

The Spanish translations of these sentences all use the same preposition (*en*), a fact that might lead you astray in English.

There is no easy solution to the challenge of using English prepositions idiomatically, but a few strategies can make it less troublesome.

Know typical examples. The **object** of the preposition *in* is often a container that encloses something; the object of the preposition *on* is often a horizontal surface that supports something touching it.

IN	The peaches are *in* the refrigerator.
	There are still some pickles *in* the jar.
ON	The peaches are *on* the table.

Learn related examples. Prepositions that are not used in typical ways may still show some similarities to typical examples.

IN	You shouldn't drive *in* a snowstorm.

Like a container, the falling snow surrounds the driver. The preposition *in* is used for many weather-related expressions.

ON	Is that a diamond ring *on* your finger?

The preposition *on* is used to describe things you wear.

Use your imagination. Mental images can help you remember figurative uses of prepositions.

IN	Michael is *in* love.

Imagine a warm bath—or a raging torrent—in which Michael is immersed.

ON	I've just read a book *on* social media.

Imagine the book sitting on a shelf labeled "Social Media."

Learn prepositions as part of a system. In identifying the location of a place or an event, the three prepositions *in*, *on*, and *at* can be used. *At* specifies the exact point in space or time; *in* is required for expanses of space or time within which a place is located or an event takes place; and *on* must be used with the names of streets (but not exact addresses) and with days of the week or month.

AT	There will be a meeting tomorrow *at* 9:30 AM *at* 160 Main Street.
IN	I arrived *in* the United States *in* January.
ON	The airline's office is *on* Fifth Avenue.
	I'll be moving to my new apartment *on* September 30.

36b   Using two-word verbs idiomatically

Some words that look like prepositions do not always function as prepositions. Consider the following sentences:

▶ The balloon rose *off* the ground.

▶ The plane took *off* without difficulty.

In the first sentence, *off* is a preposition that introduces the prepositional phrase *off the ground*. In the second sentence, *off* neither functions as a preposition nor introduces a prepositional phrase. Instead, it combines with *took* to form a two-word **verb** with its own meaning. Such a verb is called a phrasal verb, and the word *off*, when used in this way, is called an adverbial particle. Many prepositions can function as particles to form phrasal verbs.

  The verb + particle combination that makes up a phrasal verb is a single entity that cannot usually be torn apart.

▶ The plane took without difficulty. <u>off.</u>
             ^   ^

(inserted above: off)

Exceptions include some phrasal verbs that are transitive, meaning that they take a direct **object**. Some of these verbs have particles that may be separated from the verb by the object.

▶ I *picked up my baggage* at the terminal.

▶ I *picked my baggage up* at the terminal.

If a personal **pronoun** is used as the direct object, it *must* separate the verb from its particle.

▶ I picked up ~~it~~ at the terminal.
           ^

(inserted above: it)

In some idiomatic two-word verbs, the second word is a preposition. With such verbs, the preposition can never be separated from the verb.

▶ We *ran into* our neighbor on the train. [not *ran our neighbor into*]

  The combination *run + into* has a special meaning (find by chance). Therefore, *run into* is a two-word verb.

Research

Writing

Sentence
Grammar

Sentence
Style

Punctuation/
Mechanics

Language

Multilingual
Writers

Research

Documentation

37 Conducting Research

Your employer asks you to recommend the best software for a project. You need to plan a week's stay in Toronto. Your instructor assigns a term project about a musician. Each of these situations calls for research, for examining various kinds of sources—and each calls for you to assess the data you collect, synthesize your findings, and come up with an original recommendation or conclusion. Many tasks that call for research require that your work culminate in a written document—whether print or digital—that refers to and lists the sources you used.

37a Beginning the research process

For academic research assignments, once you have a topic you need to move as efficiently as possible to analyze the research assignment, articulate a research question to answer, and form a hypothesis. Then, after preliminary research, you can refine your hypothesis into a working thesis and begin your research in earnest.

Considering the context for a research project. Ask yourself what the *purpose* of the project is—perhaps to describe, survey, analyze, persuade, explain, classify, compare, or contrast. Then consider your *audience.* Who will be most interested, and what will they need to know? What assumptions might they hold? What response do you want from them?

You should also examine your own *stance* or *attitude* toward your topic. Do you feel curious, critical, confused, or some other way about it? What influences have shaped your stance?

For a research project, consider how many and what *kinds of sources* you need to find. What kinds of evidence will convince your audience? What visuals—charts, photographs, and so on—might you need? Would it help to do field research, such as interviews, surveys, or observations?

Finally, consider practical matters, such as how long your project will be, how much time it will take, and when it is due.

Formulating a research question and hypothesis. After analyzing your project's context, work from your general topic to a research question and a hypothesis.

TOPIC	Farming
NARROWED TOPIC	Small family farms in the United States
ISSUE	Making a living from a small family farm
RESEARCH QUESTION	How can small family farms in the United States successfully compete with big agriculture?
HYPOTHESIS	Small family farmers can succeed by growing specialty products that consumers want and by participating in farmers' markets and community-supported agriculture programs that forge relationships with customers.

After you have explored sources to test your hypothesis and sharpened it by reading, writing, and talking with others, you can refine it into a working thesis (2b).

WORKING THESIS	Although recent data show that small family farms are more endangered than ever, some enterprising farmers have reversed the trend by growing specialized products and connecting with consumers through farmers' markets and community-supported agriculture programs.

Planning research. Once you have formulated your hypothesis, determine what you already know about your topic and try to remember where you got your information. Consider the kinds of sources you expect to consult and the number you think you will need, how current they should be, and where you might find them.

37b Choosing among types of sources

Keep in mind some important differences among types of sources.

Primary and secondary sources. Primary sources provide you with firsthand knowledge, while secondary sources report on or

analyze the research of others. Primary sources are basic sources of raw information, including your own field research; films, works of art, or other objects you examine; literary works you read; and eyewitness accounts, photographs, news reports, and historical documents. Secondary sources are descriptions or interpretations of primary sources, such as researchers' reports, reviews, biographies, and encyclopedia articles. What constitutes a primary or secondary source depends on the purpose of your research. A film review, for instance, serves as a secondary source if you are writing about the film but as a primary source if you are studying the critic's writing.

Scholarly and popular sources. Nonacademic sources like magazines can help you get started on a research project, but you will usually want to depend more on authorities in a field, whose work generally appears in scholarly journals in print or online. The following list will help you to distinguish between scholarly and popular sources:

SCHOLARLY	POPULAR
Title often contains the word *Journal*	*Journal* usually does not appear in title
Source is available mainly through libraries and library databases	Source is generally available outside of libraries (at newsstands or from a home Internet connection)
Few or no commercial advertisements	Many advertisements
Authors are identified with academic credentials	Authors are usually journalists or reporters hired by the publication, not academics or experts
Summary or abstract appears on first page of article; articles are fairly long	No summary or abstract; articles are fairly short
Articles cite sources and provide bibliographies	Articles may include quotations but do not cite sources or provide bibliographies

SCHOLARLY

POPULAR

Older and more current sources.   Most projects can benefit from both older, historical sources and more current ones. Some older sources are classics; others are simply dated.

37c   Using library resources

Almost any research project should begin with resources in your school library.

Reference librarians.   Your library's staff—especially reference librarians—can be a valuable resource. You can talk with a librarian about your research project and get specific recommendations about databases and other helpful places to begin your research. Many libraries also have online tours and chat rooms where students can ask questions.

Catalogs.   Library catalogs can tell you whether a book is housed in the library and, if so, offer a call number that enables you to

Checklist

Effective Search Techniques

When you search online catalogs, databases, and Web sites, use carefully chosen keywords to limit the scope of your search, and be prepared to refine your search depending on what you find.

► Advanced search tools let you focus your search more narrowly—by combining terms with AND or eliminating them with NOT, by specifying dates and media types, and so on—so they may give you more relevant results.

► If you don't see an advanced search option, start with key-words. (Simply entering terms in the search box may bring up an advanced search option.) Check the first page or two of results. If you get many irrelevant options, think about how to refine your keywords to get more targeted results.

► Databases and search engines don't all refine searches the same way—for instance, some use AND, while others use the + symbol. Look for tips on making the most of the search tool you're using.

► Most libraries classify material using the *Library of Congress Subject Headings*, or LCSH. When you find a library source that seems especially relevant, be sure to use the subject headings for that source as search terms to bring up all the entries under each heading.

find the book on the shelf. Browsing through other books near the one you've found in the catalog can help you locate other works related to your topic. Catalogs also indicate whether you can find a particular periodical, either in print or in an online database, at the library.

Indexes and databases. Most college libraries subscribe to a large number of indexes and databases that students can access for free. Some databases include the full text of articles from newspapers, magazines, journals, and other works; some offer only short abstracts (summaries), which give an overview so you can decide whether to spend time finding and reading the whole text. Indexes of reviews provide information about a potential source's critical reception.

Check with a librarian for discipline-specific indexes and databases related to your topic.

Reference works. General reference works, such as encyclopedias, biographical resources, almanacs, digests, and atlases, can help you get an overview of a topic, identify subtopics, find more specialized sources, and identify keywords for searches.

Bibliographies. Bibliographies—lists of sources—in books or articles related to your topic can lead you to other valuable resources. Ask a librarian whether your library has more extensive bibliographies related to your research topic.

Other resources. Your library can help you borrow materials from other libraries (this can take time, so plan ahead). Check with reference librarians, too, about audio, video, multimedia, and art collections; government documents; and other special collections or archives that student researchers may be able to use.

37d Finding useful Internet sources

For many college students, the Internet is a favorite way of accessing information. It's true that much information—including authoritative sources identical to those your library provides—can be found online. Remember that library databases come from identifiable and professionally edited resources; you need to take special care to find out which information online is reliable and which is not (38a).

Internet searches. Research using a search tool such as Google usually begins with a keyword search (see the Checklist on the facing page). Many keyword searches bring up thousands of hits; you may find what you need on the first page or two of results, but if not, choose new keywords that lead to more specific sources.

Bookmarking tools. Today's powerful bookmarking tools can help you browse, sort, and track resources online. Social bookmarking sites allow users to tag information and share it with others. Users' tags are visible to all other users. If you find a helpful site, you can check how others have tagged it and browse similar tags for related information. You can also sort and group information with tags. Fellow users whose tags you trust can become part of your network so you can follow their sites of interest.

Web browsers can also help you bookmark online resources. However, unlike bookmarking tools in a browser, which are tied to one machine, you can use social bookmarking tools wherever you have an Internet connection.

Authoritative sources online.   Many sources online are authoritative and reliable. You can browse collections in online virtual libraries, for example, or collections housed in government sites such as the Library of Congress, the National Institutes of Health, and the U.S. Census Bureau. For current national news, consult online versions of reputable newspapers such as the *Washington Post*, or electronic sites for news services such as C-SPAN. Google Scholar can help you limit searches to scholarly works.

Some journals (such as those from Berkeley Electronic Press) and general-interest magazines (such as *Salon*) are published only online; many other print publications make at least some of their content available free on the Web.

37e   Doing field research

For many research projects, you will need to collect field data. Consider *where* you can find relevant information, *how* to gather it, and *who* might be your best providers of information.

Interviews.   Some information is best obtained by asking direct questions of other people. If you can talk with an expert—in person, on the telephone, or online—you may get information you cannot obtain through any other kind of research.

- Determine your exact purpose, and be sure it relates to your research question and your hypothesis.

- Set up the interview well in advance. Specify how long it will take, and if you wish to record the session, ask permission to do so.
- Prepare a written list of factual and open-ended questions. If the interview proceeds in a direction that seems fruitful, do not feel that you have to ask all of your prepared questions.
- Record the subject, date, time, and place of the interview.
- Thank those you interview, either in person or in a letter or email.

Observation.   Trained observers report that making a faithful record of an observation requires intense concentration and mental agility.

- Determine the purpose of the observation, and be sure it relates to your research question and hypothesis.
- Brainstorm about what you are looking for, but don't be rigidly bound to your expectations.
- Develop an appropriate system for recording data. Consider using a split notebook or page: on one side, record your observations directly; on the other, record your thoughts or interpretations.
- Record the date, time, and place of observation.

Opinion surveys.   Surveys usually depend on questionnaires. On any questionnaire, the questions should be clear and easy to understand and designed so that you can analyze the answers without difficulty. Questions that ask respondents to say *yes* or *no* or to rank items on a scale are easiest to tabulate.

- Write out your purpose, and determine the kinds of questions to ask.
- Figure out how to reach respondents.
- Draft questions that call for short, specific answers.
- Test the questions on several people, and revise questions that seem unfair, ambiguous, or too hard or time-consuming.
- Draft a cover letter or invitation email. Be sure to state a deadline.
- If you are using a print questionnaire, leave adequate space for answers.
- Proofread the questionnaire carefully.

38 Evaluating Sources, Synthesizing Sources, and Taking Notes

All research builds on the careful and sometimes inspired use of sources—that is, on research done by others. Since you want the information you glean from sources to be reliable and persuasive, you must evaluate each potential source carefully.

38a Evaluating the usefulness and credibility of potential sources

Use these guidelines to assess the usefulness of a source:

- **Your purpose.** What will this source add to your research project? Does it help you support a major point, demonstrate that you have thoroughly researched your topic, or help establish your own credibility through its authority?

- **Relevance.** Is the source closely related to your research question? You may need to read beyond the title and opening paragraph to check for relevance.

- **Publisher's credentials.** What do you know about the publisher of the source you are using? For example, is it a major newspaper known for integrity in reporting, or is it a tabloid? Is the publisher a popular source, or is it sponsored by a professional or scholarly organization?

- **Author's credentials.** Is the author an expert on the topic? An author's credentials may be presented in the article, book, or Web site, or you can search the Internet for information on the author.

- **Date of publication.** Recent sources are often more useful than older ones, particularly in fields that change rapidly. However, the most authoritative works may be older ones. The publication dates of Internet sites can often be difficult to pin down. And even for sites that include the dates of posting, remember that the material posted may have been composed some time earlier.

- **Accuracy of source.** How accurate and complete is the information in the source? How thorough is the bibliography or list of works cited that accompanies the source? Can you find other sources that corroborate what your source is saying?

- **Stance of source.** Identify the source's point of view or rhetorical stance, and scrutinize it carefully. Does the source present facts, or does it interpret or evaluate them? If it presents facts, what is included and what is omitted, and why? If it interprets or evaluates information that is not disputed, the source's stance may be obvious, but at other times you will need to think carefully about the source's goals. What does the author or sponsoring group want—to convince you of an idea? sell you something? call you to action in some way?

- **Cross-referencing.** Is the source cited in other works? If you see your source cited by others, looking at how they cite it and what they say about it can provide additional clues to its credibility.

- **Level of specialization.** General sources can be helpful as you begin your research, but you may then need the authority or currency of more specialized sources. On the other hand, extremely specialized works may be very hard to understand.

- **Audience of source.** Was the source written for the general public? specialists? advocates or opponents?

For more on evaluating Web sources and articles, see the source maps on pp. 214–17.

38b Reading and interpreting sources

After you have determined that a source is potentially useful, read it carefully and critically, asking yourself the following questions about how this research fits your writing project:

- How relevant is this material to your research question and hypothesis?

- Does the source include counterarguments that you should address?

- How persuasive is the evidence? Does it represent opposing viewpoints fairly? Will the source be convincing to your audience?

SOURCE MAP: Evaluating Web Sources

Is the sponsor credible?

1 Who is the **sponsor or publisher** of the source? See what information you can get from the URL. The domain names for government sites may end in *.gov* or *.mil* and for educational sites in *.edu*. The ending *.org* may—but does not always—indicate a nonprofit organization. If you see a tilde (~) or percent sign (%) followed by a name, or if you see a word such as *users* or *members*, the page's creator may be an individual, not an institution. In addition, check the header and footer, where the sponsor may be identified. The Web page and downloaded PDF article shown here come from a site sponsored by the nonprofit Nieman Foundation for Journalism at Harvard University.

2 Look for an *About* **page** or a link to a home page for background information on the sponsor. Is a mission statement included? What are the sponsoring organization's purpose and point of view? Does the mission statement seem balanced? What is the purpose of the site (to inform, to persuade, to advocate for a cause, to advertise, or something else)? Does the information on the site come directly from the sponsor, or is the material reprinted from another source? If it is reprinted, check the original.

Is the author credible?

3 What are the **author's credentials**? Look for information accompanying the material on the page. You can also run a search on the author to find out more. Does the author seem qualified to write about this topic?

Is the information credible and current?

4 When was the information **posted or last updated**? Is it recent enough to be useful?

5 Does the page document sources with **footnotes or links**? If so, do the sources seem credible and current? Does the author include any additional resources for further information? Look for ways to corroborate the information the author provides.

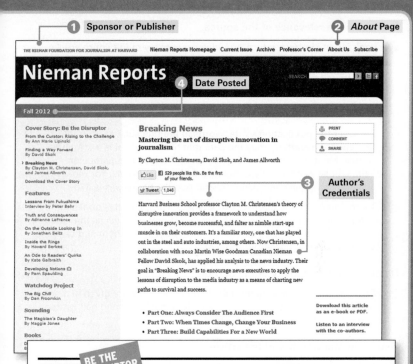

THE NIEMAN FOUNDATION FOR JOURNALISM AT HARVARD   Nieman Reports Homepage   Current Issue   Archive   Professor's Corner   About Us   Subscribe

Nieman Reports

SEARCH

Fall 2012

Cover Story: Be the Disruptor

From the Curator: Rising to the Challenge
By Ann Marie Lipinski

Finding a Way Forward
By David Skok

› Breaking News
By Clayton M. Christensen, David Skok, and James Allworth

Download the Cover Story

Features

Lessons From Fukushima
Interview by Peter Behr

Truth and Consequences
By Adrienne LaFrance

On the Outside Looking In
By Jonathan Seitz

Inside the Rings
By Howard Berkes

An Ode to Readers' Quirks
By Kate Galbraith

Developing Notions
By Pam Spaulding

Watchdog Project

The Big Chill
By Dan Froomkin

Sounding

The Magician's Daughter
By Maggie Jones

Books

Breaking News

Mastering the art of disruptive innovation in journalism

By Clayton M. Christensen, David Skok, and James Allworth

Like   529 people like this. Be the first of your friends.

Tweet   1,048

Harvard Business School professor Clayton M. Christensen's theory of disruptive innovation provides a framework to understand how businesses grow, become successful, and falter as nimble start-ups muscle in on their customers. It's a familiar story, one that has played out in the steel and auto industries, among others. Now Christensen, in collaboration with 2012 Martin Wise Goodman Canadian Nieman Fellow David Skok, has applied his analysis to the news industry. Their goal in "Breaking News" is to encourage news executives to apply the lessons of disruption to the media industry as a means of charting new paths to survival and success.

- Part One: Always Consider The Audience First
- Part Two: When Times Change, Change Your Business
- Part Three: Build Capabilities For a New World

PRINT   COMMENT   SHARE

Download this article as an e-book or PDF.

Listen to an interview with the co-authors.

COVER STORY   **BE THE DISRUPTOR**

Breaking News

Mastering the art of disruptive innovation in journalism

BY CLAYTON M. CHRISTENSEN, DAVID SKOK, AND JAMES ALLWORTH

OLD HABITS DIE HARD.

Four years after the 2008 financial crisis, traditional news organizations continue to see their newsrooms shrink or close. Those that survive remain mired in the innovator's dilemma: A false choice between today's revenues and tomorrow's digital promise. The problem is a profound one: A study in March by the Pew

This has happened before. Eighty-nine years ago, Henry Luce started Time as a weekly magazine summarizing the news. All 28 pages of the black-and-white weekly were filled with advertisements and aggregation. This wasn't just rewrites of the week's news; it was rip-and-read copy from the day's major publications—The Atlantic Monthly, The

It happened with Japanese automakers: They started with cheap subcompacts that were widely considered a joke. Now they make Lexuses that challenge the best of what Europe can offer.

It happened in the steel industry, where minimills began as a cheap, lower-quality alternative to established integrated mills, then moved their way

SOURCE MAP: Evaluating Articles

Determine the relevance of the source.

1 Look for an **abstract**, which provides a summary of the entire article. Is this source directly related to your research? Does it provide useful information and insights? Will your readers consider it persuasive support for your thesis?

Determine the credibility of the publication.

2 Consider the publication's **title**. Words in the title such as *Journal*, *Review*, and *Quarterly* may indicate that the periodical is a scholarly source. Most research projects rely on authorities in a particular field, whose work usually appears in scholarly journals. For more on distinguishing between scholarly and popular sources, see 37b.

3 Try to determine the **publisher or sponsor**. This journal is published by Johns Hopkins University Press. Academic presses such as this one generally review articles carefully before publishing them and bear the authority of their academic sponsors.

Determine the credibility of the author.

4 Evaluate the **author's credentials**. In this case, they are given in a note, which indicates that the author is a college professor and has written at least two books on related topics.

Determine the currency of the article.

5 Look at the **publication date**, and think about whether your topic and your credibility depend on your use of very current sources. Does this article's 2003 date disqualify it as a source on "contemporary Latin America"?

Determine the accuracy of the article.

6 Look at the **sources cited** by the author of the article. Here, they are documented in footnotes. Ask yourself whether the works the author has cited seem credible and current. Are any of these works cited in other articles you've considered?

In addition, consider the following questions:

- What is the article's stance or point of view? What are the author's goals? What does the author want you to know or believe?

- How does this source fit in with your other sources? Does any of the information it provides contradict or challenge other sources?

HUMAN RIGHTS QUARTERLY

 Title of Publication

Prisons and Politics in Contemporary Latin America

915

Mark Ungar*

Abstract

ABSTRACT

Despite democratization throughout Latin America, massive human rights abuses continue in the region's prisons. Conditions have become so bad that most governments have begun to enact improvements, including new criminal codes and facility decongestion. However, once in place, these reforms are undermined by chaotic criminal justice systems, poor policy administration, and rising crime rates leading to greater detention powers for the police. After describing current prison conditions in Latin America and the principal reforms to address them, this article explains how political and administrative limitations hinder the range of agencies and officials responsible for implementing those changes.

I. INTRODUCTION

Author's Credentials

Prison conditions not only constitute some of the worst human rights violations in contemporary Latin American democracies, but also reveal fundamental weaknesses in those democracies. Unlike most other human rights problems, those in the penitentiary system cannot be easily explained with authoritarian legacies or renegade officials. The systemic killing, overcrowding, disease, torture, rape, corruption, and due process abuses all occur under the state's twenty-four hour watch. Since the mid-1990s,

* Mark Ungar is Associate Professor of Political Science at Brooklyn College, City University of New York. Recent publications include the books *Elusive Reform: Democracy and the Rule of Law in Latin America* (Lynne Rienner, 2002) and *Violence and Politics: Globalization's Paradox* (Routledge, 2001) as well as articles and book chapters on democratization, policing, and judicial access. He works with Amnesty International USA and local rights groups in Latin America.

Human Rights Quarterly 25 (2003) 909–934 © 2003 by The Johns Hopkins University Press

 Publication Date

Publisher

ezuela, the jumped to agency in rs, far from the number mates form PCC)—with In the riots began in and spread s—the PCC CC leaders. nd security naffordable rgest, some ess es living in hose in the z facility of a Contra el less cells of able water, th rats and in weapons ocaine and on officials, al Guard in retribution. s protesting colony of El

a 1994).
1997.
prison (19
FELCN Prison (20 July 2000).

13. Typhus, cholera, tuberculosis, and scabies run rampant and the HIV rate may be as high as 25 percent. The warden of Retén de la Planta, where cells built for one inmate house three or four, says the prisons "are collapsing" because of insufficient budgets to train personnel. "Things fall apart and stay that way." Interview, Luis A. Lara Roche, Warden of Retén de la Planta, Caracas, Venezuela, 19 May 1995. At El Dorado prison in Bolívar state, there is one bed for every four inmates, cells are infested with vermin, and inmates lack clean bathing water and eating utensils.

14. *La Crisis Penitenciaria*, EL NACIONAL (Caracas), 2 Sept. 1988, at D2. On file with author.

Sources Cited

- Will you need to change your thesis to account for this information?
- What quotations or paraphrases from this source might you want to use?

As you read and take notes on your sources, keep in mind that you will need to present data and sources to other readers so that they can understand your point.

38c Synthesizing sources

Analysis requires you to take apart something complex (such as an article in a scholarly journal) and look closely at each part to understand how the parts fit together into an effective (or ineffective) whole. Academic writing also calls for *synthesis*—grouping similar pieces of information together and looking for patterns—so you can put your sources and your own knowledge together in an original argument. Synthesis is the flip side of analysis: you assemble the parts into a new whole.

To synthesize sources for a research project, try the following tips:

- **Don't just grab a quotation and move on.** Rather, read the material carefully. (See Chapter 3.)
- **Understand the purpose of each source.** Make sure the source is relevant and necessary to your argument.
- **Determine the important ideas in each source.** Take notes on each source (38d). Identify and summarize the key ideas.
- **Formulate a position.** Figure out how the pieces fit together. Look for patterns. After considering multiple perspectives, decide what you have to say.
- **Summon evidence to support your position.** You might use paraphrases, summaries, or direct quotations from your sources as evidence (39a), or your personal experience or prior knowledge. Keep your ideas central.
- **Consider counterarguments.** Acknowledge the existence of valid opinions that differ from yours, and try to understand them before explaining why they are incorrect or incomplete.

- **Combine your source materials effectively.** Be careful to avoid simply summarizing all of your research. Try to weave the various sources together rather than discussing each of your sources one by one.

Using sources effectively can pose challenges. A national study of first-year college writing found that student writers trying to incorporate research sometimes used sources that were not directly relevant to their point, too specific to support the larger claim being made, or otherwise ineffective. Another study showed that students tend to use sources *only* from the first one or two pages of a source, suggesting that they may not really know how relevant it is. Even after you have evaluated a source, take time to look at how well the source works in your specific situation. (If you change the focus of your work after you have begun doing research, be especially careful to check whether your sources still fit.)

38d Taking notes

While note-taking methods vary from one researcher to another, for each note you should (1) record enough information to help you recall the major points of the source; (2) put the information in the form in which you are most likely to incorporate it into your research project, whether a quotation, summary, or paraphrase; and (3) note all the information you will need to cite the source accurately. Keep a running list that includes citation information for each source in an electronic file or on note cards that you can rearrange and alter as your project takes shape. This working bibliography will simplify the process of documenting sources for your final project.

Quoting.   Quoting involves bringing a source's exact words into your text. Use an author's exact words when the wording is so memorable or expresses a point so well that you cannot improve or shorten it without weakening it, when the author is a respected authority whose opinion supports your ideas, or when an author challenges or disagrees profoundly with others in the field.

- Copy quotations carefully, with punctuation, capitalization, and spelling exactly as in the original.

- Enclose the quotation in quotation marks (23a).

- Use brackets if you introduce words of your own into the quotation or make changes in it (24b). Use ellipses if you omit words from the quotation (24f). If you later incorporate the quotation into your research project, copy it from the note precisely, including brackets and ellipses.

- Record the author's name, shortened title of the source, and page number(s) on which the quotation appeared. Make sure you have a corresponding working-bibliography entry with complete source information.

- Label the note with a subject heading, and identify it as a quotation.

Quotation-Style Note

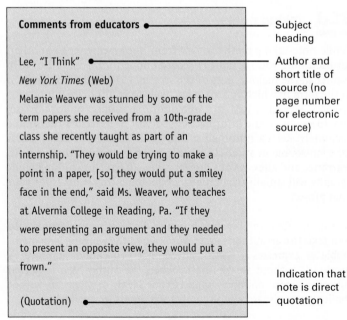

Comments from educators •————————— Subject heading

Lee, "I Think" •————————— Author and
New York Times (Web)   short title of
source (no
Melanie Weaver was stunned by some of the   page number
term papers she received from a 10th-grade for electronic
source)
class she recently taught as part of an
internship. "They would be trying to make a
point in a paper, [so] they would put a smiley
face in the end," said Ms. Weaver, who teaches
at Alvernia College in Reading, Pa. "If they
were presenting an argument and they needed
to present an opposite view, they would put a
frown."

Indication that
note is direct
(Quotation) •————————— quotation

Paraphrasing.   When you paraphrase, you're putting brief material from an author (including major and minor points, usually in the order they are presented) into *your own words and sentence structures.* If you wish to cite some of the author's words within the paraphrase, enclose them in quotation marks.

- Include all main points and any important details from the original source in the same order in which the author presents them, but in your own words. Put the original source aside to avoid following the wording too closely.
- If you want to include any language from the original, enclose it in quotation marks.
- Save your comments, elaborations, or reactions for another note.
- Record the author, shortened title, and page number(s), if the source has them, on which the original material appeared.
- Make sure you have a corresponding working-bibliography entry.
- Label the note with a subject heading, and identify it as a paraphrase to avoid confusion with a summary.
- Recheck to be sure that the words and sentence structures are your own and that they express the author's meaning accurately.

The following examples of paraphrases resemble the original material either too little or too much.

ORIGINAL

Language play, the arguments suggest, will help the development of pronunciation ability through its focus on the properties of sounds and sound contrasts, such as rhyming. Playing with word endings and decoding the syntax of riddles will help the acquisition of grammar. Readiness to play with words and names, to exchange puns and to engage in nonsense talk, promotes links with semantic development. The kinds of dialogue interaction illustrated above are likely to have consequences for the development of conversational skills. And language play, by its nature, also contributes greatly to what in recent years has been called *metalinguistic awareness*, which is turning out to be of critical importance in the development of language skills in general and of literacy skills in particular.

—David Crystal, *Language Play* (180)

UNACCEPTABLE PARAPHRASE: STRAYING FROM THE AUTHOR'S IDEAS

Crystal argues that playing with language—creating rhymes, figuring out how riddles work, making puns, playing with names, using invented words, and so on—helps children figure out a great deal about language, from the basics of pronunciation and grammar to how to carry on a conversation. Increasing their understanding of how language works in turn helps them become more interested in learning new languages and in pursuing education (180).

This paraphrase starts off well enough, but it moves away from paraphrasing the original to inserting the writer's ideas; Crystal says nothing about learning new languages or pursuing education.

UNACCEPTABLE PARAPHRASE: USING THE AUTHOR'S WORDS

Crystal suggests that language play, including rhyme, helps children improve pronunciation ability, that looking at word endings and decoding the syntax of riddles allows them to understand grammar, and that other kinds of dialogue interaction teach conversation. Overall, language play may be of critical importance in the development of language and literacy skills (180).

Because the highlighted phrases are either borrowed from the original without quotation marks or changed only superficially, this paraphrase plagiarizes.

UNACCEPTABLE PARAPHRASE: USING THE AUTHOR'S SENTENCE STRUCTURES

Language play, Crystal suggests, will improve pronunciation by zeroing in on sounds such as rhymes. Having fun with word endings and analyzing riddle structure will help a person acquire grammar. Being prepared to play with language, to use puns and talk nonsense, improves the ability to use semantics. These playful methods of communication are likely to influence a person's ability to talk to others. And language play inherently adds enormously to what has recently been known as *metalinguistic awareness*, a concept of great magnitude in developing speech abilities generally and literacy abilities particularly (180).

Here is a paraphrase of the same passage that expresses the author's ideas accurately and acceptably:

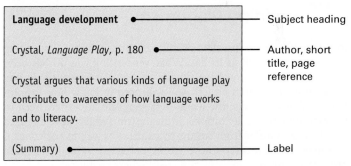

ACCEPTABLE PARAPHRASE: IN THE STUDENT WRITER'S OWN WORDS

Crystal argues that playing with language—creating rhymes, figuring out riddles, making puns, playing with names, using invented words, and so on—helps children figure out a great deal, from the basics of pronunciation and grammar to how to carry on a conversation. This kind of play allows children to understand the overall concept of how language works, a concept that is key to learning to use—and read—language effectively (180).

Summarizing. A summary is a significantly shortened version of a passage or even a whole chapter, article, film, or other work that captures main ideas *in your own words.* Unlike a paraphrase, a summary uses just enough information to record the points you wish to emphasize.

- Put the original aside to write your summary. If you later decide to include language from the original, enclose it in quotation marks.
- Record the author, shortened title, and page number(s) on which the original material appeared. For online or multimedia sources without page numbers, record any information that will help readers find the material.
- Make sure you have a corresponding working-bibliography entry.
- Label the note with a subject heading, and identify it as a summary to avoid confusion with a paraphrase.
- Recheck to be sure you have captured the author's meaning and that the words are entirely your own.

Summary Note

Language development ●	Subject heading
Crystal, *Language Play*, p. 180 ●	Author, short title, page reference
Crystal argues that various kinds of language play contribute to awareness of how language works and to literacy.	
(Summary) ●	Label

🌐 For Multilingual Writers

Identifying Sources

While some language communities and cultures expect audiences to recognize the sources of important documents and texts, thereby eliminating the need to cite them directly, conventions for writing in North America call for careful attribution of any quoted, paraphrased, or summarized material. When in doubt, explicitly identify your sources.

Annotating sources. You can annotate copies or printouts of sources you intend to use with your thoughts and questions as well as highlighting interesting quotations and key terms.

Try not to rely too heavily on copying or printing out whole pieces, however; you still need to read the material very carefully. And resist the temptation to treat copied material as notes, an action that could lead to inadvertent plagiarizing. Using a different color for text pasted from a source will help to prevent this problem.

39 Integrating Sources and Avoiding Plagiarism

In some ways, there is really nothing new under the sun, in writing and research as well as in life. Whatever writing you do has been influenced by what you have already read and experienced. As you work on your research project, you will need to know how to integrate and acknowledge the work of others. And all writers need to understand current definitions of plagiarism (which have changed over time and differ from culture to culture) as well as the concept of intellectual property—those works protected by copyright and other laws—so that they can give credit where credit is due.

39a Integrating quotations, paraphrases, and summaries

Integrate source materials into your writing with care to ensure that the integrated materials make grammatical and logical sense.

Quotations.   Because your research project is primarily your own work, limit your use of quotations to those necessary to your thesis or memorable for your readers.

Short quotations should run in with your text, enclosed by quotation marks. Longer quotations should be set off from the text (23a). Integrate all quotations into your text so that they flow smoothly and clearly into the surrounding sentences. Be sure that the sentence containing the quotation is grammatically complete, especially if you incorporate a quotation into your own words.

SIGNAL PHRASES. Introduce the quotation with a signal phrase or signal **verb**, such as those highlighted in these examples.

▶ As Eudora Welty notes, "Learning stamps you with its moments. Childhood's learning," she continues, "is made up of moments. It isn't steady. It's a pulse" (9).

▶ In her essay, Haraway strongly opposes those who condemn technology outright, arguing that we must not indulge in a "demonology of technology" (181).

Choose a signal verb that is appropriate to the idea you are expressing and that accurately characterizes the author's viewpoint. Other signal verbs include words such as *acknowledges, agrees, asserts, believes, claims, concludes, describes, disagrees, lists, objects, offers, remarks, reports, reveals, says, suggests,* and *writes.*

When you follow the Modern Language Association (MLA) style, used in the examples in this chapter, put verbs in signal phrases in the **present tense**. For *Chicago* style, use the present tense (or use the **past tense** to emphasize a point made in the past).

If you are using American Psychological Association (APA) style to describe research results, use the past tense or the **present perfect tense** (*the study* _showed_, *the study has shown*) in your signal phrase. Use the present tense to explain implications of research (*for future research, these findings* <u>*suggest*</u>).

BRACKETS AND ELLIPSES. In direct quotations, enclose in brackets any words you change or add, and indicate any deletions with ellipsis points.

▶ "There is something wrong in the [Three Mile Island] area," one farmer told the Nuclear Regulatory Commission after the plant accident ("Legacy" 33).

▶ Economist John Kenneth Galbraith pointed out that "large corporations cannot afford to compete with one another. . . . In a truly competitive market someone loses" (Key 17).

Be careful that any changes you make in a quotation do not alter its meaning. Use brackets and ellipses sparingly; too many make for difficult reading and might suggest that you have removed some of the context for the quotation.

Paraphrases and summaries. Introduce paraphrases and summaries clearly, usually with a signal phrase that includes the author of the source, as the highlighted words in the following example indicate.

▶ Professor of linguistics Deborah Tannen illustrates how communication between women and men breaks down and then suggests that a full awareness of "genderlects" can improve relationships (297).

39b Checking for excessive use of source material

Your text needs to synthesize your research in support of your own argument; it should not be a patchwork of quotations, paraphrases, and summaries from other people. You need a rhetorical stance that represents you as the author. If you cite too many sources, your own voice will disappear, a problem the following passage demonstrates:

The United States is one of the countries with the most rapid population growth. In fact, rapid population increase has been a "prominent feature of American life since the founding of the republic" (Day 31). In the past, the cause of the high rate of population growth was the combination of large-scale immigration and a high birth rate. As Day notes, "Two facts stand out in the demographic history of the United States: first, the single position as a receiver of immigrants; second, our high rate of growth from natural increase" (31).

Nevertheless, American population density is not as high as in most European countries. Day points out that the Netherlands, with a density of 906 persons per square mile, is more crowded than even the most densely populated American states (33).

Most readers will think that the source, Day, is much too prominent here and that the author of the essay is only secondary. Using three different sources rather than one in this short passage also overwhelms the writer's voice; instead, the passage should advance the writer's own argument.

39c Integrating visuals and media

Choose visuals and media wisely, whether you use video, audio, photographs, illustrations, charts and graphs, or any other kinds of images. Integrate all visuals and media smoothly into your text.

- **Does each visual or media file make a strong contribution to the message?** Purely decorative visuals and media may weaken the power of your writing.
- **Is each fair to your subject?** An obviously biased perspective may seem unfair to your audience.
- **Is each appropriate for your audience?**

While it is considered "fair use" to use such materials in an essay or other project for a college class, once that project is published on the Web, you might infringe on copyright protections if you do not ask the copyright holder for permission to use the visual or media file. If you have questions about whether your work might infringe on copyright, ask your instructor for help.

Like quotations, paraphrases, and summaries, visuals and media need to be introduced and commented on in some way.

- Refer to the visual or media element in the text *before* it appears: *As Fig. 3 demonstrates.*

- Explain or comment on the relevance of the visual or media file. This can appear *after* the visual.

- Check the documentation system you are using to make sure you label visual and media elements appropriately; MLA, for instance, asks that you number and title tables and figures (*Table 1: Average Amount of Rainfall by Region*).

- If you are posting your work publicly, make sure you have permission to use any copyrighted visuals.

39d Knowing which sources to acknowledge

As you carry out research, it is important to understand the distinction between materials that require acknowledgment (in in-text citations, footnotes, or endnotes; and in the list of works cited or bibliography) and those that do not.

Materials that do not require acknowledgment. You do not usually need to cite a source for the following:

- Common knowledge—facts that most readers are already familiar with.

- Facts available in a wide variety of sources, such as encyclopedias, almanacs, or textbooks.

- Your own findings from field research. You should, however, acknowledge people you interview as individuals rather than as part of a survey.

Materials that require acknowledgment. You should cite all of your other sources to be certain to avoid plagiarism. Follow the documentation style required (see Chapters 41–43), and list the source in a bibliography or list of works cited. Be especially careful to cite the following:

- Sources for quotations, paraphrases, and summaries that you include.
- Facts not widely known or arguable assertions.
- All visuals from any source, including your own artwork, photographs you have taken, and graphs or tables you create from data found in a source.
- Any help provided by a friend, an instructor, or another person.

39e Avoiding plagiarism

Academic integrity enables us to trust those sources we use and to demonstrate that our own work is equally trustworthy. Plagiarism is especially damaging to one's academic integrity, whether it involves inaccurate or incomplete acknowledgment of sources in citations—sometimes called unintentional plagiarism—or deliberate plagiarism that is intended to pass off one writer's work as another's.

Whether it is intentional or not, plagiarism can have serious consequences. Students who plagiarize may fail the course or be expelled. Others who have plagiarized, even inadvertently, have had degrees revoked or have been stripped of positions or awards.

Unintentional plagiarism. If your paraphrase is too close to the wording or sentence structure of a source (even if you identify the source); if after a quotation you do not identify the source (even if you include the quotation marks); or if you fail to indicate clearly the source of an idea that you did not come up with on your own, you may be accused of plagiarism even if your intent was not to plagiarize. This inaccurate or incomplete acknowledgment of one's sources often results either from carelessness or from not learning how to borrow material properly.

Take responsibility for your research and for acknowledging all sources accurately. To guard against unintentional plagiarism, photocopy or print out sources and identify the needed quotations right on the copy. You can also insert footnotes or endnotes into the text as you write.

🌐 For Multilingual Writers

Thinking about Plagiarism as a Cultural Concept

Many cultures do not recognize Western notions of plagiarism, which rest on a belief that writers can own their language and ideas. Indeed, in many cultures and communities, using the words and ideas of others without attribution is considered a sign of deep respect as well as an indication of knowledge. In academic writing in the United States, however, you should credit all materials except those that are common knowledge, that are available in a wide variety of sources, or that are your own creations or your own findings from field research.

Deliberate plagiarism. Deliberate plagiarism—such as handing in an essay written by a friend or purchased or downloaded from an essay-writing company; cutting and pasting passages directly from source materials without marking them with quotation marks and acknowledging their sources; failing to credit the source of an idea or concept in your text—is what most people think of when they hear the word *plagiarism.* This form of plagiarism is particularly troubling because it represents dishonesty and deception: those who intentionally plagiarize present someone else's hard work as their own and claim knowledge they really don't have, thus deceiving their readers.

Deliberate plagiarism is also fairly simple to spot: your instructor will be well acquainted with your writing and likely to notice any sudden shifts in the style or quality of your work. In addition, by typing a few words from a project into a search engine, your instructor can identify "matches" very easily.

40 Writing a Research Project

When you are working on a research project, there comes a time to draw the strands of your research together and articulate your conclusions in writing.

40a Drafting your text

To group the information you have collected, try arranging your notes and visuals to identify connections, main ideas, and possible organization. You may also want to develop a working outline, a storyboard, or an idea map, or you can plot out a more detailed organization in a formal outline.

For almost all research writing, drafting should begin well before the deadline in case you need to gather more information or do more drafting. Begin drafting wherever you feel most confident. If you have an idea for an introduction, begin there. If you are not sure how you want to introduce the project but do know how you want to approach one point, begin with that, and return to the introduction later.

Working title and introduction. The title and introduction set the stage for what is to come. Ideally, the title announces the subject in an intriguing or memorable way. The introduction should draw readers in and provide any background they will need to understand your discussion. You may want to open with a question, explain how you will answer it, and end with your explicit thesis statement.

Conclusion. A good conclusion helps readers know what they have learned. One effective strategy is to begin with a reference to your thesis and then expand to a more general conclusion that reminds readers why your discussion is significant. Or you may want to remind readers of your main points. Try to conclude with something that will have an impact—but avoid sounding preachy.

40b Reviewing and revising a research project

Once you've completed your draft, reread it slowly. As you do so, reconsider the project's purpose and audience, your stance and thesis, and the evidence you have gathered. Next, ask others to read and respond to your draft. Asking specific questions of your readers will result in the most helpful advice.

> ### ⊕ For Multilingual Writers
>
> **Asking Experienced Writers to Review a Thesis**
>
> You might find it helpful to ask one or two classmates who have more experience with the particular type of academic writing to look at your explicit thesis. Ask if the thesis is as direct and clear as it can be, and revise accordingly.

Once you get feedback, reread your draft very carefully, making notes for necessary changes and additions. Look closely at your support for your thesis, and gather additional information if necessary. Pay particular attention to how you have used both print and visual sources, and make sure you have full documentation for them. (For more on revising, see 2h.)

40c Preparing a list of sources

Once you have a final draft with your source materials in place, you are ready to prepare your list of sources. Create an entry for each source used in your final draft, consulting your notes and working bibliography. Then double-check your draft against your list of sources cited; be sure that you have listed every source mentioned in the in-text citations or notes and that you have omitted any sources not cited in your project. (For guidelines on documentation styles, see Chapters 41–43.)

40d Editing and proofreading

When you have revised your draft, check grammar, usage, spelling, punctuation, and mechanics. Consider the advice of spell checkers and grammar checkers carefully before accepting it. (For more information on editing, see 2i.) Proofread the final version of your project carefully. Work with a hard copy, since reading onscreen often leads to inaccuracies. Proofread once for typographical and grammatical errors and once again to make sure you haven't introduced new errors. You may find that reading the final draft backwards helps you focus on details.

Documentation

Writing

Sentence
Grammar

Sentence
Style

Punctuation/
Mechanics

Language

Multilingual
Writers

Research

Documentation

41 MLA Style

Many fields in the humanities ask students to follow Modern Language Association (MLA) style to format manuscripts and to document various kinds of sources. This chapter introduces MLA guidelines. For further reference, consult the *MLA Handbook for Writers of Research Papers*, Seventh Edition, 2009.

41a Understanding MLA citation style

Why does academic work call for very careful citation practices when writing for the general public may not? The answer is that readers of your academic work expect source citations for several reasons:

- Source citations demonstrate that you've done your homework on your topic and that you are a part of the conversation surrounding it. Careful citation shows your readers what you know, where you stand, and what you think is important.

- Source citations show your readers that you understand the need to give credit when you make use of someone else's intellectual property. Especially in academic writing, when it's better to be safe than sorry, include a citation for any source you think you might need to cite. (See 39d.)

- Source citations give explicit directions to guide readers who want to look for themselves at the works you're using.

The guidelines for MLA style help you with this last purpose, giving you instructions on exactly what information to include in your citation and how to format that information.

Types of sources. Look at the Directory to MLA Style on pp. 245–46 for guidelines on citing various types of sources, including print books, print periodicals (journals, magazines, and newspapers), digital written-word sources, and other sources (films, artwork) that consist mainly of material other than written words. A digital version of a source may include updates or corrections that the print version of the same work lacks, so MLA guidelines ask you to indicate the medium and to cite print and digital sources differently. If you can't find a model exactly like the source you've selected, see the box on p. 253.

WEB AND DATABASE SOURCES. MLA asks you to distinguish between Web sources and database sources. Individual researchers almost always gain access to articles in databases through the computer system of a school or public library that pays to subscribe. The easiest way to tell whether a source comes from a database, then, is that its information is *not* generally available to anyone with an Internet connection. Many databases are digital collections of articles that originally appeared in edited print periodicals, ensuring that an authority has vouched for the accuracy of the information. Such sources may have more credibility than free material available on the Web.

SOURCES FOR CONTENT BEYOND THE WRITTEN WORD. Figuring out which model to follow for media sources online can pose questions. Is a video interview posted on YouTube most like a work from a Web site? an online video? an interview? Talk with your instructor about any complicated sources, and remember that your ultimate goal is to make the source as accessible as possible to your readers.

Parts of citations. MLA citations appear in two parts—a brief in-text citation in parentheses in the body of your written text, and a full citation in the list of works cited, to which the in-text citation directs readers. A basic in-text citation includes the author's name and the page number (for a print source), but many variations on this format are discussed in 41c.

In the text of his research project (see 41e and the integrated media), David Craig quotes material from a print book and from an online report. He cites both parenthetically, pointing readers to entries on his list of works cited, as shown on pp. 279–80.

Explanatory notes. MLA citation style asks you to include explanatory notes for information that doesn't readily fit into your text but is needed for clarification or further explanation. In addition, MLA

advanced literacy, and for good reason. According to David Crystal, an
internationally recognized scholar of linguistics at the University of
Wales, as young children develop and learn how words string together
to express ideas, they go through many phases of language play. The
singsong rhymes and nonsensical chants of preschoolers are vital to
their learning language, and a healthy appetite for such wordplay leads
to a better command of language later in life (182).

Craig 10

*end in SAT Scores
Indicates Increased Emphasis on Math Is Yielding Results:
Reading and Writing Are Causes for Concern.* New York: College
Board, 2002. Print.

College Board. "2011 SAT Trends." *Collegeboard.org.* College Board,
14 Sept. 2011. Web. 6 Dec. 2012.

Crystal, David. *Language Play.* Chicago: U of Chicago P, 1998. Print.

The Discouraging Word. "Re: Messaging and Literacy." Message to the
author. 13 Nov. 2012. E-mail.

Ferguson, Niall. "Texting Makes U Stupid." *Newsweek* 158.12 (2011): 11.
Academic Search Premier. Web. 7 Dec. 2012.

Leibowitz, Wendy R. "Technology Transforms Writing and the
Teaching of Writing." *Chronicle of Higher Education* 26 Nov.
1999: A67-68. Print.

Lenhart, Amanda. *Teens, Smartphones, & Texting.* Washington: Pew
Internet & Amer. Life Project, 2012. PDF file.

Lenhart, Amanda, Sousan Arafeh, Aaron Smith, and Alexandra Macgill.
Writing, Technology & Teens. Washington: Pew Internet & Amer.
Life Project, 2008. Web. 6 Dec. 2012.

Lenhart, Amanda, and Oliver Lewis. *Teenage Life Online: The Rise of
the Instant-Message Generation and the Internet's Impact on*

among the young. According to the Pew Internet & American Life
Project, 85 percent of those aged 12-17 at least occasionally write
text messages, instant messages, or comments on social networking
sites (Lenhart, Arafeh, Smith, and Macgill). In 2001, the most

ashington: Pew Internet
2012.

ext-Messaging Skills Can
itor 11 Mar. 2005. Web.
10 Dec. 2012.

permits bibliographic notes for information about or evaluation of a
source, or to list multiple sources that relate to a single point. Use
superscript numbers in the text to refer readers to the notes, which
may appear as endnotes (under the heading *Notes* on a separate page
immediately before the list of works cited) or as footnotes at the bottom of each page where a superscript number appears.

EXAMPLE OF SUPERSCRIPT NUMBER IN TEXT

Although messaging relies on the written word, many messagers disregard standard writing conventions. For example, here is a snippet from an IM conversation between two teenage girls:[1]

EXAMPLE OF EXPLANATORY NOTE

1. This transcript of an IM conversation was collected on 20 Nov. 2012. The teenagers' names are concealed to protect their privacy.

41b Following MLA manuscript format

The MLA recommends the following format for the manuscript of a research paper. However, check with your instructor before preparing the final draft of a print work.

First page and title. The MLA does not require a title page. Type each of the following items on a separate line on the first page, beginning one inch from the top and flush with the left margin: your name, the instructor's name, the course name and number, and the date. Double-space between each item; then double-space again and center the title. Double-space between the title and the beginning of the text.

Margins and spacing. Leave one-inch margins at the top and bottom and on both sides of each page. Double-space the entire text, including set-off quotations, notes, and the list of works cited. Indent the first line of a paragraph one-half inch. Indent set-off quotations one inch.

Page numbers. Include your last name and the page number on each page, one-half inch below the top and flush with the right margin.

Long quotations. When quoting a long passage (more than four typed lines), set the quotation off by starting it on a new line and

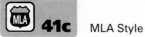

indenting each line one inch, from the left margin. Do not enclose the passage in quotation marks (23a).

Headings. MLA style allows, but does not require, headings. However, many students and instructors find them helpful. (See 2f for guidelines on using headings and subheadings.)

Visuals. Visuals (such as photographs, drawings, charts, graphs, and tables) should be placed as near as possible to the relevant text. (See 39c for guidelines on incorporating visuals into your text.) Tables should have a label and number (*Table 1*) and a clear caption. The label and caption should be aligned on the left, on separate lines. Give the source information below the table. All other visuals should be labeled *Figure* (abbreviated *Fig.*), numbered, and captioned. The label and caption should appear on the same line, followed by source information. Remember to refer to each visual in your text, indicating how it contributes to the point(s) that you are making.

41c Creating MLA in-text citations

MLA style requires a citation in the text of a writing project for every quotation, paraphrase, summary, or other material requiring documentation (see 39d). In-text citations document material from other sources with both signal phrases and parenthetical references. Parenthetical references should include the information your readers need to locate the full reference in the list of works cited at the end of the text. An in-text citation in MLA style gives the reader two kinds of information: (1) it indicates which source on the works-cited page the writer is referring to, and (2) it explains where in the source the material quoted, paraphrased, or summarized can be found, if the source has page numbers or other numbered sections.

The basic MLA in-text citation includes the author's last name either in a signal phrase introducing the source material (see 39a) or in parentheses at the end of the sentence. For print sources, it also includes the page number in parentheses at the end of the sentence.

SAMPLE CITATION USING A SIGNAL PHRASE

In his discussion of Monty Python routines, Crystal notes that the group relished "breaking the normal rules" of language (107).

SAMPLE PARENTHETICAL CITATION

A noted linguist explains that Monty Python humor often relied on "bizarre linguistic interactions" (Crystal 108).

(For digital sources without print page numbers, see model 3.)

Note in the examples on the following pages where punctuation is placed in relation to the parentheses.

DIRECTORY TO MLA STYLE

MLA style for in-text citations

1. AUTHOR NAMED IN A SIGNAL PHRASE. The MLA recommends using the author's name in a signal phrase to introduce the material and citing the page number(s) in parentheses.

> Lee claims that his comic-book creation, Thor, was "the first regularly published superhero to speak in a consistently archaic manner" (199).

2. AUTHOR NAMED IN A PARENTHETICAL REFERENCE. When you do not mention the author in a signal phrase, include the author's last name before the page number(s) in the parentheses. Use no punctuation between the author's name and the page number(s).

> The word *Bollywood* is sometimes considered an insult because it implies that Indian movies are merely "a derivative of the American film industry" (Chopra 9).

3. DIGITAL OR NONPRINT SOURCE. Give enough information in a signal phrase or in parentheses for readers to locate the source in your list of works cited. Many works found online or in electronic databases lack stable page numbers; you can omit the page number in such cases. However, if you are citing a work with stable pagination, such as an article in PDF format, include the page number in parentheses.

DIGITAL SOURCE WITHOUT STABLE PAGE NUMBERS

> As a *Slate* analysis explains, "Prominent sports psychologists get praised for their successes and don't get grief for their failures" (Engber).

DIGITAL SOURCE WITH STABLE PAGE NUMBERS

> According to Whitmarsh, the British military had experimented with using balloons for observation as far back as 1879 (328).

If the source includes numbered sections, paragraphs, or screens, include the abbreviation (*sec.*), paragraph (*par.*), or screen (*scr.*) number in parentheses.

4. TWO OR THREE AUTHORS. Use all the authors' last names in a signal phrase or in parentheses.

Gortner, Hebrun, and Nicolson maintain that "opinion leaders" influence other people in an organization because they are respected, not because they hold high positions (175).

5. FOUR OR MORE AUTHORS. Name all the authors in a signal phrase or in parentheses, or use the first author's name and *et al.* ("and others").

Similarly, as Belenky, Clinchy, Tarule, and Goldberger assert, examining the lives of women expands our understanding of human development (7).

Similarly, as Belenky et al. assert, examining the lives of women expands our understanding of human development (7).

6. ORGANIZATION AS AUTHOR. Give the group's full name or a shortened form of it in a signal phrase or in parentheses.

Any study of social welfare involves a close analysis of "the impacts, the benefits, and the costs" of its policies (Social Research Corporation iii).

7. UNKNOWN AUTHOR. Use the full title, if it is brief, in your text—or a shortened version of the title in parentheses.

One analysis defines *hype* as "an artificially engendered atmosphere of hysteria" (*Today's Marketplace* 51).

8. AUTHOR OF TWO OR MORE WORKS CITED IN THE SAME PROJECT. If your list of works cited has more than one work by the same author, include a shortened version of the title of the work you are citing in a signal phrase or in parentheses to prevent reader confusion.

Gardner shows readers their own silliness in his description of a "pointless, ridiculous monster, crouched in the shadows, stinking of dead men, murdered children, and martyred cows" (*Grendel* 2).

9. TWO OR MORE AUTHORS WITH THE SAME LAST NAME. Include the author's first *and* last names in a signal phrase or first initial and last name in a parenthetical reference.

Children will learn to write if they are allowed to choose their own subjects, James Britton asserts, citing the Schools Council study of the 1960s (37-42).

10. MULTIVOLUME WORK. In a parenthetical reference, note the volume number first and then the page number(s), with a colon and one space between them.

> Modernist writers prized experimentation and gradually even sought to
>
> blur the line between poetry and prose, according to Forster (3: 150).

If you name only one volume of the work in your list of works cited, include only the page number in the parentheses.

11. LITERARY WORK. Because literary works are usually available in many different editions, cite the page number(s) from the edition you used followed by a semicolon, and then give other identifying information that will lead readers to the passage in any edition. Indicate the act and/or scene in a play (*37; sc. 1*). For a novel, indicate the part or chapter (*175; ch. 4*).

> In utter despair, Dostoyevsky's character Mitya wonders aloud about the
>
> "terrible tragedies realism inflicts on people" (376; bk. 8, ch. 2).

For a poem, cite the part (if there is one) and line(s), separated by a period. If you are citing only line numbers, use the word *line(s)* in the first reference (*lines 33–34*).

> Whitman speculates, "All goes onward and outward, nothing collapses, /
>
> And to die is different from what anyone supposed, and luckier" (6.129-30).

For a verse play, give only the act, scene, and line numbers, separated by periods.

> The witches greet Banquo as "lesser than Macbeth, and greater" (1.3.65).

12. WORK IN AN ANTHOLOGY OR COLLECTION. For an essay, short story, or other piece of prose reprinted in an anthology, use the name of the author of the work, not the editor of the anthology, but use the page number(s) from the anthology.

> Narratives of captivity play a major role in early writing by women in the
>
> United States, as demonstrated by Silko (219).

13. SACRED TEXT. To cite a sacred text such as the Qur'an or the Bible, give the title of the edition you used, the book, and the chapter and verse (or their equivalent) separated by a period. In your text, spell out the names of books. In parenthetical references, use abbreviations for books with names of five or more letters (*Gen.* for *Genesis*).

He ignored the admonition "Pride goes before destruction, and a haughty

spirit before a fall" (*New Oxford Annotated Bible,* Prov. 16.18).

14. ENCYCLOPEDIA OR DICTIONARY ENTRY. An entry from a reference work—such as an encyclopedia or a dictionary—without an author will appear on the works-cited list under the entry's title. Enclose the entry title in quotation marks, and place it in parentheses. Omit the page number for print reference works that arrange entries alphabetically.

The term *prion* was coined by Stanley B. Prusiner from the words

proteinaceous and *infectious* and a suffix meaning *particle* ("Prion").

15. GOVERNMENT SOURCE WITH NO AUTHOR NAMED. Because entries for sources authored by government agencies will appear on your list of works cited under the name of the country (see 41d, item 73), your in-text citation for such a source should include the name of the country as well as the name of the agency responsible for the source.

To reduce the agricultural runoff into the Chesapeake Bay, the United

States Environmental Protection Agency has argued that "[h]igh nutrient

loading crops, such as corn and soybean, should be replaced with

alternatives in environmentally sensitive areas" (2-26).

16. ENTIRE WORK. Include the reference in the text, without any page numbers.

Jon Krakauer's *Into the Wild* both criticizes and admires the solitary

impulses of its young hero, which end up killing him.

17. INDIRECT SOURCE (AUTHOR QUOTING SOMEONE ELSE). Use the abbreviation *qtd. in* to indicate that you are quoting from someone else's report of a source.

As Arthur Miller says, "When somebody is destroyed everybody finally

contributes to it, but in Willy's case, the end product would be virtually

the same" (qtd. in Martin and Meyer 375).

18. TWO OR MORE SOURCES IN ONE PARENTHETICAL REFERENCE. Separate the information with semicolons.

> Economists recommend that *employment* be redefined to include unpaid
> domestic labor (Clark 148; Nevins 39).

19. VISUAL INCLUDED IN THE TEXT. When you include an image in your text, number it and include a parenthetical reference in your text (*see Fig. 2*). Number figures (photos, drawings, cartoons, maps, graphs, and charts) and tables separately. Each visual should include a caption with the figure or table number and information about the source—either a complete citation or enough information to direct readers to the works-cited entry.

> This trend is illustrated in a chart distributed by the College Board as part
> of its 2011 analysis of aggregate SAT data (see Fig. 1).

Soon after the preceding sentence, readers find the following figure and a caption referring them to the entry on the list of works cited (see 41e and the integrated media page at **bedfordstmartins.com/easy** to read the student's research paper):

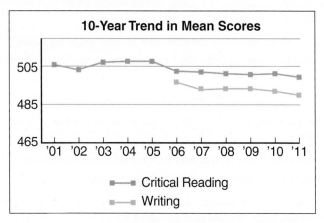

Fig. 1. Ten-year trend in mean SAT reading and writing scores (2001-2011). Source: College Board, "2011 SAT Trends."

An image that you create might appear with a caption like this:

> Fig. 4. Young women reading magazines. Personal photograph by author.

41d Creating an MLA list of works cited

A list of works cited is an alphabetical list of the sources you have referred to in your essay. (If your instructor asks you to list everything you have read as background, call the list *Works Consulted*.)

DIRECTORY TO MLA STYLE

MLA style for a list of works cited, *continued*

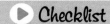 Checklist

Formatting a List of Works Cited

► Start your list on a separate page after the text of your document and any notes.

► Continue the consecutive numbering of pages.

► Center the heading *Works Cited* (not italicized or in quotation marks) one inch from the top of the page.

► Begin each entry flush with the left margin, but indent subsequent lines one-half inch. Double-space the entire list.

► List sources alphabetically by the first word. Start with the author's name, if available, or the editor's name. If no author or editor is given, start with the title.

► List the author's last name first, followed by a comma and the first name. If a source has multiple authors, subsequent authors' names appear first name first (see model 2).

► Capitalize every important word in titles and subtitles. Italicize titles of books and long works, but put titles of shorter works in quotation marks.

► In general, use a period and a space after each element of the entry; look at the models in this chapter for information on punctuating particular kinds of entries.

► For a book, list the city of publication (add a country abbreviation for non-U.S. cities that may be unfamiliar). Follow it with a colon and a shortened form of the publisher's name—omit *Co.* or *Inc.*, shorten names such as *Simon & Schuster* to *Simon*, and abbreviate *University Press* to *UP*.

► List dates of periodical publication or of access to electronic items in day, month, year order, and abbreviate months except for May, June, and July.

► Give a medium, such as *Print* or *Web*, for each entry.

► List inclusive page numbers for a part of a larger work.

Guidelines for author listings

The list of works cited is arranged alphabetically. The in-text citations in your writing point readers toward particular sources on the list.

NAME CITED IN SIGNAL PHRASE IN TEXT

Crystal explains . . .

NAME IN PARENTHETICAL CITATION IN TEXT

. . . (Crystal 107).

BEGINNING OF ENTRY ON LIST OF WORKS CITED

Crystal, David.

Models 1–5 on these facing pages explain how to arrange author names. The information that follows the name depends on the type of work you are citing—a book (models 6–27); a print periodical (models 28–34); a written text from a digital source, such as an article from a Web site or database (models 35–55); sources from art, film, comics, or other media, including live performances (models 56–71); and academic, government, and legal sources (models 72–79). Consult the model that most closely resembles the source you are using.

1. ONE AUTHOR. Put the last name first, followed by a comma, the first name (and initial, if any), and a period.

Crystal, David.

2. MULTIPLE AUTHORS. List the first author with the last name first (see model 1). Give the names of any other authors with the first name first. Separate authors' names with commas, and include the word *and* before the last person's name.

Martineau, Jane, Desmond Shawe-Taylor, and Jonathan Bate.

For four or more authors, either list all the names, or list the first author followed by a comma and *et al.* ("and others").

Lupton, Ellen, Jennifer Tobias, Alicia Imperiale, Grace Jeffers, and Randi Mates.

Lupton, Ellen, et al.

3. ORGANIZATION OR GROUP AUTHOR. Give the name of the group, government agency, corporation, or other organization listed as the author.

Getty Trust.

United States. Government Accountability Office.

4. UNKNOWN AUTHOR. When the author is not identified, begin the entry with the title, and alphabetize by the first important word. Italicize titles of books and long works, but put titles of articles and other short works in quotation marks.

"California Sues EPA over Emissions."

New Concise World Atlas.

5. TWO OR MORE WORKS BY THE SAME AUTHOR. Arrange the entries alphabetically by title. Include the author's name in the first entry, but in subsequent entries, use three hyphens followed by a period. (For the basic format for citing a book, see model 6. For the basic format for citing an article from an online newspaper, see model 38.)

Chopra, Anupama. "Bollywood Princess, Hollywood Hopeful." *New York*

Times. New York Times, 10 Feb. 2008. Web. 13 Feb. 2008.

---. *King of Bollywood: Shah Rukh Khan and the Seductive World of Indian*

Cinema. New York: Warner, 2007. Print.

Note: Use three hyphens only when the work is by *exactly* the same author(s) as the previous entry.

Print books

6. BASIC FORMAT FOR A BOOK. Begin with the author name(s). (See models 1–5.) Then include the title and subtitle, the city of publication and the publisher, the publication year, and the medium (*Print*). The source map on pp. 250–51 shows where to find this information in a typical book.

Crystal, David. *Language Play.* Chicago: U of Chicago P, 1998. Print.

Note: Place a period and a space after the name, title, and date. Place a colon after the city and a comma after the publisher, and shorten the publisher's name—omit *Co.* or *Inc.*, and abbreviate *University Press* to *UP.*

MLA SOURCE MAP: BOOKS

Take information from the book's title page and copyright page (on the reverse side of the title page), not from the book's cover or a library catalog.

1 Author. List the last name first. End with a period. For variations, see models 2–5.

2 Title. Italicize the title and any subtitle; capitalize all major words. End with a period.

3 City of publication and publisher. If more than one city is given, use the first one listed. For foreign cities, add an abbreviation of the country or province (*Cork, Ire.*). Follow it with a colon and a shortened version of the publisher's name (*Oxford UP* for *Oxford University Press*). Follow it with a comma.

4 Year of publication. If more than one copyright date is given, use the most recent one. End with a period.

5 Medium of publication. End with the medium (*Print*) followed by a period.

A citation for the book on p. 251 would look like this:

Patel, Raj. *The Value of Nothing: How to Reshape Market Society and Redefine Democracy.* New York: Picador, 2009. Print.

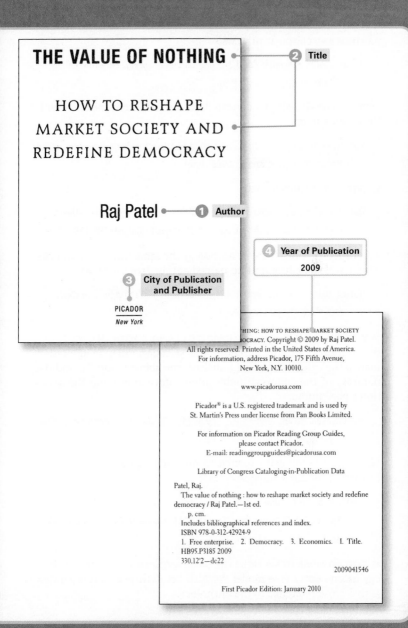

THE VALUE OF NOTHING

2 Title

HOW TO RESHAPE
MARKET SOCIETY AND
REDEFINE DEMOCRACY

Raj Patel **1** Author

4 Year of Publication
2009

3 City of Publication
and Publisher

PICADOR
New York

THING: HOW TO RESHAPE MARKET SOCIETY
OCRACY. Copyright © 2009 by Raj Patel.
All rights reserved. Printed in the United States of America.
For information, address Picador, 175 Fifth Avenue,
New York, N.Y. 10010.

www.picadorusa.com

Picador® is a U.S. registered trademark and is used by
St. Martin's Press under license from Pan Books Limited.

For information on Picador Reading Group Guides,
please contact Picador.
E-mail: readinggroupguides@picadorusa.com

Library of Congress Cataloging-in-Publication Data

Patel, Raj.
 The value of nothing : how to reshape market society and redefine
democracy / Raj Patel.—1st ed.
   p. cm.
Includes bibliographical references and index.
ISBN 978-0-312-42924-9
 1. Free enterprise. 2. Democracy. 3. Economics. I. Title.
HB95.P3185 2009
 330.12'2—dc22

2009041546

First Picador Edition: January 2010

7. AUTHOR AND EDITOR BOTH NAMED

> Bangs, Lester. *Psychotic Reactions and Carburetor Dung.* Ed. Greil Marcus.
> New York: Knopf, 1988. Print.

Note: To cite the editor's contribution instead, begin the entry with the editor's name.

> Marcus, Greil, ed. *Psychotic Reactions and Carburetor Dung.* By Lester
> Bangs. New York: Knopf, 1988. Print.

8. EDITOR, NO AUTHOR NAMED

> Wall, Cheryl A., ed. *Changing Our Own Words: Essays on Criticism, Theory,*
> *and Writing by Black Women.* New Brunswick: Rutgers UP, 1989. Print.

9. ANTHOLOGY. Cite an entire anthology the same way you would cite a book with an editor and no named author (see model 8).

> Walker, Dale L., ed. *Westward: A Fictional History of the American West.*
> New York: Forge, 2003. Print.

10. WORK IN AN ANTHOLOGY OR CHAPTER IN A BOOK WITH AN EDITOR. List the author(s) of the selection; the selection title, in quotation marks; the title of the book, italicized; the abbreviation *Ed.* and the name(s) of the editor(s); publication information; and the selection's page numbers.

> Komunyakaa, Yusef. "Facing It." *The Seagull Reader.* Ed. Joseph Kelly. New
> York: Norton, 2000. 126-27. Print.

Note: Use the following format to provide original publication information for a reprinted selection:

> Byatt, A. S. "The Thing in the Forest." *New Yorker* 3 June 2002: 80-89.
> Rpt. in *The O. Henry Prize Stories 2003.* Ed. Laura Furman. New York:
> Anchor, 2003. 3-22. Print.

11. TWO OR MORE ITEMS FROM THE SAME ANTHOLOGY. List the anthology as one entry (see model 9). Also list each selection separately with a cross-reference to the anthology.

Estleman, Loren D. "Big Tim Magoon and the Wild West." Walker 391-404.
Print.

Salzer, Susan K. "Miss Libbie Tells All." Walker 199-212. Print.

12. TRANSLATION

Bolaño, Roberto. *2666*. Trans. Natasha Wimmer. New York: Farrar, 2008.
Print.

13. BOOK WITH BOTH TRANSLATOR AND EDITOR. List the editor's and
translator's names after the title, in the order they appear on the
title page.

Kant, Immanuel. *"Toward Perpetual Peace" and Other Writings on Politics,
Peace, and History*. Ed. Pauline Kleingeld. Trans. David L. Colclasure.
New Haven: Yale UP, 2006. Print.

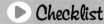 **Checklist**

Combining Parts of Models

What should you do if your source doesn't match the model
exactly? Suppose, for instance, that your source is a translated
essay that appears in the fifth edition of an anthology.

► Identify a basic model to follow. If you decide that your source
   looks most like an essay in an anthology, you would start with
   a citation that looks like model 10.

► Look for models that show the additional elements in your
   source. For this example, you would need to add elements
   of model 14 (for the translation) and model 18 (for an edition
   other than the first).

► Add new elements from other models to your basic model in
   the order indicated.

► If you still aren't sure how to arrange the pieces to create a
   combination model, ask your instructor.

14. TRANSLATION OF A SECTION OF A BOOK. If different translators have worked on various parts of the book, identify the translator of the part you are citing.

> García Lorca, Federico. *"The Little Mad Boy."* Trans. W. S. Merwin. *The*
> *Selected Poems of Federico García Lorca.* Ed. Francisco García Lorca
> and Donald M. Allen. London: Penguin, 1969. Print.

15. TRANSLATION OF A BOOK BY AN UNKNOWN AUTHOR

> *Grettir's Saga.* Trans. Denton Fox and Hermann Palsson. Toronto: U of
> Toronto P, 1974. Print.

16. BOOK IN A LANGUAGE OTHER THAN ENGLISH. Include a translation of the title in brackets, if necessary.

> Benedetti, Mario. *La borra del café [The Coffee Grind].* Buenos Aires:
> Sudamericana, 2000. Print.

17. GRAPHIC NARRATIVE. If the words and images are created by the same person, cite a graphic narrative just as you would with a book (model 6).

> Bechdel, Alison. *Are You My Mother? A Comic Drama.* New York: Houghton,
> 2012. Print.

If the work is a collaboration, indicate the author or illustrator who is most important to your research before the title of the work. List other contributors after the title, in the order of their appearance on the title page. Label each person's contribution to the work.

> Stavans, Ilan, writer. *Latino USA: A Cartoon History.* Illus. Lalo Arcaraz.
> New York: Basic, 2000. Print.

18. EDITION OTHER THAN THE FIRST

> Walker, John A. *Art in the Age of Mass Media.* 3rd ed. London: Pluto, 2001.
> Print.

19. ONE VOLUME OF A MULTIVOLUME WORK. Give the number of the volume cited after the title. Including the total number of volumes after the publication date is optional.

Ch'oe, Yong-Ho, Peter Lee, and William Theodore De Barry, eds. *Sources of Korean Tradition*. Vol. 2. New York: Columbia UP, 2000. Print. 2 vols.

20. TWO OR MORE VOLUMES OF A MULTIVOLUME WORK

Ch'oe, Yong-Ho, Peter Lee, and William Theodore De Barry, eds. *Sources of Korean Tradition*. 2 vols. New York: Columbia UP, 2000. Print.

21. PREFACE, FOREWORD, INTRODUCTION, OR AFTERWORD. After the writer's name, describe the contribution. After the title, indicate the book's author (with *By*) or editor (with *Ed.*).

Atwan, Robert. Foreword. *The Best American Essays 2002*. Ed. Stephen Jay Gould. Boston: Houghton, 2002. viii-xii. Print.

Moore, Thurston. Introduction. *Confusion Is Next: The Sonic Youth Story*. By Alec Foege. New York: St. Martin's, 1994. xi. Print.

22. ENTRY IN A REFERENCE BOOK. For a well-known encyclopedia, note the edition (if identified) and year of publication. If the entries are alphabetized, omit publication information and page number.

Kettering, Alison McNeil. "Art Nouveau." *World Book Encyclopedia*. 2002 ed. Print.

23. BOOK THAT IS PART OF A SERIES. Cite the series name (and number, if any) from the title page.

Nichanian, Marc, and Vartan Matiossian, eds. *Yeghishe Charents: Poet of the Revolution*. Costa Mesa: Mazda, 2003. Print. Armenian Studies Ser. 5.

24. REPUBLICATION (MODERN EDITION OF AN OLDER BOOK). Indicate the original publication date after the title.

Austen, Jane. *Sense and Sensibility*. 1813. New York: Dover, 1996. Print.

25. PUBLISHER'S IMPRINT. If the title page gives a publisher's imprint, hyphenate the imprint and the publisher's name.

Hornby, Nick. *About a Boy*. New York: Riverhead-Penguin Putnam, 1998. Print.

26. BOOK WITH A TITLE WITHIN THE TITLE. Do not italicize a book title within a title. For an article title within a title, italicize as usual and place the article title in quotation marks.

> Mullaney, Julie. *Arundhati Roy's* The God of Small Things: *A Reader's Guide.*
> New York: Continuum, 2002. Print.

> Rhynes, Martha. *"I, Too, Sing America": The Story of Langston Hughes.*
> Greensboro: Morgan, 2002. Print.

27. SACRED TEXT. To cite any individual published editions of sacred books, begin the entry with the title.

> *Qur'an: The Final Testament (Authorized English Version) with Arabic Text.*
> Trans. Rashad Khalifa. Fremont: Universal Unity, 2000. Print.

Print periodicals

Begin with the author name(s). (See models 1–5.) Then include the article title, the title of the periodical, the date or volume information, the page numbers, and the medium (*Print*). The source map on pp. 258–59 shows where to find this information in a sample periodical.

28. ARTICLE IN A PRINT JOURNAL. Follow the journal title with the volume number, a period, the issue number (if given), and the year (in parentheses).

> Gigante, Denise. "The Monster in the Rainbow: Keats and the Science of
> Life." *PMLA* 117.3 (2002): 433-48. Print.

29. ARTICLE IN A PRINT MAGAZINE. Provide the date from the magazine cover instead of volume or issue numbers.

> Surowiecki, James. "The Stimulus Strategy." *New Yorker* 25 Feb. 2008: 29.
> Print.

> Taubin, Amy. "All Talk?" *Film Comment* Nov.-Dec. 2007: 45-47. Print.

30. ARTICLE IN A PRINT NEWSPAPER. Include the edition (if listed) and the section number or letter (if listed).

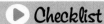

Checklist

Formatting Print Periodical Entries

▶ Put titles of articles from periodicals in quotation marks. Place the period inside the closing quotation mark.

▶ Give the title of the periodical as it appears on the magazine's or journal's cover or newspaper's front page; omit any initial *A*, *An*, or *The*. Italicize the title.

▶ For journals, include the volume number, a period, the issue number, if given, and the year in parentheses.

▶ For magazines and newspapers, give the date in this order: day (if given), month, year. Abbreviate months except for May, June, and July.

▶ List inclusive page numbers if the article appears on consecutive pages. If it skips pages, give only the first page number and a plus sign.

▶ End with the medium (*Print*).

Longman, Jeré. "Kim Jong-il, Sportsman." *New York Times* 21 Dec. 2011,

   late ed.: B12. Print.

Note: For locally published newspapers, add the city in brackets after the name if it is not part of the name: *Globe and Mail [Toronto]*.

31. ARTICLE THAT SKIPS PAGES. When an article skips pages, give only the first page number and a plus sign.

Tyrnauer, Matthew. "Empire by Martha." *Vanity Fair* Sept. 2002: 364+.

   Print.

32. EDITORIAL OR LETTER TO THE EDITOR. Include the writer's name, if given, and the title, if any, followed by a label for the work.

"California Dreaming." Editorial. *Nation* 25 Feb. 2008: 4. Print.

Galbraith, James K. "JFK's Plans to Withdraw." Letter. *New York Review of*

   Books 6 Dec. 2007: 77-78. Print.

MLA SOURCE MAP: Articles in Print Periodicals

1 **Author.** List the last name first. End with a period. For variations, see models 2–5.

2 **Article title.** Put the title and any subtitle in quotation marks; capitalize all major words. Place a period inside the closing quotation mark.

3 **Periodical title.** Italicize the title; capitalize all major words. Omit any initial *A*, *An*, or *The*.

4 **Volume and issue/Date of publication.** For journals, give the volume number and issue number (if any), separated by a period; then list the year in parentheses and follow it with a colon.

For magazines, list the day (if given), month, and year.

5 **Page numbers.** List inclusive page numbers. If the article skips pages, put the first page number and a plus sign. End with a period.

6 **Medium.** Give the medium (*Print*). End with a period.

A citation for the article on p. 259 would look like this:

Quart, Alissa. "Lost Media, Found Media: Snapshots from the Future of Writing." *Columbia Journalism Review* May/June 2008: 30-34. Print.

3 Periodical Title

COLUMBIA
JOURNALISM
REVIEW

May / June 2008 · cjr.org

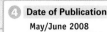
4 Date of Publication
May/June 2008

The Futu
Writ

Nonfiction's di
ALISSA QUART

Kindle isn't it,
EZRA KLEIN

UNDER THE :
A reporter reca
that got him th
CAMERON MCW

LOVE THY NE
The religion be
TIM TOWNSEND

---

2 Article Title

Lost Media,
Found Media

Snapshots from the future of writing

BY ALISSA QUART

1 Author

ALISSA QUART

If there were an ashram for people who worship contemplative long-form journalism, it would be the Nieman Conference on Narrative Journalism. This March, at the Sheraton Boston Hotel, hundreds of journalists, authors, students, and aspirants came for the weekend event. Seated on metal chairs in large conference rooms, we learned about muscular storytelling (the Q-shaped narrative structure—who knew?). We sipped cups of coffee and ate bagels and heard about reporting history through letters and public documents and how to evoke empathy for our subjects, particularly our most marginal ones. As we listened to reporters discussing great feats—exposing Walter Reed's fetid living quarters for wounded soldiers, for instance—we also renewed our pride in our profession. In short, the conference exemplified the best of the older media models, the ones that have so recently fallen into economic turmoil.

Yet even at the weekend's strongest lectures on interview techniques or the long-form profile, we couldn't ignore the digital elephant in the room. We all knew as writers that the kinds of pieces we were discussing require months of work to be both deep and refined, and that we were all hard-pressed for the time and the money to do that. It was always hard for nonfiction writers, but something seems to have changed. For those of us who believed in the value of the journalism and literary nonfiction of the past, we had

become like the people at the ashram after the guru has died.

Right now, journalism is more or less divided into two camps, which I will call Lost Media and Found Media. I went to the Nieman conference partially because I wanted to see how the forces creating this new division are affecting and afflicting the Lost Media world that I love best, not on the institutional level, but for reporters and writers themselves. This world includes people who write for all the newspapers and magazines that are currently struggling with layoffs, speedups, hiring freezes, buyouts, the death or shrinkage of film- and book-review sections, limits on expensive investigative work, the erasure of foreign bureaus, and the general narrowing of institutional ambition. It includes freelance writers competing with hordes of ever-younger competitors willing to write and publish online for free, the fade-out of established journalistic career paths, and, perhaps most crucially, a muddled sense of the meritorious, as blogs level and scramble the value and status of print publications, and of professional writers. The glamour and influence once associated with a magazine elite seem to have faded, becoming a sort of pastiche of winsome articles about yearning and boxers and dinners at Elaine's.

Found Media-ites, meanwhile, are the bloggers, the contributors to Huffington Post-type sites that aggregate blogs, as well as other work that somebody else paid for, and the new nonprofits and pay-per-article schemes that aim to save journalism from 20 percent profit-margin demands. Although these elements are often disparate, together they compose the new media landscape. In economic terms, I mean all the outlets for nonfiction writing that seem to be thriving in the new era or striving to fill niches that Lost Media is giving up in a new order. Stylistically, Found Media tends to feel spontaneous, almost accidental. It's a domain dominated by the young, where writers get points not for following traditions or burnishing them but for amateur and hybrid vigor, for creating their own venues and their own genres. It is about public expression and community—not quite John Dewey's Great Community, which the critic Eric Alterman alluded to in a recent *New Yorker* article on newspapers, but rather a fractured form of Dewey's ideal: call it Great Communities.

To be a Found Media journalist or pundit, one need not be elite, expert, or trained; one must simply produce punchy intellectual property that is in conversation with groups of

Illustration by Tomer Hanuka

5 Page Numbers
30–34

33. REVIEW

> Franklin, Nancy. "Teen Spirit." Rev. of *Glee*, by Ryan Murphy, Brad Falchuk, and Ian Brennan. *New Yorker* 10 May 2010: 72-73. Print.

> Schwarz, Benjamin. Rev. of *The Second World War: A Short History*, by R. A. C. Parker. *Atlantic Monthly* May 2002: 110-11. Print.

34. UNSIGNED ARTICLE

> "Performance of the Week." *Time* 6 Oct. 2003: 18. Print.

Digital written-word sources

Digital sources such as Web sites differ from print sources in the ease with which they can be changed, updated, or eliminated. In addition, the various electronic media do not organize their works the same way. The most commonly cited electronic sources are documents from Web sites and databases. For help determining which is which, see 41a.

35. WORK FROM A DATABASE. The basic format for citing a work from a database appears in the source map on pp. 262–63.

For a periodical article that is available in print but that you access in an online database through a library subscription service such as Academic Search Premier, begin with the author's name (if given); the title of the work, in quotation marks; the title of the periodical, italicized; and the volume/issue and date of the print version of the work (see models 28–34). Include the page numbers from the print version; if no page numbers are available, use *n. pag.* Then give the name of the online database, italicized; the medium (*Web*); and your most recent date of access.

> Collins, Ross F. "Cattle Barons and Ink Slingers: How Cow Country Journalists Created a Great American Myth." *American Journalism* 24.3 (2007): 7-29. *Communication and Mass Media Complete.* Web. 7 Feb. 2013.

36. ARTICLE FROM THE WEB SITE OF A JOURNAL. Begin an entry for an online journal article as you would one for a print journal article (see model 28). If an article does not have page numbers, use *n. pag.* End with the medium consulted (*Web*) and the date of access.

Checklist

Citing Digital Sources

When citing sources accessed online or from an electronic database, give as many of the following elements as you can find:

1. **Author.** Give the author's name, if available.

2. **Title.** Put titles of articles or short works in quotation marks. Italicize book titles.

For works from databases:

3. **Title of periodical,** italicized.

4. **Publication information.** After the volume/issue/year or date, include page numbers (or *n. pag.* if no page numbers are listed).

5. **Name of database,** italicized, if you used a subscription service such as Academic Search Premier.

For works from the Web:

3. **Title of the site,** italicized.

4. **Name of the publisher or sponsor.** This information usually appears at the bottom of the page.

5. **Date of online publication or most recent update.** This information often appears at the bottom of the page. If no date is given, use *n.d.*

6. **Medium of publication.** Use *Web*.

7. **Date of access.** Give the most recent date you accessed the source.

If you think your readers will have difficulty finding the source without a URL, put it after the period following the date of access, inside angle brackets, with a period after the closing bracket.

Gallagher, Brian. "Greta Garbo Is Sad: Some Historical Reflections on the

Paradoxes of Stardom in the American Film Industry, 1910-1960."

Images: A Journal of Film and Popular Culture 3 (1997): n. pag. Web.

7 Aug. 2013.

37. ARTICLE IN A MAGAZINE ON THE WEB. See model 29 for print publication information if the article appears in print. After the name of

Library subscriptions—such as EBSCOhost and Academic Search Premier—provide access to huge databases of articles.

1 **Author.** List the last name first. End with a period. For variations, see models 2–5.

2 **Article title.** Enclose the title and any subtitle in quotation marks.

3 **Periodical title.** Italicize it. Exclude any initial *A*, *An*, or *The*.

4 **Volume and issue/Date of publication.** List the volume and issue number, if any. Then, add the date of publication, including the day (if given), month, and year, in that order. Last, add a colon.

5 **Page numbers.** Give the inclusive page numbers. If an article has no page numbers, write *n. pag.*

6 **Database name.** Italicize the name of the database.

7 **Medium.** For an online database, use *Web*.

8 **Date of access.** Give the day, month, and year, then a period.

A citation for the article on p. 263 would look like this:

Arnett, Robert P. "*Casino Royale* and Franchise Remix: James Bond as
    Superhero." *Film Criticism* 33.3 (2009): 1-16. *Academic Search Premier.*
    Web. 16 May 2013.

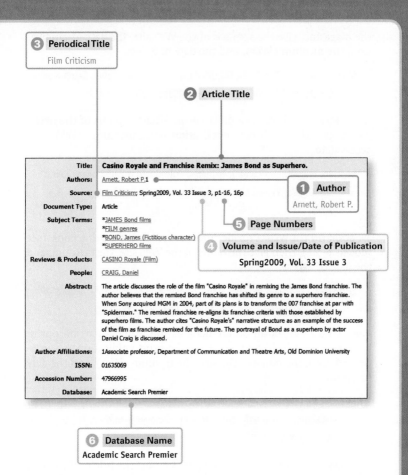

③ Periodical Title
Film Criticism

② Article Title

Title:	**Casino Royale and Franchise Remix: James Bond as Superhero.**
Authors:	Arnett, Robert P.1
Source:	Film Criticism; Spring2009, Vol. 33 Issue 3, p1-16, 16p
Document Type:	Article
Subject Terms:	*JAMES Bond films
	*FILM genres
	*BOND, James (Fictitious character)
	*SUPERHERO films
Reviews & Products:	CASINO Royale (Film)
People:	CRAIG, Daniel
Abstract:	The article discusses the role of the film "Casino Royale" in remixing the James Bond franchise. The author believes that the remixed Bond franchise has shifted its genre to a superhero franchise. When Sony acquired MGM in 2004, part of its plans is to transform the 007 franchise at par with "Spiderman." The remixed franchise re-aligns its franchise criteria with those established by superhero films. The author cites "Casino Royale's" narrative structure as an example of the success of the film as franchise remixed for the future. The portrayal of Bond as a superhero by actor Daniel Craig is discussed.
Author Affiliations:	1Associate professor, Department of Communication and Theatre Arts, Old Dominion University
ISSN:	01635069
Accession Number:	47966995
Database:	Academic Search Premier

① Author
Arnett, Robert P.

⑤ Page Numbers

④ Volume and Issue/Date of Publication
Spring2009, Vol. 33 Issue 3

⑥ Database Name
Academic Search Premier

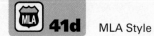

the magazine, give the sponsor of the Web site, the date of publication, the medium (*Web*), and the date of access.

> Shapiro, Walter. "The Quest for Universal Healthcare." *Salon*. Salon Media
>
> Group, 21 Feb. 2008. Web. 2 Mar. 2012.

38. ARTICLE IN A NEWSPAPER ON THE WEB. After the name of the newspaper, give the publisher, publication date, medium (*Web*), and access date.

> Bustillo, Miguel, and Carol J. Williams. "Old Guard in Cuba Keeps Reins."
>
> *Los Angeles Times*. Los Angeles Times, 25 Feb. 2008. Web. 26 Feb.
>
> 2013.

39. BOOK ON THE WEB. Provide information as for a print book (see models 6–27); then give the name of the Web site, the medium, and the date of access.

> Euripides. *The Trojan Women*. Trans. Gilbert Murray. New York: Oxford UP,
>
> 1915. *Internet Sacred Text Archive*. Web. 12 Oct. 2013.

Note: Cite a part of an online book as you would a part of a print book (see models 10 and 21). Give the print publication information (if any), the name of the site, the medium (*Web*), and the date of access.

> Riis, Jacob. "The Genesis of the Gang." *The Battle with the Slum*.
>
> New York: Macmillan, 1902. N. pag. *Bartleby.com: Great Books Online*.
>
> Web. 31 Mar. 2013.

40. POEM ON THE WEB. Include the poet's name, the title of the poem, and the print publication information (if any) as you would for part of an online book (model 39). End with the name of the site, the medium (*Web*), and the date of access.

> Dickinson, Emily. "The Grass." *Poems: Emily Dickinson*. Boston, 1891. N. pag.
>
> *Humanities Text Initiative American Verse Project*. Web. 6 Jan. 2012.

41. EDITORIAL OR LETTER IN A WEB PERIODICAL. Include the word *Editorial* or *Letter* after the author (if given) and title (if any). End with the periodical name, the sponsor of the Web site, the date of posting or most recent update, the medium, and the access date.

"The Funding Gap." Editorial. *Washington Post*. Washington Post, 5 Nov.

2003. Web. 19 Oct. 2012.

Moore, Paula. "Go Vegetarian." Letter. *New York Times*. New York Times,

25 Feb. 2008. Web. 25 Feb. 2013.

42. REVIEW IN A WEB PERIODICAL. Cite an online review as you would a print review (see model 33). End with the name of the periodical, the sponsor, the date of electronic publication, the medium, and the date of access.

Seitz, Matt Zoller. "A Modern Horror Film." Rev. of *The Social Network,* dir.

David Fincher. *Salon*. Salon Media Group, 4 Oct. 2010. Web. 24 May

2013.

43. ENTRY IN A WEB REFERENCE WORK. Cite the entry as you would an entry from a print reference work (see model 22). Follow with the name of the Web site, the sponsor, date of publication, medium, and date of access.

"Tour de France." *Encyclopaedia Britannica Online*. Encyclopaedia

Britannica, 2006. Web. 21 May 2012.

44. WORK FROM A WEB SITE. For basic information on citing a work from a Web site, see the source map on pp. 266–67. Include all of the following elements that are available: the author; the title of the work, in quotation marks; the name of the Web site, italicized; the name of the publisher or sponsor (if none is available, use *N.p.*); the date of publication (if not available, use *n.d.*); the medium (*Web*); and the date of access.

"America: A Center-Left Nation." *Media Matters for America*. Media Matters

for America, 27 May 2009. Web. 31 May 2011.

Stauder, Ellen Keck. "Darkness Audible: Negative Capability and Mark

Doty's 'Nocturne in Black and Gold.'" *Romantic Circles Praxis Series*.

U of Maryland, 2003. Web. 28 Sept. 2013.

MLA SOURCE MAP: Works from Web Sites

You may need to browse other parts of a site to find some of the following elements, and some sites may omit elements. Uncover as much information as you can.

① **Author.** List the last name first. End with a period. If no author is given, begin with the title. For variations, see models 2–5.

② **Title of work.** Enclose the title and any subtitle of the work in quotation marks.

③ **Title of Web site.** Give the title of the entire Web site, italicized.

④ **Publisher or sponsor.** Look for the sponsor's name at the bottom of the home page. If no information is available, write *N.p.* Follow it with a comma.

⑤ **Date of publication or latest update.** Give the most recent date, followed by a period. If no date is available, use *n.d.*

⑥ **Medium.** Use *Web* and follow it with a period.

⑦ **Date of access.** Give the date you accessed the work. End with a period.

A citation for the work on p. 267 would look like this:

Tønnesson, Øyvind. "Mahatma Gandhi, the Missing Laureate."

Nobelprize.org. Nobel Foundation, 1 Dec. 1999. Web. 4 May 2013.

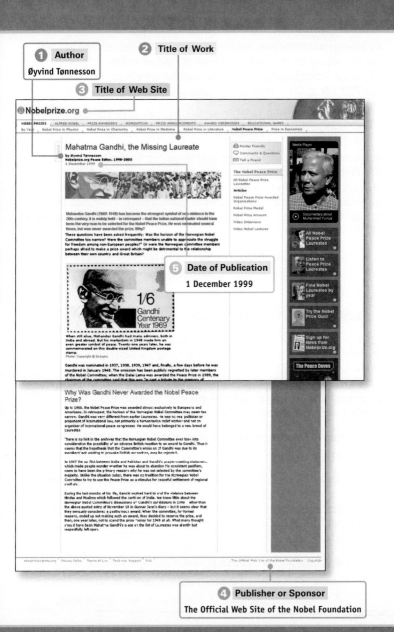

1 Author

Øyvind Tønnesson

2 Title of Work

3 Title of Web Site

Nobelprize.org

NOBEL PRIZES | ALFRED NOBEL | PRIZE AWARDERS | NOMINATION | PRIZE ANNOUNCEMENTS | AWARD CEREMONIES | EDUCATIONAL GAMES
By Year | Nobel Prize in Physics | Nobel Prize in Chemistry | Nobel Prize in Medicine | Nobel Prize in Literature | Nobel Peace Prize | Prize in Economics

Mahatma Gandhi, the Missing Laureate

by Øyvind Tønnesson
Nobelprize.org Peace Editor, 1998–2000
1 December 1999

Mohandas Gandhi (1869-1948) has become the strongest symbol of non-violence in the 20th century. It is widely held – that the Indian national leader should have been the very man to be selected for the Nobel Peace Prize. He was nominated several times, but was never awarded the prize. Why?

These questions have been asked frequently: Was the horizon of the Norwegian Nobel Committee too narrow? Were the committee members unable to appreciate the struggle for freedom among non-European peoples?" Or were the Norwegian committee members perhaps afraid to make a prize award which might be detrimental to the relationship between their own country and Great Britain?

5 Date of Publication

1 December 1999

When still alive, Mohandas Gandhi had many admirers, both in India and abroad. But his martyrdom in 1948 made him an even greater symbol of peace. Twenty-one years later, he was commemorated on this double-sized United Kingdom postage stamp.
Photo: Copyright © Scanpix

Gandhi was nominated in 1937, 1938, 1939, 1947 and, finally, a few days before he was murdered in January 1948. The omission has been publicly regretted by later members of the Nobel Committee; when the Dalai Lama was awarded the Peace Prize in 1989, the chairman of the committee said that this was "in part a tribute to the memory of

The Nobel Peace Prize

All Nobel Peace Prize
Laureates

Articles

Nobel Peace Prize Awarded
Organizations

Nobel Prize Medal

Nobel Prize Amount

Video Interviews

Video Nobel Lectures

Why Was Gandhi Never Awarded the Nobel Peace Prize?

Up to 1960, the Nobel Peace Prize was awarded almost exclusively to Europeans and Americans. In retrospect, the horizon of the Norwegian Nobel Committee may seem too narrow. Gandhi was very different from earlier Laureates. He was no real politician or proponent of international law, not primarily a humanitarian relief worker and not an organiser of international peace congresses. He would have belonged to a new breed of Laureates.

There is no hint in the archives that the Norwegian Nobel Committee ever took into consideration the possibility of an award to Gandhi. Thus it seems that the hypothesis that the Committee's omiss on of Gandhi was due to its members' not wanting to provoke British authorities, may be rejected.

In 1947 the conflict between India and Pakistan and Gandhi's prayer-meeting statement, which made people wonder whether he was about to abandon his consistent pacifism, seem to have been the primary reasons why he was not selected by the committee's majority. Unlike the situation today, there was no tradition for the Norwegian Nobel Committee to try to use the Peace Prize as a stimulus for peaceful settlement of regional conflicts.

During the last months of his life, Gandhi worked hard to end the violence between Hindus and Muslims which followed the partition of India. We know little about the Norwegian Nobel Committee's discussions on Gandhi's candidature in 1948 other than the above quoted entry of November 18 in Gunnar Jahn's diary – but it seems clear that they seriously considered a posthumous award. When the committee, for formal reasons, ended up not making such an award, they decided to reserve the prize, and then, one year later, not to spend the prize money for 1948 at all. What many thought should have been Mahatma Gandhi's place on the list of Laureates was silently but respectfully left open.

About nobelprize.org   Privacy Policy   Terms of Use   Technical Support   RSS   The Official Web Site of the Nobel Foundation   Copyright

4 Publisher or Sponsor

The Official Web Site of the Nobel Foundation

267

45. DOWNLOADED PDF FILE. If you download a PDF file instead of reading the source online, determine what kind of source it is (such as a journal article) and give the information for citing such a source. Use *PDF file* as the medium; omit the access date.

> Christenson, Clayton M., David Skok, and James Allworth. "Be the
>
> Disruptor." *Nieman Reports* 66.3 (2012): 8-23. PDF file.

46. ENTIRE WEB SITE. Follow the guidelines for a specific work from the Web, beginning with the name of the author, editor, compiler, director, narrator, or translator, followed by the title of the Web site, italicized; the name of the sponsor or publisher (if none, use *N.p.*); the date of publication or last update; the medium of publication (*Web*); and the date of access.

> Bernstein, Charles, Kenneth Goldsmith, Martin Spinelli, and Patrick Durgin,
>
> eds. *Electronic Poetry Corner.* SUNY Buffalo, 2003. Web. 26 Sept.
>
> 2013.

> *Weather.com.* Weather Channel Interactive, 2011. Web. 13 Mar. 2012.

For a personal Web site, include the name of the person who created the site; the title or (if there is no title) a description such as *Home page,* not italicized; the name of the larger site, if different from the personal site's title; the publisher or sponsor of the site (if none, use *N.p.*); the date of the last update; the medium of publication (*Web*); and the date of access.

> Ede, Lisa. Home page. *Oregon State.* Oregon State U, 2010. Web. 17 May
>
> 2013.

47. ACADEMIC COURSE WEB SITE. For a course site, include the name of the instructor, the title of the course in quotation marks, the title of the site in italics, the department (if relevant) and institution sponsoring the site, the date (or *n.d.*), the medium (*Web*), and the access date.

> Creekmur, Corey K., and Philip Lutgendorf. "Topics in Asian Cinema:
>
> Popular Hindi Cinema." *University of Iowa.* Depts. of English, Cinema,
>
> and Comparative Literature, U of Iowa, 2004. Web. 13 Mar. 2012.

For a department Web site, give the department name, the description *Dept. home page*, the institution (in italics), the site sponsor, the medium (*Web*), and the access information.

> English Dept. home page. *Amherst College.* Amherst Coll., n.d. Web. 5 Apr.
>
> 2013.

48. BLOG. For an entire blog, give the author's name; the title of the blog, italicized; the sponsor or publisher of the blog (if there is none, use *N.p.*); the date of the most recent update; the medium (*Web*); and the date of access.

> *Little Green Footballs.* Little Green Footballs, 23 Aug. 2012. Web. 23 Aug.
>
> 2012.

Note: To cite a blogger who writes under a pseudonym, begin with the pseudonym and then put the writer's real name (if you know it) in square brackets.

> Atrios [Duncan Black]. *Eschaton.* N.p., 27 June 2013. Web. 27 June
>
> 2013.

49. PUBLISHED INTERVIEW. List the person interviewed and either the title of the interview (if any) or the label *Interview* and the interviewer's name, if relevant. Then provide information about the source, following the appropriate model.

> Paretsky, Sara. Interview. *Progressive.* Progressive Magazine, 14 Jan. 2008.
>
> Web. 12 Feb. 2011.

> Taylor, Max. "Max Taylor on Winning." *Time* 13 Nov. 2000: 66. Print.

50. POST OR COMMENT ON A BLOG. Give the author's name; the title of the post or comment, in quotation marks (if there is no title, use the description *Web log post* or *Web log comment*, not italicized); the title of the blog, italicized; the sponsor of the blog (if there is none, use *N.p.*); the date of the most recent update; the medium (*Web*); and the date of access.

> Marcotte, Amanda. "Standing Up to Sexism Works." *Raw Story.* N.p.,
>
> 15 May 2013. Web. 16 May 2013.

51. ENTRY IN A WIKI. Because wiki content is collectively edited, do not include an author. Treat a wiki as you would a work from a Web site (see model 44). Check with your instructor before using a wiki as a source.

"Fédération Internationale de Football Association." *Wikipedia.* Wikimedia

Foundation, 27 June 2013. Web. 27 June 2013.

52. POSTING TO A DISCUSSION GROUP OR NEWSGROUP. Begin with the author's name and the title of the posting in quotation marks (or the words *Online posting*). Follow with the name of the Web site, the sponsor or publisher of the site (use *N.p.* if there is no sponsor), the date of publication, the medium (*Web*), and the date of access.

Daly, Catherine. "Poetry Slams." *Poetics Discussion List.* SUNY Buffalo,

29 Aug. 2003. Web. 1 Oct. 2005.

53. POSTING TO A SOCIAL NETWORKING SITE. To cite a posting on Facebook or another social networking site, include the writer's name, a description of the posting, the date of the posting, and the medium of delivery. (The MLA does not provide guidelines for citing postings on such sites; this model is based on the MLA's guidelines for citing email.)

Ferguson, Sarah. Status update. 6 Mar. 2013. Facebook posting.

54. EMAIL OR MESSAGE ON SOCIAL NETWORKING SITE. Include the writer's name; the subject line, in quotation marks (for email); *Message to* (not italicized or in quotation marks) followed by the recipient's name; the date of the message; and the medium of delivery (*E-mail*). (MLA style hyphenates *e-mail.*)

Harris, Jay. "Thoughts on Impromptu Stage Productions." Message to the

author. 16 July 2006. E-mail.

55. TWEET. Include the writer's real name, if known, with the user name (if different) in parentheses. If you don't know the real name, give just the user name. Include the entire tweet, in quotation marks. End with date and time of message and the medium (*Tweet*).

BedfordBits. "#4C12 'Think of citations as a guide for the engaged

reader.' Writing center tutor quoted by E. Kleinfeld. See http://

citationproject.net/" 23 Mar. 2012, 4:01 p.m. Tweet.

Visual, audio, multimedia, and live sources

56. FILM, DVD, OR STREAMING VIDEO. If you cite a particular person's work, start with that name. If not, start with the title; then name the director, distributor, and year of release. Other contributors, such as writers or performers, may follow the director. If you cite a DVD instead of a theatrical release, include the original film release date and the label *DVD*.

Black Swan. Dir. Darren Aronofsky. Perf. Natalie Portman. Fox Searchlight,

2010. Film.

Spirited Away. Dir. Hayao Miyazaki. 2001. Walt Disney Video, 2003. DVD.

For material streamed from a Web site, give the name of the site or database, the medium (*Web*), and the access date.

Winner, Michael, dir. *Death Wish*. Perf. Charles Bronson. Paramount, 1974.

Netflix. Web. 11 Nov. 2012.

 Checklist

Citing Sources without Models in MLA Style

To cite a source for which you cannot find a model, collect as much information as you can find—about the creator, title, sponsor, date of posting or latest update, the date you accessed the site and its location—with the goal of helping your readers find the source for themselves, if possible. Then look at the models in this section to see which one most closely matches the type of source you are using.

In an academic writing project, before citing an electronic source for which you have no model, also be sure to ask your instructor for help.

57. SHORT ONLINE VIDEO. Cite a short online video as you would a work from a Web site (see model 44).

> Weber, Jan. "As We Sow, Part 1: Where Are the Farmers?" *YouTube.*
>
> YouTube, 15 Mar. 2008. Web. 27 Sept. 2012.

58. TELEVISION OR RADIO PROGRAM. In general, begin with the title of the program, italicized. Then list important contributors (narrator, writer, director, actors); the network; the local station and city, if any; the broadcast date; and the medium. To cite a particular person's work, begin with that name. To cite a particular episode from a series, begin with the episode title, enclosed in quotation marks.

> *The American Experience: Buffalo Bill.* Writ., dir., prod. Rob Rapley. PBS.
>
> WNET, New York, 25 Feb. 2008. Television.

> "For Immediate Release." *Mad Men.* Writ. Matthew Weiner. Dir. Jennifer
>
> Getzinger. AMC. 5 May 2013. Television.

Note: For a streaming version online, give the name of the Web site, italicized. Then give the publisher or sponsor, a comma, and the date posted. End with the medium (*Web*) and the access date.

> Limbaugh, Rush. *The Rush Limbaugh Show. RushLimbaugh.com.* Premier
>
> Radio Networks, 29 Feb. 2012. Web. 2 Apr. 2012.

59. BROADCAST INTERVIEW. List the person interviewed and then the title, if any. If the interview has no title, use the label *Interview* and name the interviewer, if relevant. Then identify the source. To cite a broadcast interview, end with information about the program, the date(s) that the interview took place, and the medium.

> Revkin, Andrew. Interview with Terry Gross. *Fresh Air.* Natl. Public Radio.
>
> WNYC, New York, 14 June 2006. Radio.

Note: If you listened to an archived version online, provide the site's sponsor (if known), the date of the interview, the medium (*Web*), and the access date. For a podcast interview, see model 66.

Revkin, Andrew. Interview with Terry Gross. *Fresh Air. NPR.org.* NPR,

14 June 2006. Web. 12 Jan. 2013.

60. UNPUBLISHED OR PERSONAL INTERVIEW. List the person who was interviewed; the label *Telephone interview, Personal interview,* or *E-mail interview;* and the date the interview took place.

Freedman, Sasha. Personal interview. 10 Nov. 2011.

61. SOUND RECORDING. List the name of the person or group you wish to emphasize (such as the composer, conductor, or band); the title of the recording or composition; the artist, if appropriate; the manufacturer; and the year of issue. Give the medium (such as *CD, MP3 file,* or *LP*). If you are citing a particular song or selection, include its title, in quotation marks, before the title of the recording.

Bach, Johann Sebastian. *Bach: Violin Concertos.* Perf. Itzhak Perlman and

Pinchas Zukerman. English Chamber Orch. EMI, 2002. CD.

Sonic Youth. "Incinerate." *Rather Ripped.* Geffen, 2006. MP3 file.

Note: If you are citing instrumental music that is identified only by form, number, and key, do not underline, italicize, or enclose it in quotation marks.

Grieg, Edvard. Concerto in A minor, op. 16. Cond. Eugene Ormandy.

Philadelphia Orch. RCA, 1989. LP.

62. MUSICAL COMPOSITION. When you are not citing a specific published version, first give the composer's name, followed by the title.

Mozart, Wolfgang Amadeus. *Don Giovanni,* K527.

Mozart, Wolfgang Amadeus. Symphony no. 41 in C major, K551.

Note: Cite a published score as you would a book. If you include the date that the composition was written, do so immediately after the title.

Schoenberg, Arnold. *Chamber Symphony No. 1 for 15 Solo Instruments,*

Op. 9. 1906. New York: Dover, 2002. Print.

63. COMPUTER GAME. Include the version after the title, then the city and publisher, date, and medium.

> *Grand Theft Auto: Tales from Liberty City*. PlayStation 3 vers. New York:
>
> Rockstar Games, 2009. DVD-ROM.

Cite an online game as you would a work from a Web site (see model 44).

> *The Sims 3*. PC vers. *TheSims.com*. Electronic Arts, 2011. Web. 30 Nov. 2012.

64. LECTURE OR SPEECH. List the speaker; title, in quotation marks; sponsoring institution or group; place; and date. If the speech is untitled, use a label such as *Lecture*.

> Colbert, Stephen. Speech. White House Correspondents' Association
>
> Dinner. *YouTube*. YouTube, 29 Apr. 2006. Web. 20 May 2013.

> Eugenides, Jeffrey. Portland Arts and Lectures. Arlene Schnitzer Concert
>
> Hall, Portland, OR. 30 Sept. 2003. Lecture.

65. LIVE PERFORMANCE. List the title, appropriate names (such as writer or performer), the place, and the date. To cite a particular person's work, begin the entry with that name.

> *Anything Goes*. By Cole Porter. Perf. Klea Blackhurst. Shubert Theater,
>
> New Haven. 7 Oct. 2003. Performance.

66. PODCAST (STREAMING). Include all of the following that are relevant and available: the speaker, the title of the podcast, the title of the program, the host or performers, the title of the site, the site's sponsor, the date of posting, the medium (*Web*), and the access date. (This model is based on MLA guidelines for a short work from a Web site. For a downloaded podcast, see model 67.)

> "Seven Arrested in U.S. Terror Raid." *Morning Report*. Host Krishnan
>
> Guru-Murthy. *4 Radio*. Channel 4 News, 23 June 2006. Web.
>
> 27 June 2012.

67. DIGITAL FILE. A citation for a file that you can download—one that exists independently, not only on a Web site—begins with citation information required for the type of source (a photograph or sound recording, for example). For the medium, indicate the type of file (*MP3 file, JPEG file*).

> *Officers' Winter Quarters, Army of Potomac, Brandy Station.* Mar. 1864.
>
> > Prints and Photographs Div., Lib. of Cong. TIFF file.
>
> "Return to the Giant Pool of Money." *This American Life.* Narr. Ira Glass.
>
> > NPR, 25 Sept. 2009. MP3 file.

68. WORK OF ART OR PHOTOGRAPH. List the artist or photographer; the work's title, italicized; the date of composition (if unknown, use *n.d.*); and the medium of composition (*Oil on canvas, Bronze*). Then cite the name of the museum or other location and the city. To cite a reproduction in a book, add the publication information. To cite artwork found online, omit the medium of composition, and after the location, add the title of the database or Web site, italicized; the medium consulted (*Web*); and the date of access.

> Chagall, Marc. *The Poet with the Birds.* 1911. Minneapolis Inst. of Arts.
>
> > *artsmia.org.* Web. 6 Oct. 2013.
>
> *General William Palmer in Old Age.* 1810. Oil on canvas. National Army
>
> > Museum, London. *White Mughals: Love and Betrayal in Eighteenth-Century*
> >
> > *India.* By William Dalrymple. New York: Penguin, 2002. 270. Print.
>
> Kahlo, Frida. *Self-Portrait with Cropped Hair.* 1940. Oil on canvas. Museum
>
> > of Mod. Art, New York.

69. MAP OR CHART. Cite a map or chart as you would a book or a short work within a longer work, and include the word *Map* or *Chart* after the title. Add the medium of publication. For an online source, end with the date of access.

> "Australia." Map. *Perry-Castañeda Library Map Collection.* U of Texas, 1999.
>
> > Web. 4 Nov. 2012.
>
> *California.* Map. Chicago: Rand, 2002. Print.

70. CARTOON OR COMIC STRIP. List the artist's name; the title (if any) of the cartoon or comic strip, in quotation marks; the label *Cartoon* or

Comic strip; and the usual publication information for a print periodical (see models 28–31) or a work from a Web site (model 44).

> Johnston, Lynn. "For Better or Worse." Comic strip. *FBorFW.com*. Lynn
>
> Johnston Publications, 30 June 2006. Web. 20 July 2006.

> Lewis, Eric. "The Unpublished Freud." Cartoon. *New Yorker* 11 Mar. 2002: 80.
>
> Print.

71. ADVERTISEMENT. Include the label *Advertisement* after the name of the item or organization being advertised.

> Microsoft. Advertisement. *Harper's* Oct. 2003: 2-3. Print.

> Microsoft. Advertisement. *New York Times*. New York Times, 11 Nov. 2003.
>
> Web. 11 Nov. 2003.

Academic, government, and legal sources (including digital versions)

If an online version is not shown here, use the appropriate model for the source and then end with the medium and date of access.

72. REPORT OR PAMPHLET. Follow the guidelines for either a print book (models 6–27) or an online book (model 39).

> Allen, Katherine, and Lee Rainie. *Parents Online*. Washington: Pew Internet
>
> & Amer. Life Project, 2002. Print.

> Environmental Working Group. *Dead in the Water*. Washington:
>
> Environmental Working Group, 2006. Web. 24 Apr. 2011.

73. GOVERNMENT PUBLICATION. Begin with the author, if identified. Otherwise, start with the name of the government, followed by the agency. For congressional documents, cite the number, session, and house of Congress (*S* for Senate, *H* for House of Representatives); the type (*Report, Resolution, Document*) in abbreviated form; and the number. End with the publication information. The print publisher is often the Government Printing Office (GPO). For online versions, follow the models for a work from a Web site (model 44) or an entire Web site (model 46).

Gregg, Judd. *Report to Accompany the Genetic Information Act of 2003*. US 108th Cong., 1st sess. S. Rept. 108-22. Washington: GPO, 2003. Print.

Kinsella, Kevin, and Victoria Velkoff. *An Aging World: 2001*. US Bureau of the Census. Washington: GPO, 2001. Print.

United States. Centers for Disease Control and Prevention. "FluView Interactive." *Centers for Disease Control and Prevention*. Centers for Disease Control and Prevention, Dec. 2012. Web. 7 Mar. 2013.

74. PUBLISHED PROCEEDINGS OF A CONFERENCE. Cite proceedings as you would a book.

Cleary, John, and Gary Gurtler, eds. *Proceedings of the Boston Area Colloquium in Ancient Philosophy 2002*. Boston: Brill Academic, 2003. Print.

75. DISSERTATION. Enclose the title in quotation marks. Add the label *Diss.*, the school, and the year the work was accepted.

Paris, Django. "Our Culture: Difference, Division, and Unity in Multicultural Youth Space." Diss. Stanford U, 2008. Print.

Note: Cite a published dissertation as a book, adding the identification *Diss.* and the university after the title.

76. DISSERTATION ABSTRACT. Cite as you would an unpublished dissertation (see model 75). For the abstract of a dissertation using *Dissertation Abstracts International* (*DAI*), include the *DAI* volume, year, and page number.

Huang-Tiller, Gillian C. "The Power of the Meta-Genre: Cultural, Sexual, and Racial Politics of the American Modernist Sonnet." Diss. U of Notre Dame, 2000. *DAI* 61 (2000): 1401. Print.

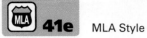
77. UNPUBLISHED LETTER. Cite a published letter as a work in an anthology (see model 10). If the letter is unpublished, follow this form, with *MS* (for *manuscript*) as the medium:

Anzaldúa, Gloria. Letter to the author. 10 Sept. 2002. MS.

78. MANUSCRIPT OR OTHER UNPUBLISHED WORK. List the author's name; the title (if any) or a description of the material; the form of the material (such as *TS* for *typescript*) and any identifying numbers; and the name and location of the library or research institution housing the material, if applicable.

Woolf, Virginia. "The Searchlight." N.d. TS. Ser. III, Box 4, Item 184.

　Papers of Virginia Woolf, 1902-1956. Smith Coll., Northampton.

79. LEGAL SOURCE. To cite a court case, give the names of the first plaintiff and defendant, the case number, the name of the court, and the date of the decision. To cite an act, give the name of the act followed by its Public Law (*Pub. L.*) number, the date the act was enacted, and its Statutes at Large (*Stat.*) cataloging number.

Eldred v. Ashcroft. No. 01-618. Supreme Ct. of the US. 15 Jan. 2003. Print.

Museum and Library Services Act of 2003. Pub. L. 108-81. 25 Sept. 2003.

　Stat. 117.991. Print.

Note: You do not need an entry on the list of works cited when you cite articles of the U.S. Constitution and laws in the U.S. Code.

41e A sample student research project, MLA style

Excerpts from a brief research essay by David Craig appear on the following pages. David followed the MLA guidelines described in this chapter. To read his complete project, go to the integrated media page at **bedfordstmartins.com/easy**.

1/2"

1"

Craig 1

David Craig

Professor Turkman

English 219

15 December 2012

Messaging: The Language of Youth Literacy

The English language is under attack. At least, that is what
many people seem to believe. From concerned parents to local
librarians, everyone seems to have a negative comment on the state
of youth literacy today. They fear that the current generation of
grade school students will graduate with an extremely low level of
literacy, and they point out that although language education hasn't
changed, kids are having more trouble reading and writing than in
the past. When asked about the cause of this situation, many adults
pin the blame on technologies such as texting and instant messaging,
arguing that electronic shortcuts create and compound undesirable
reading and writing habits and discourage students from learning
conventionally correct ways to use language. But although the
arguments against messaging are passionate, evidence suggests that
they may not hold up.

The disagreements about messaging shortcuts are profound,
even among academics. John Briggs, an English professor at the
University of California, Riverside, says, "Americans have always
been informal, but now the informality of precollege culture is so
ubiquitous that many students have no practice in using language
in any formal setting at all" (qtd. in McCarroll). Such objections are
not new; Sven Birkerts of Mount Holyoke College argued in 1999
that "[students] read more casually. They strip-mine what they
read" online and consequently produce "quickly generated, casual
prose" (qtd. in Leibowitz A67). However, academics are also among
the defenders of texting and instant messaging (IM), with some
suggesting that messaging may be a beneficial force in the

Name,
instructor,
course, date
aligned at
left

Title
centered

Opens with
attention-
getting
statement

Background
on the
problem
of youth
literacy

Thesis
statement

Quotation
used as
evidence

Annotations indicate effective choices or MLA-style formatting.

Craig 10

Heading
centered

Works Cited

Report

Carnahan, Kristin, and Chiara Coletti. *Ten-Year Trend in SAT Scores Indicates Increased Emphasis on Math Is Yielding Results: Reading and Writing Are Causes for Concern.* New York: College Board, 2002. Print.

Graph
source

College Board. "2011 SAT Trends." *Collegeboard.org.* College Board, 14 Sept. 2011. Web. 6 Dec. 2012.

Print book

Crystal, David. *Language Play.* Chicago: U of Chicago P, 1998. Print.

Email

The Discouraging Word. "Re: Messaging and Literacy." Message to the author. 13 Nov. 2012. E-mail.

Article from
database

Ferguson, Niall. "Texting Makes U Stupid." *Newsweek* 158.12 (2011): 11. *Academic Search Premier.* Web. 7 Dec. 2012.

Print
newspaper
article

Leibowitz, Wendy R. "Technology Transforms Writing and the Teaching of Writing." *Chronicle of Higher Education* 26 Nov. 1999: A67-68. Print.

Downloaded
PDF file

Lenhart, Amanda. *Teens, Smartphones, & Texting.* Washington: Pew Internet & Amer. Life Project, 2012. PDF file.

Online report

Lenhart, Amanda, Sousan Arafeh, Aaron Smith, and Alexandra Macgill. *Writing, Technology & Teens.* Washington: Pew Internet & Amer. Life Project, 2008. Web. 6 Dec. 2012.

Subsequent
lines of
each entry
indented

Lenhart, Amanda, and Oliver Lewis. *Teenage Life Online: The Rise of the Instant-Message Generation and the Internet's Impact on Friendships and Family Relationships.* Washington: Pew Internet & Amer. Life Project, 2001. Web. 6 Dec. 2012.

Online
newspaper
article

McCarroll, Christina. "Teens Ready to Prove Text-Messaging Skills Can Score SAT Points." *Christian Science Monitor* 11 Mar. 2005. Web. 10 Dec. 2012.

42 APA Style

Chapter 42 discusses the basic formats prescribed by the American Psychological Association (APA), guidelines that are widely used for research in the social sciences. For further reference, consult the *Publication Manual of the American Psychological Association,* Sixth Edition (2010).

42a Understanding APA citation style

Why does academic work call for very careful citation practices when writing for the general public may not? The answer is that readers of academic work expect source citations for several reasons:

- Source citations demonstrate that you've done your homework on your topic and that you are a part of the conversation surrounding it.

- Source citations show that you understand the need to give credit when you make use of someone else's intellectual property. (See Chapter 39.)

- Source citations give explicit directions to guide readers who want to look for themselves at the works you're using.

The guidelines for APA style tell you exactly what information to include in your citation and how to format that information.

Types of sources. Look at the Directory to APA Style on pp. 290–91 for guidelines on citing various types of sources—print books (or parts of print books), print periodicals (journals, magazines, and newspapers), and digital written-word sources (an online article or a book on an e-reader). A digital version of a source may include updates or corrections that the print version lacks, so it's important to provide the correct information for readers. For sources that consist mainly of material other than written words—such as a film, song, or artwork—consult the "other sources" section of the directory. And if you can't find a model exactly like the source you've selected, see the box on p. 293.

ARTICLES FROM WEB AND DATABASE SOURCES. You need a subscription to look through most databases, so individual researchers almost always gain access to articles in databases through the computer system of a school or public library that pays to subscribe. The easiest way to tell whether a source comes from a database, then, is that its information is *not* generally available for free. Many databases are digital collections of articles that originally appeared in edited print periodicals, ensuring that an authority has vouched for the accuracy of the information. Such sources often have more credibility than free material available on the Web.

Parts of citations. APA citations appear in two parts of your text—a brief in-text citation in the body of your written text and a full citation in the list of references, to which the in-text citation directs readers. The most straightforward in-text citations include the author's name, the publication year, and the page number, but many variations on this basic format are discussed in 42c.

In the text of her research essay (see 42e and the integrated media), Tawnya Redding includes a paraphrase of material from an online journal that she accessed through the publisher's Web site. She cites the authors' names and the year of publication in a parenthetical reference, pointing readers to the entry for "Baker, F., & Bor, W. (2008)" in her references list, shown on p. 313.

Content notes. APA style allows you to use content notes, either at the bottom of the page or on a separate page at the end of the text, to expand or supplement your text. Indicate such notes in the text by superscript numerals ([1]). Double-space all entries. Indent the first line of each note five spaces, but begin subsequent lines at the left margin.

SUPERSCRIPT NUMBER IN TEXT

The age of the children involved in the study was an important factor in the selection of items for the questionnaire.[1]

FOOTNOTE

[1]Marjorie Youngston Forman and William Cole of the Child Study Team provided great assistance in identifying appropriate items for the questionnaire.

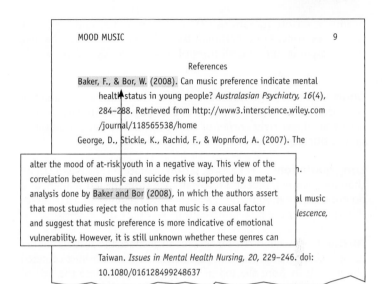

MOOD MUSIC 9

References

Baker, F., & Bor, W. (2008). Can music preference indicate mental
health status in young people? *Australasian Psychiatry, 16*(4),
284–288. Retrieved from http://www3.interscience.wiley.com
/journal/118565538/home

George, D., Stickle, K., Rachid, F., & Wopnford, A. (2007). The

alter the mood of at-risk youth in a negative way. This view of the
correlation between music and suicide risk is supported by a meta-
analysis done by Baker and Bor (2008), in which the authors assert
that most studies reject the notion that music is a causal factor
and suggest that music preference is more indicative of emotional
vulnerability. However, it is still unknown whether these genres can

Taiwan. *Issues in Mental Health Nursing, 20,* 229–246. doi:
10.1080/016128499248637

42b Following APA manuscript format

The following formatting guidelines are adapted from the APA recommendations for preparing manuscripts for publication in journals. However, check with your instructor before preparing the final
draft of a print text.

Title page. APA does not provide specific title-page guidelines.
Center the title and include your name, the course name and number, the instructor's name, and the date. If your instructor wants you
to include a running head, place it flush left on the first line. Write
the words *Running head*, a colon, and a short version of the title (fifty
characters or fewer, including spaces) using all capital letters. On the
same line, flush with the right margin, type the number *1*.

Margins and spacing. Leave margins of at least one inch at
the top and bottom and on both sides of the page. Do not justify
the right margin. Double-space the entire text, including any

headings, set-off quotations (23a), content notes, and the list of references. Indent one-half inch from the left margin for the first line of a paragraph and all lines of a quotation over forty words long.

Short title and page numbers.   Place the running head and the short title in the upper left corner of each page. Place the page number in the upper right corner of each page, in the same position as on the title page.

Long quotations.   For a long, set-off quotation (one having more than forty words), indent it one-half inch from the left margin, and do not use quotation marks. Place the page reference in parentheses one space after the final punctuation.

Abstract.   If your instructor asks for an abstract, the abstract should go immediately after the title page, with the word *Abstract* centered about an inch from the top of the page. Double-space the text of the abstract. In most cases, a one-paragraph abstract of about one hundred words will be sufficient to introduce readers to your topic and provide a brief summary of your major thesis and supporting points.

Headings.   Headings are used within the text of many APA-style projects. In a text with only one or two levels of headings, center the main headings; italicize the subheadings and position them flush with the left margin. Capitalize all major words; however, do not capitalize **articles**, short **prepositions**, and **coordinating conjunctions** unless they are the first word or follow a colon.

Visuals.   Tables should be labeled *Table*, numbered, and captioned. All other visuals (such as charts, graphs, photographs, and drawings) should be labeled *Figure*, numbered, and captioned with a description and the source information. Remember to refer to each visual in your text, stating how it contributes to the point(s) you are making. Tables and figures should generally appear near the relevant text; check with your instructor for guidelines on the placement of visuals.

42c Creating APA in-text citations

An in-text citation in APA style always indicates which source on the references page the writer is referring to, and it explains in what year the material was published; for quoted material, the in-text citation also indicates where in the source the quotation can be found.

Note that APA style generally calls for using the past tense or present perfect tense for signal verbs: *Baker (2003) showed* or *Baker (2003) has shown.* Use the present tense only to discuss results (*the experiment demonstrates*) or widely accepted information (*researchers agree*).

1. BASIC FORMAT FOR A QUOTATION. Generally, use the author's name in a signal phrase to introduce the cited material, and place the date, in parentheses, immediately after the author's name. The page number, preceded by p., appears in parentheses after the quotation.

> Gitlin (2001) pointed out that "political critics, convinced that the media are rigged against them, are often blind to other substantial reasons why their causes are unpersuasive" (p. 141).

DIRECTORY TO APA STYLE

APA style for in-text citations

If the author is not named in a signal phrase, place the author's name, the year, and the page number in parentheses after the quotation: (Gitlin, 2001, p. 141). For a long, set-off quotation (more than forty words), place the page reference in parentheses one space after the final quotation.

For quotations from works without page numbers, you may use paragraph numbers, if the source includes them, preceded by the abbreviation *para.*

> Driver (2007) has noticed "an increasing focus on the role of land" in
> policy debates over the past decade (para. 1).

2. BASIC FORMAT FOR A PARAPHRASE OR SUMMARY. Include the author's last name and the year as in model 1, but omit the page or paragraph number unless the reader will need it to find the material in a long work.

> Gitlin (2001) has argued that critics sometimes overestimate the influence
> of the media on modern life.

3. TWO AUTHORS. Use both names in all citations. Use *and* in a signal phrase, but use an ampersand (&) in a parentheses.

> Babcock and Laschever (2003) have suggested that many women do
> not negotiate their salaries and pay raises as vigorously as their male
> counterparts do.

> A recent study has suggested that many women do not negotiate their
> salaries and pay raises as vigorously as their male counterparts do (Babcock
> & Laschever, 2003).

4. THREE TO FIVE AUTHORS. List all the authors' names for the first reference.

> Safer, Voccola, Hurd, and Goodwin (2003) reached somewhat different
> conclusions by designing a study that was less dependent on subjective
> judgment than were previous studies.

In subsequent references, use just the first author's name followed by *et al.*

Based on the results, Safer et al. (2003) determined that the apes took significant steps toward self-expression.

5. SIX OR MORE AUTHORS. Use only the first author's name and *et al.* in every citation.

As Soleim et al. (2002) demonstrated, advertising holds the potential for manipulating "free-willed" consumers.

6. CORPORATE OR GROUP AUTHOR. If the name of the organization or corporation is long, spell it out the first time you use it, followed by an abbreviation in brackets. In later references, use the abbreviation only.

FIRST CITATION	(Centers for Disease Control and Prevention [CDC], 2006)
LATER CITATIONS	(CDC, 2006)

7. UNKNOWN AUTHOR. Use the title or its first few words in a signal phrase or in parentheses. A book's title is italicized, as in the following example; an article's title is placed in quotation marks.

The employment profiles for this time period substantiated this trend (*Federal Employment,* 2001).

8. TWO OR MORE AUTHORS WITH THE SAME LAST NAME. Include the authors' initials in each citation.

S. Bartolomeo (2000) conducted the groundbreaking study on teenage childbearing.

9. TWO OR MORE WORKS BY AN AUTHOR IN A SINGLE YEAR. Assign lowercase letters (*a, b,* and so on) alphabetically by title, and include the letters after the year.

Gordon (2004b) examined this trend in more detail.

10. TWO OR MORE SOURCES IN ONE PARENTHETICAL REFERENCE. List any sources by different authors in alphabetical order by the authors' last names, separated by semicolons: (Cardone, 1998; Lai, 2002).

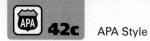
List works by the same author in chronological order, separated by commas: (Lai, 2000, 2002).

11. SOURCE REPORTED IN ANOTHER SOURCE. Use the phrase *as cited in* to indicate that you are reporting information from a secondary source. Name the original source in a signal phrase, but list the secondary source in your list of references.

> Amartya Sen developed the influential concept that land reform was necessary for "promoting opportunity" among the poor (as cited in Driver, 2007, para. 2).

12. PERSONAL COMMUNICATION. Cite any personal letters, email messages, electronic postings, telephone conversations, or interviews as shown. Do not include personal communications in the reference list.

> R. Tobin (personal communication, November 4, 2006) supported his claims about music therapy with new evidence.

13. ELECTRONIC DOCUMENT. Cite a Web or electronic document as you would a print source, using the author's name and date.

> Link and Phelan (2005) argued for broader interventions in public health that would be accessible to anyone, regardless of individual wealth.

The APA recommends the following for electronic sources without names, dates, or page numbers:

AUTHOR UNKNOWN
Use a shortened form of the title in a signal phrase or in parentheses (see model 7). If an organization is the author, see model 6.

DATE UNKNOWN
Use the abbreviation *n.d.* (for "no date") in place of the year: (*Hopkins, n.d.*).

NO PAGE NUMBERS
Many works found online or in electronic databases lack stable page numbers. (Use the page numbers for an electronic work in a format, such as PDF, that has stable pagination.) If paragraph numbers are included in such a source, use the abbreviation *para.*: (*Giambetti, 2006,*

para. 7). If no paragraph numbers are included but the source includes headings, give the heading and identify the paragraph in the section:

> Jacobs and Johnson (2007) have argued that "the South African media is
> still highly concentrated and not very diverse in terms of race and class"
> (South African Media after Apartheid, para. 3).

14. TABLE OR FIGURE REPRODUCED IN THE TEXT. Number figures (graphs, charts, illustrations, and photographs) and tables separately.

For a table, place the label (*Table 1*) and an informative heading (*Hartman's Key Personality Traits*) above the table; below, provide information about its source.

Table 1
Hartman's Key Personality Traits

Trait category	Color			
	Red	Blue	White	Yellow
Motive	Power	Intimacy	Peace	Fun
Strengths	Loyal to tasks	Loyal to people	Tolerant	Positive
Limitations	Arrogant	Self-righteous	Timid	Uncommitted

Note: Adapted from *The Hartman Personality Profile,* by N. Hayden. Retrieved February 24, 2009, from http://students.cs.byu.edu/~nhayden/Code/index.php

For a figure, place the label (*Figure 3*) and a caption indicating the source below the image. If you do not cite the source of the table or figure elsewhere in your text, you do not need to include the source on your list of references.

42d Creating an APA list of references

The alphabetical list of the sources cited in your document is called *References.* If your instructor asks that you list everything you have read—not just the sources you cite—call the list *Bibliography.*

All the entries in this section of the book use hanging indent format, in which the first line aligns on the left and the subsequent lines indent one-half inch or five spaces. This is the customary APA format.

Guidelines for author listings

List authors' last names first, and use only initials for first and middle names. The in-text citations in your text point readers toward particular sources in your list of references (see 42c).

NAME CITED IN SIGNAL PHRASE IN TEXT

Driver (2007) has noted . . .

NAME IN PARENTHETICAL CITATION IN TEXT

. . . (Driver, 2007).

BEGINNING OF ENTRY IN LIST OF REFERENCES

Driver, T. (2007).

Models 1–5 below explain how to arrange author names. The information that follows the name of the author depends on the type of work you are citing—a book (models 6–15), a print periodical (models 16–23), a digital written-word source (models 24–34), or another kind of source (models 35–48).

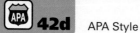
> ▶ **Checklist**

Formatting a List of References

▶ Start your list on a new page after the text of your document but before appendices or notes. Continue consecutive page numbers.

▶ Center the heading *References* one inch from the top of the page.

▶ Begin each entry flush with the left margin, but indent subsequent lines one-half inch or five spaces. Double-space the entire list.

▶ List sources alphabetically by author's last name. If no author is given, alphabetize the source by the first word of the title other than *A*, *An*, or *The*. If the list includes two or more works by the same author, list them in chronological order.

▶ Italicize titles and subtitles of books and periodicals. Do not italicize titles of articles, and do not enclose them in quotation marks.

▶ For titles of books and articles, capitalize only the first word of the title and the subtitle and any proper nouns or proper adjectives.

▶ For titles of periodicals, capitalize all major words.

1. ONE AUTHOR. Give the last name, a comma, the initial(s), and the date in parentheses.

Zimbardo, P. G. (2009).

2. MULTIPLE AUTHORS. List up to seven authors, last name first, with commas separating authors' names and an ampersand (&) before the last author's name.

Walsh, M. E., & Murphy, J. A. (2003).

Note: For a work with more than seven authors, list the first six, then an ellipsis (. . .), and then the final author's name.

3. CORPORATE OR GROUP AUTHOR

Resources for Rehabilitation. (2003).

> ▶ **Checklist**

Combining Parts of Models

What should you do if your source doesn't match the model exactly? Suppose, for instance, that your source is a translation of a republished book with an editor.

▶ Identify a basic model to follow. If you decide that your source looks most like a republished book, for example, start with a citation that looks like model 13.

▶ Look for models that show additional elements in your source. For this example, you would need elements of model 9 (for the translation) and model 7 (for the editor).

▶ Add new elements from other models to your basic model in the order that makes the most sense to you.

▶ If you still aren't sure how to arrange the pieces to create a combination model, ask your instructor.

4. UNKNOWN AUTHOR. Begin with the work's title. Italicize book titles, but do not italicize article titles or enclose them in quotation marks. Capitalize only the first word of the title and subtitle (if any) and proper nouns and proper adjectives.

Safe youth, safe schools. (2009).

5. TWO OR MORE WORKS BY THE SAME AUTHOR. List works by the same author in chronological order. Repeat the author's name in each entry.

Goodall, J. (1999).

Goodall, J. (2002).

If the works appeared in the same year, list them alphabetically by title, and assign lowercase letters (*a*, *b*, etc.) after the dates.

Shermer, M. (2002a). On estimating the lifetime of civilizations. *Scientific American, 287*(2), 33.

Shermer, M. (2002b). Readers who question evolution. *Scientific American, 287*(1), 37.

Print books

6. BASIC FORMAT FOR A BOOK. Begin with the author name(s). (See models 1–5.) Then include the publication year, title and subtitle, city of publication, country or state abbreviation, and publisher. The source map on pp. 296–97 shows where to find this information in a typical book.

> Levick, S. E. (2003). *Clone being: Exploring the psychological and social dimensions.* Lanham, MD: Rowman & Littlefield.

7. EDITOR. For a book with an editor but no author, list the source under the editor's name.

> Dickens, J. (Ed.). (1995). *Family outing: A guide for parents of gays, lesbians and bisexuals.* London, England: Peter Owen.

To cite a book with an author and an editor, place the editor's name, with a comma and the abbreviation *Ed.*, in parentheses after the title.

> Austin, J. (1995). *The province of jurisprudence determined.* (W. E. Rumble, Ed.). Cambridge, England: Cambridge University Press.

8. SELECTION IN A BOOK WITH AN EDITOR

> Burke, W. W., & Nourmair, D. A. (2001). The role of personality assessment in organization development. In J. Waclawski & A. H. Church (Eds.), *Organization development: A data-driven approach to organizational change* (pp. 55–77). San Francisco, CA: Jossey-Bass.

9. TRANSLATION

> Al-Farabi, A. N. (1998). *On the perfect state* (R. Walzer, Trans.). Chicago, IL: Kazi.

10. EDITION OTHER THAN THE FIRST

> Moore, G. S. (2002). *Living with the earth: Concepts in environmental health science* (2nd ed.). New York, NY: Lewis.

11. MULTIVOLUME WORK WITH AN EDITOR

Barnes, J. (Ed.). (1995). *Complete works of Aristotle* (Vols. 1–2). Princeton, NJ: Princeton University Press.

Note: If you are citing just one volume of a multivolume work, list that volume, not the complete span of volumes, in parentheses after the title.

12. ARTICLE IN A REFERENCE WORK

Dean, C. (1994). Jaws and teeth. In *The Cambridge encyclopedia of human evolution* (pp. 56–59). Cambridge, England: Cambridge University Press.

If no author is listed, begin with the title.

13. REPUBLISHED BOOK

Piaget, J. (1952). *The language and thought of the child.* London, England: Routledge & Kegan Paul. (Original work published 1932)

14. INTRODUCTION, PREFACE, FOREWORD, OR AFTERWORD

Klosterman, C. (2007). Introduction. In P. Shirley, *Can I keep my jersey?: 11 teams, 5 countries, and 4 years in my life as a basketball vagabond* (pp. v–vii). New York, NY: Villard-Random House.

15. BOOK WITH A TITLE WITHIN THE TITLE. Do not italicize or enclose in quotation marks a title within a book title.

Klarman, M. J. (2007). *Brown v. Board of Education and the civil rights movement.* New York, NY: Oxford University Press.

Print periodicals

Begin with the author name(s). (See models 1–5.) Then include the publication date (year only for journals, and year, month, and day for all other periodicals); the article title; the periodical

APA SOURCE MAP: Books

Take information from the book's title page and copyright page (on the reverse side of the title page), not from the book's cover or a library catalog.

1 **Author.** List all authors' last names first, and use only initials for first and middle names. For more about citing authors, see models 1–5.

2 **Publication year.** Enclose the year of publication in parentheses.

3 **Title.** Italicize the title and any subtitle. Capitalize only the first word of the title and the subtitle and any proper nouns or proper adjectives.

4 **City and state of publication, and publisher.** List the city of publication and the country or state abbreviation, a colon, and the publisher's name, dropping any *Inc.*, *Co.*, or *Publishers*.

A citation for the book on p. 297 would look like this:

Tsutsui, W. (2004). *Godzilla on my mind: Fifty years of the king of monsters.* New York, NY: Palgrave Macmillan.

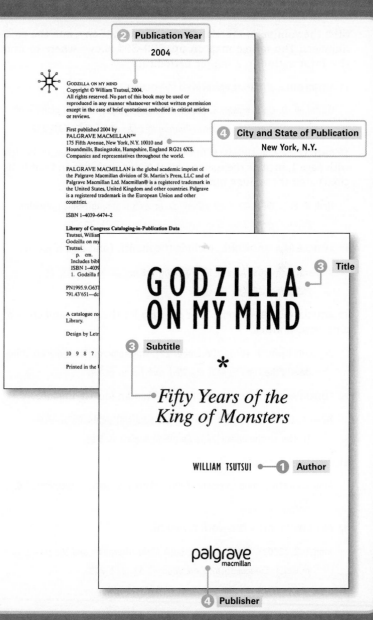

2 Publication Year

2004

GODZILLA ON MY MIND
Copyright © William Tsutsui, 2004.
All rights reserved. No part of this book may be used or
reproduced in any manner whatsoever without written permission
except in the case of brief quotations embodied in critical articles
or reviews.

First published 2004 by
PALGRAVE MACMILLAN™
175 Fifth Avenue, New York, N.Y. 10010 and
Houndmills, Basingstoke, Hampshire, England RG21 6XS.
Companies and representatives throughout the world.

4 City and State of Publication

New York, N.Y.

PALGRAVE MACMILLAN is the global academic imprint of
the Palgrave Macmillan division of St. Martin's Press, LLC and of
Palgrave Macmillan Ltd. Macmillan® is a registered trademark in
the United States, United Kingdom and other countries. Palgrave
is a registered trademark in the European Union and other
countries.

ISBN 1–4039–6474–2

Library of Congress Cataloging-in-Publication Data
Tsutsui, William
Godzilla on my
Tsutsui.
   p.   cm.
   Includes bibl
   ISBN 1–4039
   1. Godzilla f

PN1995.9.G637
791.43'651—dc

A catalogue re
Library.

Design by Letr

10 9 8 7

Printed in the

GODZILLA® ON MY MIND

3 Title

*

3 Subtitle

*Fifty Years of the
King of Monsters*

WILLIAM TSUTSUI ● **1 Author**

palgrave
macmillan

4 Publisher

297

title; the volume number and issue number, if any; and the page numbers. The source map on pp. 300–301 shows where to find this information in a sample periodical.

16. ARTICLE IN A JOURNAL PAGINATED BY VOLUME

O'Connell, D. C., & Kowal, S. (2003). Psycholinguistics: A half century of

monologism. *The American Journal of Psychology, 116,* 191–212.

17. ARTICLE IN A JOURNAL PAGINATED BY ISSUE. If each issue begins with page 1, include the issue number (in parentheses and not italicized) after the volume number (italicized).

Hall, R. E. (2000). Marriage as vehicle of racism among women of color.

Psychology: A Journal of Human Behavior, 37(2), 29–40.

18. ARTICLE IN A MAGAZINE. Include the month (and day, if given).

Ricciardi, S. (2003, August 5). Enabling the mobile work force. *PC*

Magazine, 22, 46.

19. ARTICLE IN A NEWSPAPER. Use *p.* or *pp.* for the page number(s) of a newspaper article.

Reynolds Lewis, K. (2011, December 22). Why some business owners think

now is the time to sell. *The New York Times,* p. B5.

20. EDITORIAL OR LETTER TO THE EDITOR. Add an identifying label.

Zelneck, B. (2003, July 18). Serving the public at public universities

[Letter to the editor]. *The Chronicle Review,* p. B18.

21. UNSIGNED ARTICLE

Annual meeting announcement. (2003, March). *Cognitive Psychology, 46,*

227.

22. REVIEW. Identify the work reviewed.

Ringel, S. (2003). [Review of the book *Multiculturalism and the therapeutic*

process]. *Clinical Social Work Journal, 31,* 212–213.

23. PUBLISHED INTERVIEW. Identify the person interviewed.

> Smith, H. (2002, October). [Interview with A. Thompson]. *The Sun,* pp. 4–7.

Digital written-word sources

Updated guidelines for citing digital resources are maintained at the APA's Web site (www.apa.org).

24. ARTICLE FROM AN ONLINE PERIODICAL. Give the author, date, title, and publication information as you would for a print document. Include both the volume and issue numbers for all journal articles. If the article has a digital object identifier (DOI), include it. If there is no DOI, write *Retrieved from* and the URL for the periodical's home page or for the article (if the article is difficult to find from the home page). For newspaper articles accessible from a searchable Web site, give the site URL only.

> Barringer, F. (2008, February 7). In many communities, it's not easy going green. *The New York Times.* Retrieved from http://www.nytimes.com

> Cleary, J. M., & Crafti, N. (2007). Basic need satisfaction, emotional eating, and dietary restraint as risk factors for recurrent overeating in a community sample. *E-Journal of Applied Psychology, 2*(3), 27–39. Retrieved from http://ojs.lib.swin.edu.au/index.php/ejap/article /view/90/116

25. ARTICLE FROM A DATABASE. Give the author, date, title, and publication information as you would for a print document. Include both the volume and issue numbers for all journal articles. If the article has a DOI, include it. If there is no DOI, write *Retrieved from* and the URL of the journal's home page (not the URL of the database). The source map on pp. 304–5 shows where to find this information for a typical article from a database.

> Hazleden, R. (2003, December). Love yourself: The relationship of the self with itself in popular self-help texts. *Journal of Sociology, 39*(4), 413–428. Retrieved from http://jos.sagepub.com

APA SOURCE MAP: Articles from Print Periodicals

1 **Author.** List all authors' last names first, and use only initials for first and middle names. For more about citing authors, see models 1–5.

2 **Publication date.** Enclose the date in parentheses. For journals, use only the year. For magazines and newspapers, use the year, a comma, the month (spelled out), and the day, if given.

3 **Article title.** Do not italicize or enclose article titles in quotation marks. Capitalize only the first word of the article title and subtitle and any proper nouns or proper adjectives.

4 **Periodical title.** Italicize the periodical title (and subtitle, if any), and capitalize all major words. Follow the periodical title with a comma.

5 **Volume and issue numbers.** Give the volume number (italicized) and, without a space in between, the issue number (if given) in parentheses. Follow with a comma.

6 **Page numbers.** Give the inclusive page numbers of the article. For newspapers only, include the abbreviation *p.* ("page") or *pp.* ("pages") before the page numbers. End the citation with a period.

A citation for the periodical article on p. 301 would look like this:

Etzioni, A. (2006). Leaving race behind: Our growing Hispanic population creates a golden opportunity. *The American Scholar, 75*(2), 20–30.

The AMERICAN SCHOLAR

Spring 2006 | Vol. 75, No. 2

The AMERICAN SCHOLAR

Leaving Race Behind

Our growing Hispanic population creates a golden opportunity

AMITAI ETZIONI

For a subscription to THE AMERICAN SCHOLAR, a quarterly publication of the Phi Beta Kappa Society, $48 two years, $69 three years; international subscriptions, additional. Newsstand Services. For more information about advertising please contact: THE AMERICAN SCHOLAR, a quarterly publication of the Phi Beta Kappa Society, 16... scholar@pbk.org. Manuscripts... AMERICAN SCHOLAR assumes no... Periodical postage paid at W... P.O. Box 354, Mt. Morris, IL. additional revenues, the Phi... deleted should send their na...

S ome years ago the United States government asked me what my race was. I was reluctant to respond because my 50 years of practicing sociology—and some powerful personal experiences—have underscored for me what we all know to be true, that racial divisions bedevil America, just as they do many other societies across the world. Not wanting to encourage these divisions, I refused to check off one of the specific racial options on the U.S. Census form and instead marked a box labeled "Other." I later found out that the federal government did not accept such an attempt to de-emphasize race, by me or by some 6.75 million other Americans who tried it. Instead the government assigned me to a racial category, one it chose for me. Learning this made me conjure up what I admit is a far-fetched association. I was in this place once before. When I was a Jewish child in Nazi Germany in the early 1930s, many Jews who saw themselves as good Germans wanted to "pass" as Aryans. But the Nazi regime would have none of it. Never mind, they told these Jews, *we determine* who is Jewish and who is not. A similar practice prevailed in the Old South, where if you had one drop of African blood you were a Negro, disregarding all other facts and considerations, including how you saw yourself.

You might suppose that in the years since my little Census-form protest

~ Amitai Etzioni is University Professor at George Washington University and the author of *The Monochrome Society*.

Checklist

Citing Digital Sources

When citing sources accessed online or from an electronic database, include as many of the following elements as you can find:

▶ **Author.** Give the author's name, if available.

▶ **Publication date.** Include the date of electronic publication or of the latest update, if available. When no publication date is available, use *n.d.* ("no date").

▶ **Title.** If the source is not from a larger work, italicize the title.

▶ **Print publication information.** For articles from online journals, magazines, or reference databases, give the publication title and other publishing information as you would for a print periodical (see models 16–23).

▶ **Retrieval information.** For a work from a database, do the following: if the article has a DOI (digital object identifier), include that number after the publication information; do not include the name of the database. If there is no DOI, write *Retrieved from* followed by the URL for the journal's home page (not the database URL). For a work found on a Web site, write *Retrieved from* and include the URL. If the work seems likely to be updated, include the retrieval date. If the URL is longer than one line, break it only before a punctuation mark; do not break *http://*.

Morley, N. J., Ball, L. J., & Ormerod, T. C. (2006). How the detection of
insurance fraud succeeds and fails. *Psychology, Crime, & Law, 12*(2),
163–180. doi:10.1080/10683160512331316325

26. **ABSTRACT FOR AN ONLINE ARTICLE.** Include a label.

Gudjonsson, G. H., & Young, S. (2010). Does confabulation in memory
predict suggestibility beyond IQ and memory? [Abstract].
Personality & Individual Differences, 49(1), 65–67. doi: 10.1016
/j.paid.2010.03.014

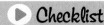 **Checklist**

Citing Sources without Models in APA Style

You may need to cite a source for which you cannot find a model in APA style. If so, collect as much information as you can find about the creator, title, sponsor, date, and so on, with the goal of helping readers find the source for themselves. Then look at the models in this section to see which one most closely matches the type of source you are using.

In an academic writing project, before citing an electronic source for which you have no model, also be sure to ask your instructor's advice.

27. REPORT OR LONG DOCUMENT FROM A WEB SITE. Include all of the following information that you can find: the author's name; the publication date (or *n.d.* if no date is available); the title of the document, italicized; and *Retrieved from* and the URL. Provide your date of access only if an update seems likely. The source map on pp. 308–9 shows where to find this information for a report from a Web site.

Nice, M. L., & Katzev, R. (n.d.). *Internet romances: The frequency and*

 nature of romantic on-line relationships. Retrieved from http://www

 .publicpolicyresearch.net/papers.html

28. CHAPTER OR SECTION OF A WEB DOCUMENT. Follow model 27. After the chapter or section title, type *In* and give the document title, with identifying information, if any, in parentheses. End with the date of access (if needed) and the URL.

Salamon, Andrew. (n.d.). War in Europe. In *Childhood in times of war*

 (chap. 2). Retrieved April 11, 2008, from http://remember.org

 /jean

29. SHORT WORK FROM A WEB SITE. Include the name of the work (with no italics) and the name of the site, italicized.

Zimbardo, P. G. (2013). Constructing the experiment. *Stanford Prison*

 Experiment. Retrieved from http://www.prisonexp.org/psychology/5

APA SOURCE MAP: Articles from Databases

① **Author.** Include the author's name as you would for a print source. List all authors' last names first, and use initials for first and middle names. For more about citing authors, see models 1–5.

② **Publication date.** Enclose the date in parentheses. For journals, use only the year. For magazines and newspapers, use the year, a comma, the month, and the day if given.

③ **Article title.** Capitalize only the first word of the article title and the subtitle and any proper nouns or proper adjectives.

④ **Periodical title.** Italicize the periodical title.

⑤ **Volume and issue number.** For journals and magazines, give the volume number (italicized) and the issue number (in parentheses).

⑥ **Page numbers.** For journals only, give inclusive page numbers.

⑦ **Retrieval information.** If the article has a DOI (digital object identifier), include that number after the publication information; do not include the name of the database. If there is no DOI, write *Retrieved from* followed by the URL of the journal's home page (not the database URL).

A citation for the article on p. 305 would look like this:

Knobloch-Westerwick, S., & Crane, J. (2012). A losing battle: Effects of prolonged exposure to thin-ideal images on dieting and body satisfaction. *Communication Research, 39*(1), 79–102. doi:10.1177/0093650211400596

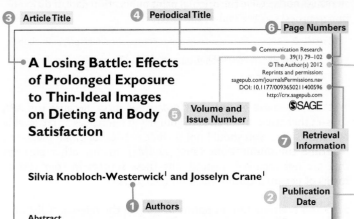

3 Article Title

4 Periodical Title

6 Page Numbers

Communication Research
39(1) 79–102
© The Author(s) 2012
Reprints and permission:
sagepub.com/journalsPermissions.nav
DOI: 10.1177/0093650211400596
http://crx.sagepub.com
$SAGE

A Losing Battle: Effects of Prolonged Exposure to Thin-Ideal Images on Dieting and Body Satisfaction

5 Volume and Issue Number

7 Retrieval Information

Silvia Knobloch-Westerwick[1] and Josselyn Crane[1]

1 Authors

2 Publication Date

Abstract

The present study examined prolonged exposure effects of thin-ideal media messages. College-aged females participated in seven online sessions over 10 days including a baseline measures session, five daily measures, and a posttest. Two experimental groups viewed magazine pages with thin-ideal imagery. One of those groups was induced to engage in social comparisons with the thin-ideal models. The control group viewed messages with body-neutral images of women. Prolonged exposure to thin-ideal messages led to greater body satisfaction. This finding was attributed to the fact that the experimental groups reported more dieting behaviors. A mediation analysis showed that the impact of thin-ideal message exposure on body satisfaction was mediated by dieting.

Keywords

body dissatisfaction, body image, dieting, prolonged exposure, social comparison

Idealized body images in the media have been linked to unrealistic body shape aspirations and body dissatisfaction (see meta-analysis by Grabe, Ward, & Hyde, 2008), which, in turn, have been linked to numerous pathological problems, including depression, obesity, dieting, and eating disorders (e.g., Johnson & Wardle, 2005; Neumark-Sztainer, Paxton, Hannan, Haines, & Story, 2006; Ricciardelli & McCabe, 2001). However, another meta-analysis by Holmstrom (2004) found that the longer the media exposure, the *better* the individuals felt about their body. This inconsistency indicates that the factors and processes at work have not yet been fully understood and captured by the research at hand and deserve further investigation. Social comparison theory is the theoretical framework that has guided much

[1]The Ohio State University

Corresponding Author:
Silvia Knobloch-Westerwick, The Ohio State University, 154 N Oval Mall, Columbus, OH 43210
Email: knobloch-westerwick.1@osu.edu

30. ONLINE BOOK. Give the original print publication date, if different, in parentheses at the end of the entry.

> Russell, B. (2008). *The analysis of mind*. Retrieved from http://onlinebooks
> .library.upenn.edu/webbin/gutbook/lookup?num=2529 (Original work
> published 1921)

31. EMAIL MESSAGE OR REAL-TIME COMMUNICATION. Because the APA stresses that any sources cited in your list of references be retrievable by your readers, you should not include entries for email messages, real-time communications (such as IMs), or any other postings that are not archived. Instead, cite these sources in your text as forms of personal communication (see p. 288).

32. ONLINE POSTING. List an online posting in the references list only if you are able to retrieve the message from an archive. Provide the author's name, the date of posting, and the subject line. Include other identifying information in square brackets. Then, end with the retrieval statement and the URL of the archived message.

> Troike, R. C. (2001, June 21). Buttercups and primroses [Electronic mailing
> list message]. Retrieved from http://listserv.linguistlist.org/archives
> /ads-l.html

> Wittenberg, E. (2001, July 11). Gender and the Internet [Newsgroup
> message]. Retrieved from news://comp.edu.composition

33. BLOG (WEB LOG) POST

> Spaulding, P. (2010, April 27). Who believes in a real America? [Web
> log post]. Retrieved from http://pandagon.net/index.php
> /site/2010/04

34. WIKI ENTRY. Use the date of posting, if there is one, or *n.d.* for "no date" if there is none. Include the retrieval date because wiki content can change frequently.

> Happiness. (2007, June 14). Retrieved March 24, 2008, from PsychWiki:
> http://www.psychwiki.com/wiki/Happiness

Other sources (including online versions)

35. GOVERNMENT PUBLICATION

Office of the Federal Register. (2003). *The United States government manual 2003/2004.* Washington, DC: U.S. Government Printing Office.

Cite an online government document as you would a printed government work, adding the URL. If there is no date, use *n.d.*

U.S. Public Health Service. (1999). *The surgeon general's call to action to prevent suicide.* Retrieved from http://www.mentalhealth.org/suicideprevention/calltoaction.asp

36. DATA SET

U.S. Department of Education, Institute of Education Sciences. (2009). *NAEP state comparisons* [Data set]. Retrieved from http://nces.ed.gov/nationsreportcard/statecomparisons/

37. DISSERTATION. If you retrieved the dissertation from a database, give the database name and the accession number, if one is assigned.

Lengel, L. L. (1968). *The righteous cause: Some religious aspects of Kansas populism.* Retrieved from ProQuest Digital Dissertations. (6900033)

If you retrieve a dissertation from a Web site, give the type of dissertation and the institution after the title, and provide a retrieval statement.

Meeks, M. G. (2006). *Between abolition and reform: First-year writing programs, e-literacies, and institutional change* (Doctoral dissertation, University of North Carolina). Retrieved from http://dc.lib.unc.edu/etd/

38. TECHNICAL OR RESEARCH REPORT. Give the report number, if available, in parentheses after the title.

McCool, R., Fikes, R., & McGuinness, D. (2003). *Semantic Web tools for enhanced authoring* (Report No. KSL-03-07). Retrieved from www.ksl.stanford.edu/KSL_Abstracts/KSL-03-07.html

1 **Author.** If one is given, include the author's name (see models 1–5). List last names first, and use only initials for first names. The site's sponsor may be the author. If no author is identified, begin the citation with the title of the document.

2 **Publication date.** Enclose the date of publication or latest update in parentheses. Use *n.d.* ("no date") when no publication date is available.

3 **Title of work.** Italicize the title. Capitalize only the first word of the title and subtitle and any proper nouns or proper adjectives.

4 **Retrieval information.** Write *Retrieved from* and include the URL. For a report from an organization's Web site, identify the organization in the retrieval statement. If the work seems likely to be updated, include the retrieval date.

A citation for the Web document on p. 309 would look like this:

Parker, K., & Wang, W. (2013, March 14). *Modern parenthood: Roles of moms and dads converge as they balance work and family.* Retrieved from the Pew Research Center Web site: http://www.pewsocialtrends .org/2013/03/14/modern-parenthood-roles-of-moms-and-dads -converge-as-they-balance-work-and-family/

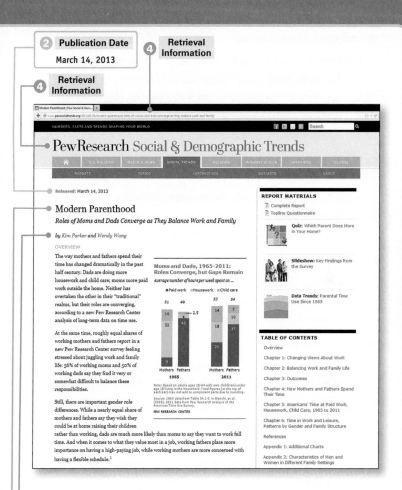

Publication Date

March 14, 2013

Retrieval Information

Retrieval Information

1 Author

Kim Parker and Wendy Wang

3 Title of Work

39. CONFERENCE PROCEEDINGS

> Robertson, S. P., Vatrapu, R. K., & Medina, R. (2009). YouTube and
> Facebook: Online video "friends" social networking. In *Conference
> proceedings: YouTube and the 2008 election cycle* (pp. 159–176).
> Amherst, MA: University of Massachusetts. Retrieved from http://
> scholarworks.umass.edu/jitpc2009

40. PAPER PRESENTED AT A MEETING OR SYMPOSIUM, UNPUBLISHED. Cite the month of the meeting if it is available.

> Jones, J. G. (1999, February). *Mental health intervention in mass casualty
> disasters.* Paper presented at the Rocky Mountain Region Disaster
> Mental Health Conference, Laramie, WY.

41. POSTER SESSION

> Barnes Young, L. L. (2003, August). *Cognition, aging, and dementia.* Poster
> session presented at the 2003 Division 40 APA Convention, Toronto,
> Ontario, Canada.

42. PRESENTATION SLIDES

> Mader, S. (2007, March 27). *The Zen aesthetic* [Presentation slides].
> Retrieved from http://www.slideshare.net/slmader/the-zen-aesthetic

43. FILM, VIDEO, DVD, OR BLU-RAY. Begin with the director, the producer, and other relevant contributors.

> Bigelow, K. (Director, Producer), Boal, M. (Producer), & Ellison, M.
> (Producer). (2012). *Zero dark thirty* [Motion picture]. United States:
> Annapurna.

If you watched the film in another medium, such as on a DVD or Blu-ray disc, indicate the medium in brackets. If the DVD or Blu-ray and the film were not released in the same year, put *Original release* and the year in parentheses at the end of the entry.

> Hitchcock, A. (Director, Producer). (2010). *Psycho* [Blu-ray]. United
> States: Universal. (Original release 1960.)

44. ONLINE (STREAMING) AUDIO OR VIDEO FILE

Klusman, P. (2008, February 13). An engineer's guide to cats [Video file].
  Retrieved from http://www.youtube.com/watch?v=mHXBL6bzAR4

Koenig, S. (2013, January 25). Petticoats in a twist [Audio file]. Retrieved
  from http://www.thisamericanlife.org/radio-archives/episode/485
  /surrogates

45. TELEVISION PROGRAM, SINGLE EPISODE

Imperioli, M. (Writer), & Buscemi, S. (Director). (2002). Everybody hurts
  [Television series episode]. In D. Chase (Executive Producer), *The
  Sopranos*. New York, NY: Home Box Office.

46. TELEVISION SERIES

Abrams, J. J., Lieber, J., & Lindelof, D. (2004). *Lost*. [Television series].
  New York, NY: WABC.

47. PODCAST (DOWNLOADED AUDIO FILE)

Noguchi, Yugi. (2010, 24 May). BP hard to pin down on oil spill claims.
  [Audio podcast]. *NPR morning edition*. Retrieved from http://www
  .npr.org

48. RECORDING

The Avalanches. (2001). Frontier psychiatrist. On *Since I left you* [CD].
  Los Angeles, CA: Elektra/Asylum Records.

42e A sample student writing project, APA style

On the following pages are excerpts from a paper by Tawnya Redding that conforms to the APA guidelines described in this chapter.
To read her complete project, go to the integrated media page at
bedfordstmartins.com/easy.

MOOD MUSIC   3

Full title
centered

Paragraphs
indented

Background
information
about review
supplied

Questions
focus
reader's
attention

Boldface
headings
help organize
review

Paren-
thetical
references
follow APA
style

Mood Music: Music Preference and the Risk for Depression and
Suicide in Adolescents

    Music is a significant part of American culture. Since the
explosion of rock and roll in the 1950s, there has been a concern
for the effects that music may have on listeners, and especially
on young people. The genres most likely to come under suspicion
in recent decades have included heavy metal, country, and blues.
These genres have been suspected of having adverse effects on the
mood and behavior of young listeners. But can music really alter
the disposition and create self-destructive behaviors in listeners?
And if so, which genres and aspects of those genres are responsible?
The following review of the literature will establish the correlation
between potentially problematic genres of music such as heavy metal
and country and depression and suicide risk. First, correlational
studies concerning music preference and suicide risk will be discussed,
followed by a discussion of the literature concerning the possible
reasons for this link. Finally, studies concerning the effects of music
on mood will be discussed. Despite the link between genres such as
heavy metal and country and suicide risk, previous research has been
unable to establish the causal nature of this link.

The Correlation Between Music and Depression and Suicide Risk

    Studies over the past two decades have set out to answer
this question by examining the correlation between youth music
preference and risk for depression and suicide. A large portion of
these studies have focused on heavy metal and country music as
the main genre culprits associated with youth suicidality and
depression (Lacourse, Claes, & Villeneuve, 2001; Scheel & Westefeld,
1999; Stack & Gundlach, 1992). Stack and Gundlach (1992) examined
the radio airtime devoted to country music in 49 metropolitan
areas and found that the higher the percentages of country

Annotations indicate effective choices or APA-style formatting.

MOOD MUSIC 9

References

Baker, F., & Bor, W. (2008). Can music preference indicate mental health status in young people? *Australasian Psychiatry, 16*(4), 284–288. Retrieved from http://www3.interscience.wiley.com /journal/118565538/home

George, D., Stickle, K., Rachid, F., & Wopnford, A. (2007). The association between types of music enjoyed and cognitive, behavioral, and personality factors of those who listen. *Psychomusicology, 19*(2), 32–56.

Lacourse, E., Claes, M., & Villeneuve, M. (2001). Heavy metal music and adolescent suicidal risk. *Journal of Youth and Adolescence, 30*(3), 321–332.

Lai, Y. (1999). Effects of music listening on depressed women in Taiwan. *Issues in Mental Health Nursing, 20,* 229–246. doi: 10.1080/016128499248637

Martin, G., Clark, M., & Pearce, C. (1993). Adolescent suicide: Music preference as an indicator of vulnerability. *Journal of the American Academy of Child and Adolescent Psychiatry, 32,* 530–535.

Scheel, K., & Westefeld, J. (1999). Heavy metal music and adolescent suicidality: An empirical investigation. *Adolescence, 34*(134), 253–273.

Siedliecki, S., & Good, M. (2006). Effect of music on power, pain, depression and disability. *Journal of Advanced Nursing, 54*(5), 553–562. doi: 10.1111/j.1365-2648.2006.03860.x

Smith, J. L., & Noon, J. (1998). Objective measurement of mood change induced by contemporary music. *Journal of Psychiatric & Mental Health Nursing, 5,* 403–408.

Stack, S. (2000). Blues fans and suicide acceptability. *Death Studies, 24,* 223–231.

Stack, S., & Gundlach, J. (1992). The effect of country music on suicide. *Social Forces, 71*(1), 211–218. Retrieved from http:// socialforces.unc.edu/

References begin on new page

Journal article from a database, no DOI

Print journal article

Journal article from a database with DOI

43 *Chicago* Style

The style guide of the University of Chicago Press has long been used in history as well as in other areas of the arts and humanities. The Sixteenth Edition of *The Chicago Manual of Style* (2010) provides a complete guide to *Chicago* style, including two systems for citing sources. This chapter presents the notes and bibliography system.

43a Understanding *Chicago* citation style

Why does academic work call for very careful citation practices when writing for the general public may not? The answer is that readers of academic work expect source citations for several reasons:

- Source citations demonstrate that you've done your homework on your topic and that you are a part of the conversation surrounding it.

- Source citations show that you understand the need to give credit when you make use of someone else's intellectual property. (See Chapter 39.)

- Source citations give explicit directions to guide readers who want to look for themselves at the works you're using.

Guidelines from *The Chicago Manual of Style* will tell you exactly what information to include in your citation and how to format that information.

Types of sources. Look at the Directory to *Chicago* Style on p. 318. You will need to be careful to tell your readers whether you read a print version or a digital version of a source that consists mainly of written words. Digital magazine and newspaper articles may include updates or corrections that the print version lacks; digital books may not number pages or screens the same way the print book does. If you are citing a source with media elements—such as a film, song, or artwork—consult the "other sources" section of the directory. And if you can't find a model exactly like the source you've selected, see the box on p. 325.

ARTICLES FROM WEB AND DATABASE SOURCES. You need a subscription to look through most databases, so individual researchers almost always gain access to articles in databases through the computer system of a school or public library that pays to subscribe. The easiest way to tell whether a source comes from a database, then, is that its information is *not* generally available free to anyone with an Internet connection. Many databases are digital collections of articles that originally appeared in edited print periodicals, ensuring that an authority has vouched for the accuracy of the information. Such sources may have more credibility than free material available on the Web.

Parts of citations. Citations in *Chicago* style will appear in three places in your text—a note number in the text marks the material from the source, a footnote or an endnote includes information to identify the source (or information about supplemental material), and the bibliography provides the full citation.

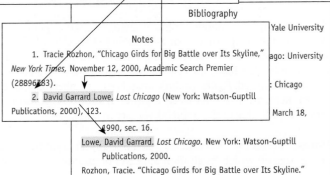

Chicago is a city for the working man. Nowhere is this more evident than in its architecture. David Garrard Lowe, author of *Lost Chicago,* notes that early Chicagoans "sought reality, not fantasy, and the reality of America as seen from the heartland did not include the pavilions of princes or the castles of kings,"² The inclination toward unadorned, sturdy buildings began in the late nineteenth century

Bibliography

Yale University

Notes

1. Tracie Rozhon, "Chicago Girds for Big Battle over Its Skyline," *New York Times,* November 12, 2000, Academic Search Premier (28896783).

ago: University

: Chicago

2. David Garrard Lowe, *Lost Chicago* (New York: Watson-Guptill Publications, 2000), 123.

March 18,

1990, sec. 16.

Lowe, David Garrard. *Lost Chicago.* New York: Watson-Guptill Publications, 2000.

Rozhon, Tracie. "Chicago Girds for Big Battle over Its Skyline."

43b Following *Chicago* manuscript format

Title page.   About halfway down the title page, center the full title of your project and your name. Unless otherwise instructed, at the bottom of the page also list the course name, the instructor's name, and the date submitted. Do not type a number on this page. Check to see if your instructor has a preference on whether to count the title page as part of the text (if so, the first text page will be page 2) or as part of the frontmatter (if so, the first text page will be page 1).

Margins and spacing.   Leave one-inch margins at the top, bottom, and sides of your pages. Double-space the entire text, including block quotations, notes, and bibliography.

Page numbers.   Number all pages (except the title page) in the upper right-hand corner. Also use a short title or your name before page numbers.

Long quotations.   For a long quotation, indent one-half inch (or five spaces) from the left margin and do not use quotation marks. *Chicago* defines a long quotation as one hundred words or eight lines, though you may set off shorter quotes for emphasis (23a).

Headings.   *Chicago* style allows, but does not require, headings. Many students and instructors find them helpful.

Visuals.   Visuals (photographs, drawings, charts, graphs, and tables) should be placed as near as possible to the relevant text. (See 39c for guidelines on incorporating visuals into your text.) Tables should be labeled *Table,* numbered, and captioned. All other visuals should be labeled *Figure* (abbreviated *Fig.*), numbered, and captioned. Remember to refer to each visual in your text, pointing out how it contributes to the point(s) you are making.

Notes.   Notes can be footnotes (each one appearing at the bottom of the page on which its citation appears) or endnotes (in a list on a separate page at the end of the text). (Check your instructor's preference.) Indent the first line of each note one-half inch and begin with a number, a period, and one space before the first word. All remaining lines of the entry are flush with the left margin. Single-space footnotes and endnotes, with a double space between each entry.

Use superscript numbers ([1]) to mark citations in the text. Place the superscript number for each note just after the relevant quotation, sentence, clause, or phrase. Type the number after any punctuation mark except the dash, and do not leave a space before the superscript. Number citations sequentially throughout the text. When you use signal phrases to introduce source material, note that *Chicago* style requires you to use the present tense (*citing Bebout's studies, Meier points out . . .*).

IN THE TEXT

> Sweig argues that Castro and Che Guevara were not the only key players in the Cuban Revolution of the late 1950s.[19]

IN THE FIRST NOTE REFERRING TO THE SOURCE

> 19. Julia Sweig, *Inside the Cuban Revolution* (Cambridge, MA: Harvard University Press, 2002), 9.

After giving complete information the first time you cite a work, shorten additional references to that work: list only the author's last name, a comma, a short version of the title, a comma, and the page number. If you refer to the same source cited in the previous note, you can use the Latin abbreviation *Ibid.* ("in the same place") instead of the name and title.

IN FIRST AND SUBSEQUENT NOTES

> 19. Julia Sweig, *Inside the Cuban Revolution* (Cambridge, MA: Harvard University Press, 2002), 9.
>
> 20. Ibid., 13.
>
> 21. Ferguson, "Comfort of Being Sad," 63.
>
> 22. Sweig, *Cuban Revolution*, 21.

DIRECTORY TO *CHICAGO* STYLE

Chicago style for notes and bibliographic entries

Bibliography. Begin the list of sources on a separate page after the main text and any endnotes. Continue numbering the pages consecutively. Center the title *Bibliography* (without underlining, italics, or quotation marks) one inch below the top of the page. Double-space, and then begin each entry at the left margin. Indent the second and subsequent lines of each entry one-half inch, or five spaces.

List sources alphabetically by authors' last names or by the first major word in the title if the author is unknown. See p. 339 for an example of a *Chicago*-style bibliography.

In the bibliographic entry, include the same information as in the first note for that source, but omit the page reference. Give the *first* author's last name first, followed by a comma and the first name; separate the main elements of the entry with periods rather than commas; and do not enclose the publication information for books in parentheses.

IN THE BIBLIOGRAPHY

Sweig, Julia. *Inside the Cuban Revolution*. Cambridge, MA: Harvard
University Press, 2002.

43c Creating *Chicago* notes and bibliographic entries

The following examples demonstrate how to format both notes and bibliographic entries according to *Chicago* style. The note, which is numbered, appears first; the bibliographic entry, which is not numbered, appears below the note.

Print and digital books

For the basic format for citing a print book, see the source map on pp. 322–23. The note for a book typically includes five elements: author's name, title and subtitle, city of publication and publisher, year, and page number(s) or electronic locator information for the information in the note. The bibliographic entry usually includes all these elements but the page number (and does include a URL or other locator if the book is digitally published), but it is styled differently: commas separate major elements of a note, but a bibliographic entry uses periods.

1. ONE AUTHOR

1. Nell Irvin Painter, *The History of White People* (New York: W. W. Norton, 2010), 119.

Painter, Nell Irvin. *The History of White People.* New York: W. W. Norton, 2010.

2. MULTIPLE AUTHORS

2. Margaret Macmillan and Richard Holbrooke, *Paris 1919: Six Months That Changed the World* (New York: Random House, 2003), 384.

Macmillan, Margaret, and Richard Holbrooke. *Paris 1919: Six Months That Changed the World.* New York: Random House, 2003.

With more than three authors, you may give the first-listed author followed by *et al.* in the note. In the bibliography, list all the authors' names.

2. Stephen J. Blank et al., *Conflict, Culture, and History: Regional Dimensions* (Miami: University Press of the Pacific, 2002), 276.

Blank, Stephen J., Lawrence E. Grinter, Karl P. Magyar, Lewis B. Ware, and Bynum E. Weathers. *Conflict, Culture, and History: Regional Dimensions.* Miami: University Press of the Pacific, 2002.

3. ORGANIZATION AS AUTHOR

3. World Intellectual Property Organization, *Intellectual Property Profile of the Least Developed Countries* (Geneva: World Intellectual Property Organization, 2002), 43.

World Intellectual Property Organization. *Intellectual Property Profile of the Least Developed Countries.* Geneva: World Intellectual Property Organization, 2002.

4. UNKNOWN AUTHOR

    4. *Broad Stripes and Bright Stars* (Kansas City, MO: Andrews McMeel, 2002), 10.

Broad Stripes and Bright Stars. Kansas City, MO: Andrews McMeel, 2002.

5. ONLINE BOOK

    5. Dorothy Richardson, *Long Day: The Story of a New York Working Girl, as Told by Herself* (1906; UMDL Texts, 2010), 159, http://quod.lib .umich.edu/cgi/t/text/text-idx?c=moa;idno=AFS7156.0001.001.

Richardson, Dorothy. *Long Day: The Story of a New York Working Girl, as Told by Herself.* 1906. UMDL Texts, 2010. http://quod.lib.umich.edu /cgi/t/text/text-idx?c=moa;idno=AFS7156.0001.001.

6. ELECTRONIC BOOK (E-BOOK)

    6. Manal M. Omar, *Barefoot in Baghdad* (Naperville, IL: Sourcebooks, 2010), Kindle edition, ch. 4.

Omar, Manal M. *Barefoot in Baghdad.* Naperville, IL: Sourcebooks, 2010. Kindle edition.

7. EDITED BOOK WITH NO AUTHOR

    7. James H. Fetzer, ed., *The Great Zapruder Film Hoax: Deceit and Deception in the Death of JFK* (Chicago: Open Court, 2003), 56.

Fetzer, James H., ed. *The Great Zapruder Film Hoax: Deceit and Deception in the Death of JFK.* Chicago: Open Court, 2003.

8. EDITED BOOK WITH AUTHOR

    8. Leopold von Ranke, *The Theory and Practice of History,* ed. Georg G. Iggers (New York: Routledge, 2010), 135.

von Ranke, Leopold. *The Theory and Practice of History.* Edited by Georg G. Iggers. New York: Routledge, 2010.

CHICAGO SOURCE MAP: Books

Take information from the book's title page and copyright page (on the reverse side of the title page), not from the book's cover or a library catalog. Look carefully at the differences in punctuation between the note and the bibliographic entry.

1 **Author.** In a note, list the author(s) first name first. In a bibliographic entry, list the first author last name first. List other authors first name first.

2 **Title.** Italicize the title and subtitle and capitalize all major words.

3 **City of publication and publisher.** List the city (and country or state abbreviation for an unfamiliar city) followed by a colon. In a note only, city, publisher, and year appear in parentheses. Drop *Inc.*, *Co.*, *Publishing*, or *Publishers*. Follow with a comma.

4 **Publication year.** In a bibliographic entry only, end with a period.

5 **Page number.** In a note only, end with the page number and a period.

Citations for the book on p. 323 would look like this:
ENDNOTE

    1. Alex von Tunzelmann, *Red Heat: Conspiracy, Murder, and the Cold War in the Caribbean* (New York: Picador, 2011), 178.

BIBLIOGRAPHIC ENTRY

von Tunzelmann, Alex. *Red Heat: Conspiracy, Murder, and the Cold War in the Caribbean.* New York: Picador, 2011.

Publication Year

2011

RED HEAT

Title

CONSPIRACY, MURDER, AND THE COLD WAR IN THE CARIBBEAN

ALEX VON TUNZELMANN

Author

PICADOR

HENRY HOLT AND COMPANY

NEW YORK

Publisher and City of Publication

9. SELECTION IN AN ANTHOLOGY OR CHAPTER IN A BOOK WITH AN EDITOR

9. Denise Little, "Born in Blood," in *Alternate Gettysburgs,* ed. Brian Thomsen and Martin H. Greenberg (New York: Berkley Publishing Group, 2002), 245.

Give the inclusive page numbers of the selection or chapter in the bibliographic entry.

Little, Denise. "Born in Blood." In *Alternate Gettysburgs.* Edited by Brian Thomsen and Martin H. Greenberg, 242–55. New York: Berkley Publishing Group, 2002.

10. INTRODUCTION, PREFACE, FOREWORD, OR AFTERWORD

10. Robert B. Reich, introduction to *Making Work Pay: America after Welfare,* ed. Robert Kuttner (New York: New Press, 2002), xvi.

Reich, Robert B. Introduction to *Making Work Pay: America after Welfare,* vii–xvii. Edited by Robert Kuttner. New York: New Press, 2002.

11. TRANSLATION

11. Suetonius, *The Twelve Caesars,* trans. Robert Graves (London: Penguin Classics, 1989), 202.

Suetonius. *The Twelve Caesars.* Translated by Robert Graves. London: Penguin Classics, 1989.

12. EDITION OTHER THAN THE FIRST

12. Dee Brown, *Bury My Heart at Wounded Knee: An Indian History of the American West,* 4th ed. (New York: Owl Books, 2007), 12.

Brown, Dee. *Bury My Heart at Wounded Knee: An Indian History of the American West,* 4th ed. New York: Owl Books, 2007.

13. MULTIVOLUME WORK

13. John Watson, *Annals of Philadelphia and Pennsylvania in the Olden Time,* vol. 2 (Washington, DC: Ross & Perry, 2003), 514.

Watson, John. *Annals of Philadelphia and Pennsylvania in the Olden Time.*
Vol. 2. Washington, DC: Ross & Perry, 2003.

14. REFERENCE WORK. In a note, use *s.v.,* the abbreviation for the Latin *sub verbo* ("under the word") to help your reader find the entry. Do not list reference works such as encyclopedias or dictionaries in your bibliography.

14. *Encyclopedia Britannica,* s.v. "carpetbagger."

15. WORK WITH A TITLE WITHIN THE TITLE. Use quotation marks around any title within a book title.

15. John A. Alford, *A Companion to "Piers Plowman"* (Berkeley: University of California Press, 1988), 195.

Alford, John A. *A Companion to "Piers Plowman."* Berkeley: University of California Press, 1988.

16. SACRED TEXT. Do not include sacred texts in the bibliography.

16. Luke 18:24–25 (New International Version)

16. Qur'an 7:40–41

 Checklist

Citing Sources without Models in *Chicago* Style

To cite a source for which you cannot find a model, collect as much information as you can find—about the creator, title, date of creation or update, and location of the source—with the goal of helping your readers find the source for themselves, if possible. Then look at the models in this section to see which one most closely matches the type of source you are using.

In an academic writing project, before citing an electronic source for which you have no model, also be sure to ask your instructor's advice.

17. SOURCE QUOTED IN ANOTHER SOURCE. Identify both the original and the secondary source.

> 17. Frank D. Millet, "The Filipino Leaders," *Harper's Weekly,* March 11, 1899, quoted in Richard Slotkin, *Gunfighter Nation: The Myth of the Frontier in Twentieth-Century America* (New York: HarperCollins, 1992), 110.

> Millet, Frank D. "The Filipino Leaders." *Harper's Weekly,* March 11, 1899. Quoted in Richard Slotkin, *Gunfighter Nation: The Myth of the Frontier in Twentieth-Century America* (New York: HarperCollins, 1992), 110.

Print and digital periodicals

The note for an article in a periodical typically includes the author's name, the article title, and the periodical title. The format for other information, including the volume and issue numbers (if any) and the date of publication, as well as the page number(s) to which the note refers, varies according to the type of periodical and whether you consulted it in print, on the Web, or in a database. In a bibliographic entry for a journal or magazine article from a database or a print periodical, also give the inclusive page numbers.

18. ARTICLE IN A PRINT JOURNAL

> 18. Karin Lützen, "The Female World: Viewed from Denmark," *Journal of Women's History* 12, no. 3 (2000): 36.

> Lützen, Karin. "The Female World: Viewed from Denmark." *Journal of Women's History* 12, no. 3 (2000): 34–38.

19. ARTICLE IN AN ONLINE JOURNAL. Give the DOI if there is one. If not, include the article URL. If page numbers are provided, include them as well.

> 19. Jeffrey J. Schott, "America, Europe, and the New Trade Order," *Business and Politics* 11, no. 3 (2009), doi:10.2202/1469-3569.1263.

> Schott, Jeffrey J. "America, Europe, and the New Trade Order." *Business and Politics* 11, no. 3 (2009). doi:10.2202/1469-3569.1263.

20. JOURNAL ARTICLE FROM A DATABASE. For basic information on citing a periodical article from a database in *Chicago* style, see the source map on pp. 328–29.

20. W. Trent Foley and Nicholas J. Higham, "Bede on the Britons," *Early Medieval Europe* 17, no. 2 (2009), 157, doi:10.1111/j.1468-0254.2009.00258.x.

Foley, W. Trent, and Nicholas J. Higham. "Bede on the Britons." *Early Medieval Europe* 17, no. 2 (2009). 154–85. doi:10.1111/j.1468-0254.2009.00258.x.

21. ARTICLE IN A PRINT MAGAZINE

21. Terry McDermott, "The Mastermind: Khalid Sheikh Mohammed and the Making of 9/11," *New Yorker,* September 13, 2010, 42.

McDermott, Terry. "The Mastermind: Khalid Sheikh Mohammed and the Making of 9/11." *New Yorker,* September 13, 2010, 38–51.

22. ARTICLE IN AN ONLINE MAGAZINE

22. Tracy Clark-Flory, "Educating Women Saves Kids' Lives," *Salon,* September 17, 2010, http://www.salon.com/life/broadsheet/2010/09/17/education_women/index.html.

Clark-Flory, Tracy. "Educating Women Saves Kids' Lives." *Salon,* September 17, 2010. http://www.salon.com/life/broadsheet/2010/09/17/education_women/index.html.

23. MAGAZINE ARTICLE FROM A DATABASE

23. Sami Yousafzai and Ron Moreau, "Twisting Arms in Afghanistan," *Newsweek,* November 9, 2009, 8, Academic Search Premier (44962900).

Yousafzai, Sami, and Ron Moreau. "Twisting Arms in Afghanistan." *Newsweek,* November 9, 2009. 8. Academic Search Premier (44962900).

CHICAGO SOURCE MAP: Articles from Databases

1 **Author.** In a note, list the author(s) first name first. In the bibliographic entry, list the first author last name first, comma, first name; list other authors first name first.

2 **Article title.** Enclose the title and subtitle (if any) in quotation marks, and capitalize major words. In the notes section, put a comma before and after the title. In the bibliography, put a period before and after.

3 **Periodical title.** Italicize the title and subtitle, and capitalize all major words. For a magazine or newspaper, follow with a comma.

4 **Volume and issue numbers (for journals) and date.** For journals, follow the title with the volume number, a comma, the abbreviation *no.*, and the issue number; enclose the publication year in parentheses and follow with a comma (in a note) or with a period (in a bibliography). For other periodicals, give the month and year or month, day, and year, not in parentheses, followed by a comma.

5 **Page numbers.** In a note, give the page where the information is found. In the bibliographic entry, give the page range.

6 **Retrieval information.** Provide the article's DOI, if one is given, the name of the database and an accession number, or a "stable or persistent" URL for the article in the database. Because you provide stable retrieval information, you do not need to identify the electronic format of the work (i.e., PDF, as in the example shown here). End with a period.

Citations for the journal article on p. 329 would look like this:
ENDNOTE

1. Daniel Herda, "How Many Immigrants? Foreign-Born Population Innumeracy in Europe," *Public Opinion Quarterly* 74, no. 4 (2010), 677. doi:10.1093/poq/nfq013.

BIBLIOGRAPHIC ENTRY

Daniel Herda. "How Many Immigrants? Foreign-Born Population
Innumeracy in Europe." *Public Opinion Quarterly* 74, no. 4 (2010).
674–95. doi:10.1093/poq/nfq013.

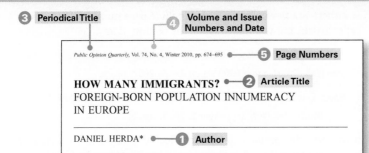

❸ Periodical Title

❹ Volume and Issue Numbers and Date

Public Opinion Quarterly, Vol. 74, No. 4, Winter 2010, pp. 674–695 ●── **❺ Page Numbers**

HOW MANY IMMIGRANTS? ●──❷ **Article Title**
FOREIGN-BORN POPULATION INNUMERACY IN EUROPE

DANIEL HERDA* ●──❶ **Author**

Abstract Individuals frequently perceive immigrant and minority population sizes to be much larger than they are in reality. To date, little is understood about the extent or causes of this phenomenon, known as innumeracy, which may have consequences for inter-group relations. However, before the literature can assess these consequences, a better understanding of the development of these misperceptions is needed. The extant literature focuses only on the United States and lacks a clear understanding of how innumeracy arises. Drawing from the 2002 European Social Survey (ESS), this study attempts to make sense of this phenomenon by proposing and testing a framework that views innumeracy among majority group members as developing in two ways: as cognitive mistakes and emotional responses. I establish the existence and extent of the phenomenon across 21 European nations, test new key predictors such as media exposure and socio-economic status, and find independent associations with cognitive and emotional factors using multi-level regression analyses.

When asked to estimate the size of minority populations, survey respondents frequently over-estimate. Research on this curious phenomenon, dubbed innumeracy,[1] indicates that a substantial proportion of majority group members perceive minority populations as much larger than they are in reality (Paulos

DANIEL HERDA is a Ph.D. candidate in the Department of Sociology, University of California–Davis, Davis, CA, USA. The author would like to thank Mary Jackman, Dina Okamoto, Diane Felmlee, Brad Jones, Xiaoling Shu, Golnaz Komaie, Danielle Presti, the editors and anonymous reviewers for their helpful advice on this research. The data used in this study were provided by Norwegian Social Sciences Data Service and are available for download at http://ess.nsd.uib.no/. An earlier version of this research was presented at the 2009 annual meeting of the Pacific Sociological Association in San Diego, CA, USA. *Address correspondence to Daniel Herda, University of California–Davis, One Shields Avenue, Davis, CA 95616-8701, USA; e-mail: deherda@ucdavis.edu.

❻ Retrieval Information

1. While the term innumeracy is very general, I use it to specifically refer to the over-estimation of the immigrant population size.

doi: 10.1093/poq/nfq013   Advance Access published on March 29, 2010

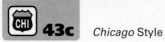

24. ARTICLE IN A NEWSPAPER. Do not include page numbers for a newspaper article, but you may include the section, if any.

> 24. Caroline E. Mayer, "Wireless Industry to Adopt Voluntary
> Standards," *Washington Post,* September 9, 2003, sec. E.

> Mayer, Caroline E. "Wireless Industry to Adopt Voluntary Standards."
> *Washington Post,* September 9, 2003, sec. E.

If you provide complete documentation of a newspaper article in a note, you may not need to include it in the bibliography. Check your instructor's preference.

25. ARTICLE IN AN ONLINE NEWSPAPER. If the URL for the article is very long, use the URL for the newspaper's home page.

> 25. Andrew C. Revkin, "Arctic Melt Unnerves the Experts," *New York
> Times,* October 2, 2007, http://www.nytimes.com.

> Revkin, Andrew C. "Arctic Melt Unnerves the Experts." *New York Times,*
> October 2, 2007. http://www.nytimes.com.

26. NEWSPAPER ARTICLE FROM A DATABASE

> 26. Demetria Irwin, "A Hatchet, Not a Scalpel, for NYC Budget Cuts,"
> *New York Amsterdam News,* November 13, 2008, Academic Search Premier
> (35778153).

> Irwin, Demetria. "A Hatchet, Not a Scalpel, for NYC Budget Cuts." *New
> York Amsterdam News,* November 13, 2008. Academic Search Premier
> (35778153).

27. BOOK REVIEW. After the information about the book under review, give publication information for the appropriate kind of source (see models 18–26).

> 27. Arnold Relman, "Health Care: The Disquieting Truth," review of
> *Tracking Medicine: A Researcher's Quest to Understand Health Care,* by John
> E. Wennberg, *New York Review of Books* 57, no. 14 (2010), 45.

Relman, Arnold. "Health Care: The Disquieting Truth." Review of
*Tracking Medicine: A Researcher's Quest to Understand Health
Care,* by John E. Wennberg. *New York Review of Books* 57,
no. 14 (2010), 45–48.

Online sources

In general, include the author (if given); the title of a work from a
Web site (in quotation marks); the name of the site (in italics, if
the site is an online publication, but otherwise neither italicized
nor in quotation marks); the sponsor of the site, if different from
the name of the site or name of the author; the date of publication
or most recent update; and a URL. If the online source does not
indicate when it was published or last modified, or if your instructor requests an access date, place it before the URL.

For basic information on citing works from Web sites in *Chicago*
style, see the source map on pp. 334–35.

28. WEB SITE

> 28. Rutgers School of Arts and Sciences, *The Rutgers Oral History
> Archive,* 2010, http://oralhistory.rutgers.edu/.

Rutgers School of Arts and Sciences. *The Rutgers Oral History Archive.*
2010. http://oralhistory.rutgers.edu/.

29. WORK FROM A WEB SITE

> 29. Rose Cohen, "My First Job," *The Triangle Factory Fire,* Cornell
> University School of Industrial and Labor Relations, 2005, http://www.ilr
> .cornell.edu/trianglefire/texts/.

Cohen, Rose. "My First Job." *The Triangle Factory Fire.* Cornell University
School of Industrial and Labor Relations. 2005. http://www.ilr
.cornell.edu/trianglefire/texts/.

30. BLOG (WEB LOG) POST. Treat a blog post as a short work from a
Web site (see model 29).

30. Jai Arjun Singh, "On the Road in the USSR," *Jabberwock* (blog), November 29, 2007, http://jaiarjun.blogspot.com/2007/11 /on-road-in-ussr.html.

Chicago recommends that blog posts appear in the notes section only, not in the bibliography, unless the blog is cited frequently. Check your instructor's preference. A bibliography reference to an entire blog would look like this:

Singh, Jai Arjun. *Jabberwock* (blog). http://jaiarjun.blogspot.com/.

31. EMAIL AND OTHER PERSONAL COMMUNICATIONS. Cite email messages and other personal communications, such as letters and telephone calls, in the text or in a note only, not in the bibliography. (*Chicago* style recommends hyphenating *e-mail*.)

31. Kareem Adas, e-mail message to author, February 11, 2013.

32. PODCAST. Treat a podcast as a short work from a Web site (see model 29) and give as much of the following information as you can find: the author or speaker, the title or a description of the podcast, the title of the site, the site sponsor (if different from the author or site name), the type of podcast or file format, the date of posting or access, and the URL.

32. Barack Obama, "Weekly Address: A Solar Recovery," *The White House,* podcast video, July 3, 2010, http://www.whitehouse.gov /photos-and-video/video/weekly-address-a-solar-recovery.

Obama, Barack. "Weekly Address: A Solar Recovery." *The White House.* Podcast video. July 3, 2010. http://www.whitehouse .gov/photos-and-video/video/weekly-address-a-solar -recovery.

33. ONLINE AUDIO OR VIDEO. Treat an online audio or video source as a short work from a Web site (see model 29). If the source is downloadable, give the medium or file format before the URL (see model 32).

33. Alyssa Katz, "Did the Mortgage Crisis Kill the American Dream?" YouTube video, 4:32, posted by NYCRadio, June 24, 2009, http://www.youtube.com/watch?v=uivtwjwd_Qw.

Katz, Alyssa. "Did the Mortgage Crisis Kill the American Dream?"
YouTube video, 4:32. Posted by NYCRadio. June 24, 2009.
http://www.youtube.com/watch?v=uivtwjwd_Qw.

Other sources

34. PUBLISHED OR BROADCAST INTERVIEW

34. Nina Totenberg, interview by Charlie Rose, *The Charlie Rose Show,*
PBS, June 29, 2010.

Totenberg, Nina. Interview by Charlie Rose. *The Charlie Rose Show.* PBS,
June 29, 2010.

Interviews you conduct are considered personal communications
(see model 31).

35. VIDEO OR DVD

35. Edward Norton and Edward Furlong, *American History X,* directed
by Tony Kaye (1998; Los Angeles: New Line Studios, 2002), DVD.

Norton, Edward, and Edward Furlong. *American History X.* Directed by Tony
Kaye, 1998. Los Angeles: New Line Studios, 2002. DVD.

36. SOUND RECORDING

36. Paul Robeson, *The Collector's Paul Robeson,* recorded 1959,
Monitor MCD-61580, 1989, compact disc.

Robeson, Paul. *The Collector's Paul Robeson.* Recorded 1959. Monitor
MCD-61580, 1989, compact disc.

37. WORK OF ART. Begin with the artist's name and the title of the work. If you viewed the work in person, give the medium, the date, and the name of the place where you saw it.

37. Mary Cassatt, *The Child's Bath,* oil on canvas, 1893, The Art
Institute of Chicago, Chicago, IL.

Cassatt, Mary. *The Child's Bath.* Oil on canvas, 1893. The Art Institute of
Chicago, Chicago, IL.

CHICAGO SOURCE MAP: Works from Web Sites

1 **Author.** In a note, list the author(s) first name first. In a bibliographic entry, list the first author last name first, comma, first name; list additional authors first name first. Note that the host may serve as the author.

2 **Document title.** Enclose the title in quotation marks, and capitalize all major words. In a note, put a comma before and after the title. In the bibliography, put a period before and after.

3 **Title of Web site.** Capitalize all major words. If the site's title is analogous to a book or periodical title, italicize it. In the notes section, put a comma after the title. In the bibliography, put a period after the title.

4 **Sponsor of site.** If the sponsor is the same as the author or site title, you may omit it. End with a comma (in the note) or a period (in the bibliographic entry).

5 **Date of publication or last modification.** If no date is available, or if your instructor requests it, include your date of access (with the word *accessed*).

6 **Retrieval information.** Give the URL for the Web site. If you are required to include a date of access, put the word *accessed* and the date in parentheses after the URL. End with a period.

Citations for the Web site on p. 335 would look like this:
ENDNOTE

1. Rebecca Edwards, "The Populist Party," *1896: The Presidential Campaign: Cartoons & Commentary,* Vassar College, 2000, http://projects .vassar.edu/1896/populists.html.

BIBLIOGRAPHIC ENTRY

Edwards, Rebecca. "The Populist Party." *1896: The Presidential Campaign: Cartoons & Commentary.* Vassar College. 2000. http://projects.vassar .edu/1896/populists.html.

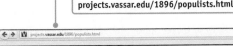

The Populist Party ●—**2** Document Title

The Rise of Populism

The People's Party (or Populist Party, as it was widely known) was much younger than the Democratic and Republican Parties, which had been founded before the Civil War. Agricultural areas in the West and South had been hit by economic depression years before industrial areas. In the 1880s, as drought hit the wheat-growing areas of the Great Plains and prices for Southern cotton sunk to new lows, many tenant farmers fell into deep debt. This exacerbated long-held grievances against railroads, lenders, grain-elevator owners, and others with whom farmers did business. By the early 1890s, as the depression worsened, some industrial workers shared these farm families' views on labor and the trusts.

In 1890 Populists won control of the Kansas state legislature, and Kansan **William Peffer** became the party's first U.S. Senator. Peffer, with his long white beard, was a humorous figure to many Eastern journalists and politicians, who saw little evidence of Populism in their states and often treated the party as a joke. Nonetheless, Western and Southern Populists gained support rapidly. In 1892 the national party was officially founded through a merger of the Farmers' Alliance and the Knights of Labor. In that year the Populist presidential candidate, James B. Weaver, won over one million votes. Between 1892 and 1896, however, the party failed to make further gains, in part because of fraud, intimidation, and violence by Southern Democrats.

By 1896 the Populist organization was in even more turmoil than that of Democrats. Two main factions had appeare[...]

organiz[...]

"fused"[...]

third pa[...]

3 Title of Web Site

Homepage

5 Date of Publication

1 Author

4 Sponsor of Site

335

If you refer to a reproduction, give the publication information.

> 37. Mary Cassatt, *The Child's Bath,* oil on canvas, 1893, on *Art Access,* The Art Institute of Chicago, August 2004, http://www.artic.edu /artaccess/AA_Impressionist/pages/IMP_6.shtml#.

> Cassatt, Mary. *The Child's Bath.* Oil on canvas, 1893. On *Art Access,* The Art Institute of Chicago. August 2004. http://www.artic.edu/artaccess /AA_Impressionist/pages/IMP_6.shtml#.

38. PAMPHLET, REPORT, OR BROCHURE. Information about the author or publisher may not be readily available, but give enough information to identify your source.

> 38. Jamie McCarthy, *Who Is David Irving?* (San Antonio, TX: Holocaust History Project, 1998).

> McCarthy, Jamie. *Who Is David Irving?* San Antonio, TX: Holocaust History Project, 1998.

39. GOVERNMENT DOCUMENT

> 39. U.S. House Committee on Ways and Means, *Report on Trade Mission to Sub-Saharan Africa,* 108th Cong., 1st sess. (Washington, DC: Government Printing Office, 2003), 28.

> U.S. House Committee on Ways and Means. *Report on Trade Mission to Sub-Saharan Africa.* 108th Cong., 1st sess. Washington, DC: Government Printing Office, 2003.

43d A sample student research essay, *Chicago* style

On the following pages are excerpts from an essay by Amanda Rinder that conforms to the *Chicago* guidelines described in this chapter. To read her complete project, go to the integrated media page at **bedfordstmartins.com/easy**.

Rinder 2

First page
of body text
is p. 2

Refers to
each figure
by number

Only one city has the "Big Shoulders" described by Carl Sandburg: Chicago (fig. 1). So renowned are its skyscrapers and celebrated building style that an entire school of architecture is named for Chicago. Presently, however, the place that Frank Sinatra called "my kind of town" is beginning to lose sight of exactly what kind of town it is. Many of the buildings that give Chicago its distinctive character are being torn down in order to make room for new growth. Both preserving the classics and encouraging new creation are important; the combination of these elements gives Chicago architecture its unique flavor. Witold Rybczynski, a professor of urbanism, told Tracie Rozhon of the *New York Times,* "Of all the cities we can think of . . . we associate Chicago with new things, with building new. Combining that with preservation is a difficult task, a tricky thing. It's hard to find the middle ground in Chicago."[1] Yet finding a middle ground is essential if the city is to retain the original character that sets it apart from the rest. In order to

Thesis
introduced

Double-
spaced text

Source
cited using
superscript
numeral

Fig. 1. Chicago skyline, circa 1940s. (Postcard courtesy of Minnie Dangburg.)

Figure
caption
includes
number,
short title,
and source

Annotations indicate effective choices or *Chicago*-style formatting.

Rinder 9

Notes

Newspaper article in database

1. Tracie Rozhon, "Chicago Girds for Big Battle over Its Skyline," *New York Times,* November 12, 2000, Academic Search Premier (28896783).

Book

2. David Garrard Lowe, *Lost Chicago* (New York: Watson-Guptill Publications, 2000), 123.

3. *Columbia Encyclopedia,* Sixth Ed., s.v. "Louis Sullivan."

4. Daniel Bluestone, *Constructing Chicago* (New Haven: Yale University Press, 1991), 105.

Indirect source

5. Alan J. Shannon, "When Will It End?" *Chicago Tribune,* September 11, 1987, quoted in Karen J. Dilibert, *From Landmark to Landfill* (Chicago: Chicago Architectural Foundation, 2000), 11.

6. Steve Kerch, "Landmark Decisions," *Chicago Tribune,* March 18, 1990, sec. 16.

7. John W. Stamper, *Chicago's North Michigan Avenue* (Chicago: University of Chicago Press, 1991), 215.

Newspaper article online

8. Alf Siewers, "Success Spoiling the Magnificent Mile?" *Chicago Sun-Times,* April 9, 1995, http://www.sun-times.com/.

9. Paul Gapp, "McCarthy Building Puts Landmark Law on a Collision Course with Developers," *Chicago Tribune,* April 20, 1986, quoted in Karen J. Dilibert, *From Landmark to Landfill* (Chicago: Chicago Architectural Foundation, 2000), 4.

Reference to previous source

10. Ibid.

11. Rozhon, "Chicago Girds for Big Battle."

Second reference to source

12. Kerch, "Landmark Decisions."

13. Robert Bruegmann, *The Architects and the City* (Chicago: University of Chicago Press, 1997), 443.

Rinder 10

Bibliography

Bluestone, Daniel. *Constructing Chicago*. New Haven: Yale University
Press, 1991.

Bruegmann, Robert. *The Architects and the City*. Chicago: University of
Chicago Press, 1997.

Dilibert, Karen J. *From Landmark to Landfill*. Chicago: Chicago
Architectural Foundation, 2000.

Kerch, Steve. "Landmark Decisions." *Chicago Tribune,* March 18, 1990,
sec. 16.

Lowe, David Garrard. *Lost Chicago*. New York: Watson-Guptill
Publications, 2000.

Rozhon, Tracie. "Chicago Girds for Big Battle over Its Skyline." *New
York Times,* November 12, 2000. Academic Search Premier
(28896783).

Siewers, Alf. "Success Spoiling the Magnificent Mile?" *Chicago
Sun-Times,* April 9, 1995. http://www.sun-times.com/.

Stamper, John W. *Chicago's North Michigan Avenue*. Chicago: University
of Chicago Press, 1991.

Bibliography
starts on
new page

Book

Pamphlet

Newspaper
article

Article from
database

Bibliography
entries use
hanging
indent and
are not
numbered

Glossary of Usage

Conventions of usage might be called the "good manners" of discourse. And just as manners vary from culture to culture and time to time, so do conventions of usage. Matters of usage, like other language choices you must make, depend on what your purpose is and on what is appropriate for a particular audience at a particular time.

a, an Use *a* with a word that begins with a consonant (*a* book), a consonant sound such as "y" or "w" (*a* euphoric moment, *a* one-sided match), or a sounded *h* (*a* hemisphere). Use *an* with a word that begins with a vowel (*an* umbrella), a vowel sound (*an* X-ray), or a silent *h* (*an* honor).

accept, except The verb *accept* means "receive" or "agree to." *Except* is usually a preposition that means "aside from" or "excluding." *All the plaintiffs except Mr. Kim decided to accept the settlement.*

advice, advise The noun *advice* means "opinion" or "suggestion"; the verb *advise* means "offer advice." *Doctors advise everyone not to smoke, but many people ignore the advice.*

affect, effect As a verb, *affect* means "influence" or "move the emotions of"; as a noun, it means "emotions" or "feelings." *Effect* is a noun meaning "result"; less commonly, it is a verb meaning "bring about." *The storm affected a large area. Its effects included widespread power failures. The drug effected a major change in the patient's affect.*

aggravate The formal meaning is "make worse." *Having another mouth to feed aggravated their poverty.* In academic and professional writing, avoid using *aggravate* to mean "irritate" or "annoy."

all ready, already *All ready* means "fully prepared." *Already* means "previously." *We were all ready for Lucy's party when we learned that she had already left.*

all right, alright Avoid the spelling *alright*.

all together, altogether *All together* means "all in a group" or "gathered in one place." *Altogether* means "completely" or "everything considered." *When the board members were all together, their mutual distrust was altogether obvious.*

allude, elude *Allude* means "refer indirectly." *Elude* means "avoid" or "escape from." *The candidate did not even <u>allude</u> to her opponent. The suspect <u>eluded</u> the police for several days.*

allusion, illusion An *allusion* is an indirect reference. An *illusion* is a false or misleading appearance. *The speaker's <u>allusion</u> to the Bible created an <u>illusion</u> of piety.*

a lot Avoid the spelling *alot*.

already See *all ready, already*.

alright See *all right, alright*.

altogether See *all together, altogether*.

among, between In referring to two things or people, use *between*. In referring to three or more, use *among*. *The relationship <u>between</u> the twins is different from that <u>among</u> the other three children.*

amount, number Use *amount* with quantities you cannot count; use *number* for quantities you can count. *A small <u>number</u> of volunteers cleared a large <u>amount</u> of brush.*

an See *a, an*.

and/or Avoid this term except in business or legal writing. Instead of *fat and/or protein*, write *fat, protein, or both*.

any body, anybody, any one, anyone *Anybody* and *anyone* are pronouns meaning "any person." *<u>Anyone</u> [or <u>anybody</u>] would enjoy this film. Any body* is an adjective modifying a noun. *<u>Any body</u> of water has its own ecology. Any one* is two adjectives or a pronoun modified by an adjective. *Customers could buy only two sale items at <u>any one</u> time. The winner could choose <u>any one</u> of the prizes.*

anyplace In academic and professional discourse, use *anywhere* instead.

anyway, anyways In writing, use *anyway*, not *anyways*.

apt, liable, likely *Likely to* means "probably will," and *apt to* means "inclines or tends to." In many instances, they are interchangeable. *Liable* often carries a more negative sense and is also a legal term meaning "obligated" or "responsible."

as Avoid sentences in which it is not clear if *as* means "when" or "because." For example, does *Carl left town <u>as</u> his father was* *arriving* mean "at the same time as his father was arriving" or "because his father was arriving"?

as, as if, like In academic and professional writing, use *as* or *as if* instead of *like* to introduce a clause. *The dog howled <u>as if</u>* [not *like*] *it were in pain. She did <u>as</u>* [not *like*] *I suggested.*

assure, ensure, insure *Assure* means "convince" or "promise"; its direct object is usually a person or persons. *She <u>assured</u> voters she would not raise taxes. Ensure* and *insure* both mean "make certain," but *insure* usually refers specifically to protection against financial loss. *When the city rationed water to <u>ensure</u> that the supply would last, the Browns could no longer afford to <u>insure</u> their car-wash business.*

as to Do not use *as to* as a substitute for *about. Karen was unsure <u>about</u>* [not *as to*] *Bruce's intentions.*

at, where See *where.*

awhile, a while Always use *a while* after a preposition such as *for, in,* or *after. We drove <u>awhile</u> and then stopped for <u>a while</u>.*

bad, badly Use *bad* after a linking verb such as *be, feel,* or *seem.* Use *badly* to modify an action verb, an adjective, or another verb. *The hostess felt <u>bad</u> because the dinner was <u>badly</u> prepared.*

bare, bear Use *bare* to mean "uncovered" and *bear* to refer to the animal or to mean "carry" or "endure": *The walls were <u>bare</u>. The emptiness was hard to <u>bear</u>.*

because of, due to Use *due to* when the effect, stated as a noun, appears before the verb *be. His illness was <u>due to</u> malnutrition.* (*Illness,* a noun, is the effect.) Use *because of* when the effect is stated as a clause. *He was sick <u>because of</u> malnutrition.* (*He was sick,* a clause, is the effect.)

being as, being that In academic or professional writing, use *because* or *since* instead of these expressions. *<u>Because</u>* [not *being as*] *Romeo killed Tybalt, he was banished to Padua.*

beside, besides *Beside* is a preposition meaning "next to." *Besides* can be a preposition meaning "other than" or an adverb meaning "in addition." *No one <u>besides</u> Francesca would sit <u>beside</u> him.*

between See *among, between.*

brake, break *Brake* means "to stop" and also refers to a stopping mechanism: *Check the <u>brakes</u>. Break* means "fracture" or an interruption: *The coffee <u>break</u> was too short.*

breath, breathe *Breath* is a noun; *breathe*, a verb. "*Breathe*," said the nurse, so June took a deep *breath*.

bring, take Use *bring* when an object is moved from a farther to a nearer place; use *take* when the opposite is true. *Take the box to the post office; bring back my mail.*

but that, but what Avoid using these as substitutes for *that* in expressions of doubt. *Hercule Poirot never doubted that* [not *but that*] *he would solve the case.*

but yet Do not use these words together. *He is strong but* [not *but yet*] *gentle.*

can, may *Can* refers to ability and *may* to possibility or permission. *Since I can ski the slalom well, I may win the race.*

can't hardly *Hardly* has a negative meaning; therefore, *can't hardly* is a double negative. This expression is commonly used in some varieties of English but is not used in academic English. *Tim can* [not *can't*] *hardly wait.*

can't help but This expression is not used in academic English. Use *I can't help going* rather than *I can't help but go.*

censor, censure *Censor* means "remove that which is considered offensive." *Censure* means "formally reprimand." *The newspaper censored stories that offended advertisers. The legislature censured the official for misconduct.*

compare to, compare with *Compare to* means "regard as similar." *Jamie compared the loss to a kick in the head. Compare with* means "examine to find differences or similarities." *Compare Tim Burton's films with David Lynch's.*

complement, compliment *Complement* means "go well with." *Compliment* means "praise." *Guests complimented her on how her earrings complemented her gown.*

comprise, compose *Comprise* means "contain." *Compose* means "make up." *The class comprises twenty students. Twenty students compose the class.*

conscience, conscious *Conscience* means "a sense of right and wrong." *Conscious* means "awake" or "aware." *Lisa was conscious of a guilty conscience.*

consensus of opinion Use *consensus* instead of this redundant phrase. *The family consensus was to sell the old house.*

consequently, subsequently *Consequently* means "as a result"; *subsequently* means "then." *He quit, and subsequently his wife lost her job; consequently, they had to sell their house.*

continual, continuous *Continual* means "repeated at regular or frequent intervals." *Continuous* means "continuing or connected without a break." *The damage done by continuous erosion was increased by the continual storms.*

could of *Have,* not *of,* should follow *could, would, should,* or *might.* *We could have [not of] invited them.*

criteria, criterion *Criterion* means "standard of judgment" or "necessary qualification." *Criteria* is the plural form. *Image is the wrong criterion for choosing a president.*

data *Data* is the plural form of the Latin word *datum,* meaning "fact." Although *data* is used informally as either singular or plural, in academic or professional writing, treat *data* as plural. *These data indicate that fewer people are smoking.*

different from, different than *Different from* is generally preferred in academic and professional writing, although both of these phrases are widely used. *Her lab results were no different from [not than] his.*

discreet, discrete *Discreet* means "tactful" or "prudent." *Discrete* means "separate" or "distinct." *The leader's discreet efforts kept all the discrete factions unified.*

disinterested, uninterested *Disinterested* means "unbiased." *Uninterested* means "indifferent." *Finding disinterested jurors was difficult. She was uninterested in the verdict.*

distinct, distinctive *Distinct* means "separate" or "well defined." *Distinctive* means "characteristic." *Germany includes many distinct regions, each with a distinctive accent.*

doesn't, don't *Doesn't* is the contraction for *does not.* Use it with *he, she, it,* and singular nouns. *Don't* stands for *do not;* use it with *I, you, we, they,* and plural nouns.

due to See *because of, due to.*

each other, one another Use *each other* in sentences involving two subjects and *one another* in sentences involving more than two.

effect See *affect, effect.*

elicit, illicit The verb *elicit* means "draw out." The adjective *illicit* means "illegal." *The police <u>elicited</u> from the criminal the names of others involved in <u>illicit</u> activities.*

elude See *allude, elude.*

emigrate from, immigrate to *Emigrate from* means "move away from one's country." *Immigrate to* means "move to another country." *We <u>emigrated from</u> Norway in 1999. We <u>immigrated to</u> the United States.*

ensure See *assure, ensure, insure.*

enthused, enthusiastic Use *enthusiastic* rather than *enthused* in academic and professional writing.

equally as good Replace this redundant phrase with *equally good* or *as good.*

every day, everyday *Everyday* is an adjective meaning "ordinary." *Every day* is an adjective and a noun, meaning "each day." *I wore <u>everyday</u> clothes almost <u>every day</u>.*

every one, everyone *Everyone* is a pronoun. *Every one* is an adjective and a pronoun, referring to each member of a group. *Because he began after <u>everyone</u> else, David could not finish <u>every one</u> of the problems.*

except See *accept, except.*

explicit, implicit *Explicit* means "directly or openly expressed." *Implicit* means "indirectly expressed or implied." *The <u>explicit</u> message of the ad urged consumers to buy the product, while the <u>implicit</u> message promised popularity if they did so.*

farther, further *Farther* refers to physical distance. *How much <u>farther</u> is it to Munich? Further* refers to time or degree. *I want to avoid <u>further</u> delays.*

fewer, less Use *fewer* with nouns that can be counted. Use *less* with general amounts that you cannot count. *The world needs <u>fewer</u> bombs and <u>less</u> hostility.*

finalize *Finalize* is a pretentious way of saying "end" or "make final." *We <u>closed</u> [not finalized] the deal.*

firstly, secondly, etc. *First, second,* etc., are more common in U.S. English.

flaunt, flout *Flaunt* means to "show off." *Flout* means to "mock" or "scorn." *The drug dealers <u>flouted</u> authority by <u>flaunting</u> their wealth.*

former, latter *Former* refers to the first and *latter* to the second of two things previously mentioned. *Kathy and Anna are athletes; the <u>former</u> plays tennis, and the <u>latter</u> runs.*

further See *farther, further.*

good, well *Good* is an adjective and should not be used as a substitute for the adverb *well. Gabriel is a <u>good</u> host who cooks <u>well</u>.*

good and *Good and* is colloquial for "very"; avoid it in academic and professional writing.

hanged, hung *Hanged* refers to executions; *hung* is used for all other meanings.

hardly See *can't hardly.*

herself, himself, myself, yourself Do not use these reflexive pronouns as subjects or as objects unless they are necessary. *Jane and I* [not *myself*] *agree. They invited John and me* [not *myself*].

he/she, his/her Better solutions for avoiding sexist language are to write out *he or she,* to eliminate pronouns entirely, or to make the subject plural. Instead of writing *Everyone should carry his/her driver's license,* try *<u>Drivers</u> should carry <u>their</u> licenses* or *<u>People</u> should carry <u>their</u> driver's licenses.*

himself See *herself, himself, myself, yourself.*

hisself Use *himself* instead in academic or professional writing.

hopefully *Hopefully* is often used informally to mean "it is hoped," but its formal meaning is "with hope." *Sam watched the roulette wheel <u>hopefully</u>* [not *Hopefully, Sam will win*].

hung See *hanged, hung.*

illicit See *elicit, illicit.*

illusion See *allusion, illusion.*

immigrate to See *emigrate from, immigrate to.*

impact Some readers object to the colloquial use of *impact* or *impact on* as a verb meaning "affect." *Population control may reduce* [not *impact*] *world hunger.*

implicit See *explicit, implicit.*

imply, infer To *imply* is to suggest indirectly. To *infer* is to guess or conclude on the basis of an indirect suggestion. *The note implied they were planning a small wedding; we inferred we would not be invited.*

inside of, outside of Use *inside* and *outside* instead. *The class regularly met outside* [not *outside of*] *the building.*

insure See *assure, ensure, insure.*

interact, interface *Interact* is a vague word meaning "do something that somehow involves another person." *Interface* is computer jargon; when used as a verb, it means "discuss" or "communicate." Avoid both verbs in academic and professional writing.

irregardless, regardless *Irregardless* is a double negative. Use *regardless.*

is when, is where These vague expressions are often incorrectly used in definitions. *Schizophrenia is a psychotic condition in which* [not *is when* or *is where*] *a person withdraws from reality.*

its, it's *Its* is the possessive form of *it. It's* is a contraction for *it is* or *it has. It's important to observe the rat before it eats its meal.*

kind, sort, type These singular nouns should be modified with *this* or *that*, not *these* or *those*, and followed by other singular nouns, not plural nouns. *Wear this kind of dress* [not *those kind of dresses*].

kind of, sort of In formal writing, avoid these colloquialisms. *Amy was somewhat* [not *kind of*] *tired.*

know, no Use *know* to mean "understand." *No* is the opposite of *yes.*

later, latter *Later* means "after some time." *Latter* refers to the second of two items named. *Juan and Chad won all their early matches, but the latter was injured later in the season.*

latter See *former, latter* and *later, latter.*

lay, lie *Lay* means "place" or "put." Its main forms are *lay, laid, laid.* It generally has a direct object, specifying what has been placed. *She laid her books on the desk.* *Lie* means "recline" or "be positioned" and does not take a direct object. Its main forms are *lie, lay, lain.* *She lay awake until two.*

leave, let *Leave* means "go away." *Let* means "allow." *Leave alone* and *let alone* are interchangeable. *Let me leave now, and leave [or let] me alone from now on!*

lend, loan In academic and professional writing, do not use *loan* as a verb; use *lend* instead. *Please lend me your pen so that I may fill out this application for a loan.*

less See *fewer, less.*

let See *leave, let.*

liable See *apt, liable, likely.*

lie See *lay, lie.*

like See *as, as if, like.*

likely See *apt, liable, likely.*

literally *Literally* means "actually" or "exactly as stated." Use it to stress the truth of a statement that might otherwise be understood as figurative. Do not use *literally* as an intensifier in a figurative statement. *Mirna was literally at the edge of her seat* may be accurate, but *Mirna is so hungry that she could literally eat a horse* is not.

loan See *lend, loan.*

loose, lose *Lose* is a verb meaning "misplace." *Loose* is an adjective that means "not securely attached." *Sew on that loose button before you lose it.*

lots, lots of Avoid these informal expressions meaning "much" or "many" in academic or professional discourse.

man, mankind Replace these terms with *people, humans, humankind, men and women,* or similar wording.

may See *can, may.*

may be, maybe *May be* is a verb phrase. *Maybe* is an adverb that means "perhaps." *He may be the head of the organization, but maybe someone else would handle a crisis better.*

media *Media* is the plural form of the noun *medium* and takes a plural verb. *The media are [not is] obsessed with scandals.*

might of See *could of.*

moral, morale A *moral* is a succinct lesson. *The moral of the story is that generosity is rewarded.* *Morale* means "spirit" or "mood." *Office morale was low.*

myself See *herself, himself, myself, yourself.*

no See *know, no.*

nor, or Use *either* with *or* and *neither* with *nor.*

number See *amount, number.*

off, of Use *off* without *of.* *The spaghetti slipped off [not off of] the plate.*

OK, O.K., okay All are acceptable spellings, but avoid the term in academic and professional discourse.

on account of Use this substitute for *because of* sparingly or not at all.

one another See *each other, one another.*

or See *nor, or.*

outside of See *inside of, outside of.*

owing to the fact that Avoid this and other wordy expressions for *because.*

passed, past Use *passed* to mean "went by" or "received a passing grade": *The marching band passed the reviewing stand.* Use *past* to refer to a time before the present: *Historians study the past.*

per Use the Latin *per* only in standard technical phrases such as *miles per hour.* Otherwise, find English equivalents. *As mentioned in [not As per] the latest report, the country's average food consumption each day [not per day] is only 2,000 calories.*

percent, percentage Use *percent* with a specific number; use *percentage* with an adjective such as *large* or *small.* *Last year, 80 percent of the members were female. A large percentage of the members are women.*

plenty *Plenty* means "enough" or "a great abundance." *They told us America was a land of plenty.* Colloquially, it is used to mean "very," a usage you should avoid in academic and professional writing. *He was very [not plenty] tired.*

plus *Plus* means "in addition to." *Your salary plus mine will cover our expenses.* In academic writing, do not use *plus* to mean "besides" or "moreover." *That dress does not fit me. Besides [not Plus], it is the wrong color.*

precede, proceed *Precede* means "come before"; *proceed* means "go forward." *Despite the storm that* precede*d the ceremony, the wedding* proceed*ed on schedule.*

pretty Except in informal situations, avoid using *pretty* as a substitute for "rather," "somewhat," or "quite." *Bill was* quite *[not pretty] disagreeable.*

principal, principle When used as a noun, *principal* refers to a head official or an amount of money; when used as an adjective, it means "most significant." *Principle* means "fundamental law or belief." *Albert went to the* principal *and defended himself with the* principle *of free speech.*

proceed See *precede, proceed.*

quotation, quote *Quote* is a verb, and *quotation* is a noun. *He* quote*d the president, and the* quotation *[not quote] was preserved in history books.*

raise, rise *Raise* means "lift" or "move upward." (Referring to children, it means "bring up.") It takes a direct object; someone raises something. *The guests* raised *their glasses to toast. Rise* means "go upward." It does not take a direct object; something rises by itself. *She saw the steam* rise *from the pan.*

rarely ever Use *rarely* by itself, or use *hardly ever. When we were poor, we* rarely *went to the movies.*

real, really *Real* is an adjective, and *really* is an adverb. Do not substitute *real* for *really.* In academic and professional writing, do not use *real* or *really* to mean "very." *The old man walked* very *[not real or really] slowly.*

reason is because Use either *the reason is that* or *because*—not both. *The* reason *the copier stopped* is that *[not is because] the paper jammed.*

reason why Avoid this expression in formal writing. *The* reason *[not reason why] this book is short is market demand.*

regardless See *irregardless, regardless.*

respectfully, respectively *Respectfully* means "with respect." *Respectively* means "in the order given." *Karen and David are,* respectively, *a juggler and an acrobat. The children treated their grandparents* respectfully.

rise See *raise, rise.*

set, sit *Set* usually means "put" or "place" and takes a direct object. *Sit* refers to taking a seat and does not take an object. <u>*Set*</u> *your cup on the table, and* <u>*sit*</u> *down.*

should of See *could of.*

since Be careful not to use *since* ambiguously. In <u>*Since*</u> *I broke my leg, I've stayed home,* the word *since* might be understood to mean either "because" or "ever since."

sit See *set, sit.*

so In academic and professional writing, avoid using *so* alone to mean "very." Instead, follow *so* with *that* to show how the intensified condition leads to a result. *Aaron was* <u>*so*</u> *tired* <u>*that*</u> *he fell asleep at the wheel.*

someplace Use *somewhere* instead in academic and professional writing.

some time, sometime, sometimes *Some time* refers to a length of time. *Please leave me* <u>*some time*</u> *to dress. Sometime* means "at some indefinite later time." <u>*Sometime*</u> *I will take you to London. Sometimes* means "occasionally." <u>*Sometimes*</u> *I eat sushi.*

sort See *kind, sort, type.*

sort of See *kind of, sort of.*

stationary, stationery *Stationary* means "standing still"; *stationery* means "writing paper." *When the bus was* <u>*stationary*</u>, *Pat took out* <u>*stationery*</u> *and wrote a note.*

subsequently See *consequently, subsequently.*

supposed to, used to Be careful to include the final *-d* in these expressions. *He is* <u>*supposed to*</u> *attend.*

sure, surely Avoid using *sure* as an intensifier. Instead, use *certainly. I was* <u>*certainly*</u> *glad to see you.*

take See *bring, take.*

than, then Use *than* in comparative statements. *The cat was bigger* <u>*than*</u> *the dog.* Use *then* when referring to a sequence of events. *I won, and* <u>*then*</u> *I cried.*

that, which A clause beginning with *that* singles out the item being described. *The book* <u>*that*</u> *is on the table is a good one* specifies the book on the table as opposed to some other book. A clause beginning with *which* may or may not single out the item, although some writers use *which* clauses only to add more information about an item being described. *The book, which is on the table, is a good one* contains a *which* clause between the commas. The clause simply adds extra, nonessential information about the book; it does not specify which book.

theirselves Use *themselves* instead in academic and professional writing.

then See *than, then*.

thorough, threw, through *Thorough* means "complete": *After a thorough inspection, the restaurant reopened. Threw* is the past tense of *throw*, and *through* means "in one side and out the other": *He threw the ball through a window*.

to, too, two *To* generally shows direction. *Too* means "also." *Two* is the number. *We, too, are going to the meeting in two hours*. Avoid using *to* after *where*. *Where are you flying* [not *flying to*]?

two See *to, too, two*.

type See *kind, sort, type*.

uninterested See *disinterested, uninterested*.

unique Some people argue that *unique* means "one and only" and object to usage that suggests it means merely "unusual." In formal writing, avoid constructions such as *quite unique*.

used to See *supposed to, used to*.

very Avoid using *very* to intensify a weak adjective or adverb; instead, replace the adjective or adverb with a stronger, more precise, or more colorful word. Instead of *very nice*, for example, use *kind, warm, sensitive, endearing*, or *friendly*.

way, ways When referring to distance, use *way*. *Graduation was a long way* [not *ways*] *off*.

well See *good, well*.

where Use *where* alone, not with words such as *at* and *to*. *Where are you going* [not *going to*]?

which See *that, which*.

who, whom Use *who* if the word is the subject of the clause and *whom* if the word is the object of the clause. *Monica, <u>who</u> smokes incessantly, is my godmother.* (*Who* is the subject of the clause; the verb is *smokes.*) *Monica, <u>whom</u> I saw last winter, lives in Tucson.* (*Whom* is the object of the verb *saw.*)

who's, whose *Who's* is a contraction for *who is* or *who has.* <u>*Who's*</u> *on the patio? Whose* is a possessive form. <u>*Whose*</u> *sculpture is in the garden?* <u>*Whose*</u> *is on the patio?*

would of See *could of.*

yet See *but yet.*

your, you're *Your* shows possession. *Bring <u>your</u> sleeping bag along. You're* is the contraction for *you are.* <u>*You're*</u> *in the wrong sleeping bag.*

yourself See *herself, himself, myself, yourself.*

Acknowledgments

PHOTO CREDITS

p. 41, (fourth image down) Sovfoto/UIG via Getty Images

p. 54, *Mother Jones* and Emmanuel Saez/University of California–Berkeley

p. 172, Fontshop.com

p. 207, (top left) *Michigan Quarterly Review*; (top right) Reproduced with permission. Copyright © 2013 Scientific American, a division of Nature America, Inc. All rights reserved; (bottom left) Courtesy of *Ecology and Sociology*; (bottom right) Salon .com

p. 215, Nieman Foundation for Journalism at Harvard

p. 217, Mark Ungar, "Prisons and Politics in Contemporary Latin America." *Human Rights Quarterly* 25:4 (2003), pp. 909, 915. © 2003 Johns Hopkins University Press. Reprinted with permission of Johns Hopkins University Press.

p. 251, Copyright and title pages from *The Value of Nothing* by Raj Patel. Copyright © 2009 by Picador. Reprinted by permission of Picador.

p. 259, Courtesy of Alissa Quart and *Columbia Journalism Review*

p. 263, EBSCOhost

p. 267, Nobelprize.org; Scanpix/Sipa USA

p. 297, William M. Tsutsui, *Godzilla on My Mind*. Published 2004, Palgrave Macmillan. Reproduced with permission of Palgrave Macmillan.

p. 301, From *The American Scholar*, Volume 75, No. 2, Spring 2006. Copyright © 2006 by The Phi Beta Kappa Society and by Amitai Etzioni.

p. 305, Silvia Knobloch-Westerwick and Josselyn Crane. "A Losing Battle: Effects of Prolonged Exposure to Thin-Ideal Images on Dieting and Body Satisfaction." *Communication Research* (Volume 39, Issue 1), p. 79, Copyright © 2012 by SAGE Publications, Inc. Reprinted by Permission.

p. 309, Pew Research Center

p. 323, Title and copyright pages from the book *Red Heat* by Alex von Tunzelmann, Copyright © 2011 by Alex von Tunzelmann. Title and copyright pages Copyright © 2011 by Henry Holt and Company, LLC. Reprinted by permission of Henry Holt and Company, LLC.

p. 329, Daniel Herda, "How Many Immigrants? Foreign-Born Population Innumeracy in Europe." *Public Opinion Quarterly*, Vol. 74 (4): 674–695 (2010), p. 674, by permission of Oxford University Press.

p. 335, Rebecca Edwards

INTEGRATED MEDIA

Chicago-style project, Amanda Rinder

p. 5, Courtesy College of Architecture and the Arts, University of Illinois at Chicago

Critical analysis, Shuqiao Song

p. 2, Digital Image © 2013 Museum Associates/LACMA. Licensed by Art Resource, NY. © 2013. C. Herscovici, London/Artists Rights Society (ARS), New York LLC.

pp. 3, 5, 6, From *Fun Home: A Family Tragicomic* by Alison Bechdel. Copyright © 2006 by Alison Bechdel. Reprinted by permission of Houghton Mifflin Harcourt Publishing Company. All rights reserved.

Index

with Glossary of Terms

Words in blue are followed by a definition. **Boldface** terms in definitions are themselves defined elsewhere in this index.

A

a, an, 191–93, 341
abbreviations, 137–38, 153–54
  APA style, 286–88, 294–95, 298, 300
  Chicago style, 320, 325, 328
  MLA style, 248
  texting, avoiding, 26
absolute concepts, 93
abstracts
  APA style, 284
  evaluating, 216
abstract words, 175
academic essentials, 12–15
academic writing. *See also* writing projects
  authority in, 19–20, 53, 67
  clarity and directness in, 20–21
  genres of, 65–66, 189–90
  social writing versus, 18–19
  standard English for, 168–69
  style for, 20
  timed essay examination, 24–25
accept, except, 178, 341
acknowledging sources, 227–28

active voice, 82 The form of a **verb** when the **subject** performs the action: *Lata sang the chorus.*

  for conciseness, 118
  shifts to passive, 121–22

AD, CE, 154
addresses. *See also* URLs
  commas in, 133
  numbers in, 155
ad hominem fallacy, 55

adjective, 91–93 A word that modifies, quantifies, identifies, or describes a **noun** or words acting as a noun.

  absolute concepts, 93
  adverb versus, 91–92
  capitalization of, 151
  clauses, commas with, 129
  comparative and superlative, 93
  compound, 10, 158
  coordinate, 131
  hyphen with, 158
  after linking verb, 91–92
  with plural noun, 92
  proper, 151
adjective suffixes, 185

adverb, 91–93 A word that qualifies, modifies, limits, or defines a **verb**, an **adjective**, another adverb, or a **clause**, frequently answering the question *where? when? how? why? to what extent?* or *under what conditions?*

  absolute concepts, 93
  adjective versus, 91–92
  clauses, commas with, 130
  comparative and superlative, 93
  conjunctive, 104, 132, 136
  hyphen with, 158
adverbial particles, 202
advice, advise, 341

comma splice, 8–9, 103–6 An error
in formal writing resulting from
joining two **independent clauses**
with only a comma.

comparative, 93 The *-er* or *more*
form of an **adjective** or **adverb**
used to compare two things (*happier, more quickly*).

conciseness Using the fewest
possible words to make a point
effectively.

conjunction A word or words
joining **words**, **phrases**, or **clauses**.
See **coordinating conjunction; correlative conjunction; subordinating
conjunction**

conjunctive adverb, 104, 132, 136
A word (such as *consequently,
moreover,* or *nevertheless*) that
modifies an **independent clause**
following another independent
clause. A conjunctive adverb

faulty sentence structure, 6–7, 110–12 A common writing problem in which a sentence begins with one grammatical pattern and switches to another (also called "mixed structure").

fragment, 10, 106–8 A group of words that is not a complete sentence but is punctuated as one. Usually a fragment lacks a **subject**, a **verb**, or both, or it is a **dependent clause**.

fused (run-on) sentences, 8, 103–6 Sometimes called a "run-on," a

P

participle, 76–80, 196–97 A word
formed from the **base form** of a
verb. The present participle always
ends in *-ing* (*going*). The past participle ends in *-ed* (*ruined*) unless
the verb is **irregular**. A participle
can function as an **adjective** (*the
singing frog, a ruined shirt*) or form
part of a **verb phrase** (*You have
ruined my shirt*).

parts of speech The eight
grammatical categories describing
how words function in a sentence
(**adjectives, adverbs, conjunctions,
interjections, nouns, prepositions,
pronouns, verbs**).

passive voice, 82–83, 118 The form
of a **verb** when the **subject** is being
acted on, not acting: *The batter
was hit by a pitch.*

past tense, 80 The **tense** of a **verb**
that indicates an action or condition has already happened: *They
arrived yesterday.*

sentence errors. *See also* Top Twenty
  comma splices, 8–9, 103–6
  compound structures, inconsistent, 111
  faulty predication, 111
  faulty structure, 6–7, 110–12
  fragments, 10, 106–8
  fused (run-on) sentences, 8, 103–6
  incomplete comparisons, 112
  missing words, 6–7, 111–12, 120–21
  shifts, 7, 121–23
  subordination, excessive, 115–16
sentence fragments. *See* fragment
sentence structure
  faulty, 6–7, 110–12
  for multilingual writers, 189–90
  simplifying, 117–18
series. *See* items in a series
set, sit, 80, 352
several, both, 191–92
sexist language, 101, 165–66
she, her, 97–103
she/he, 347
shifts
  in discourse, 122
  in person, 122
  in tone and diction, 122–23
  in varieties of English, 168–69
  in verb tense, 7, 121
  in voice, 121–22
should of, could of, 345
sic (so), 146
signal phrases, 225–26
  APA style, 285
  Chicago style, 317
  MLA style, 238–39
signpost language, 62–63
silent *e*, 179
similes, 175

simple tenses, 81–82 The past (*It happened*), present (*Things fall apart*), and future (*You will succeed*) forms of **verbs**.

since, 352
single quotation marks, 141
singular forms, 9, 84, 101
sit, set, 80, 352
slang, 26, 144, 164, 169, 171
slashes, 142, 148
slides, PowerPoint, 63–64
so, 352. *See also* coordinating conjunctions
social bookmarking sites, 210
social media
  citing in APA style, 306
  citing in *Chicago* style, 332
  citing in MLA style, 270–71
  writing for, 18–19, 61
social sciences, evidence for, 67
some, enough, 191–92
somebody, someone, something. See indefinite pronoun
someplace, 352
some time, sometime, sometimes, 352
sort, type, kind, 348
sort of, kind of, 348
source maps
  APA style
    articles from databases, 304–5
    articles from periodicals, 300–301
    books, 296–97
    works from Web sites, 308–9
  Chicago style
    articles from databases, 328–29
    books, 322–23
    works from Web sites, 334–35

subject The **noun** or **pronoun**
and related words that indicate
who or what a sentence is about.
The simple subject is the noun or
pronoun: *The timid gray <u>mouse</u> ran
away.* The complete subject is the
simple subject and its modifiers:
<u>The timid gray mouse</u> ran away.
See also topic.

For Multilingual Writers

Throughout *EasyWriter*, boxed tips offer help on the following topics for writers whose first language is not English.

For High School Writers

Revision Symbols

Numbers in bold refer to sections of this book.

abbr	abbreviation **26a**	pass	inappropriate passive **7e, 18b**
ad	adjective/adverb **9**	ref	unclear pronoun reference **11c**
agr	agreement **8, 11b**		
awk	awkward	run-on	run-on (fused) sentence **12**
cap	capitalization **25**		
case	case **11a**	sexist	sexist language **11b, 30b**
cliché	cliché **32d**		
com	incomplete comparison **14d**	shift	shift **18**
		slang	slang **32a**
concl	weak conclusion	sp	spelling **32f**
cs	comma splice **12**	sum	summarize **39a**
def	define	trans	transition
dm	dangling modifier **10c**	verb	verb form **7**
doc	documentation **41–43**	vs	verb sequence **7d**
emph	emphasis unclear	vt	verb tense **7c–d**
ex	example needed	wc	word choice **32**
frag	sentence fragment **13**	wrdy	wordy **16**
fs	fused sentence **12**	wv	weak verb **16d**
hyph	hyphen **28**	ww	wrong word **32b**
inc	incomplete construction **14**	. ? !	period, question mark, exclamation point **21**
it	italics **27**	,	comma **19**
jarg	jargon **32a**	;	semicolon **20**
lc	lower case **25**	,	apostrophe **22**
lv	language variety **31**	" "	quotation marks **23**
mix	mixed construction **14, 18**	( ) [ ] –	parentheses, brackets, dash **24**
mm	misplaced modifier **10a**	: / …	colon, slash, ellipses **24**
ms	manuscript form **41b, 42b, 43b**	^	insert
no ,	no comma **19i**	~	transpose
num	number **26b**	⌣	close up
¶	paragraph	X	delete
//	faulty parallelism **17**		
para	paraphrase **39a**		